University of Michigan Studies

HUMANISTIC SERIES

VOLUME XXII

A PAPYRUS CODEX OF THE SHEPHERD OF HERMAS

A PAPYRUS CODEX OF THE SHEPHERD OF HERMAS

(SIMILITUDES 2–9)

WITH

A FRAGMENT OF THE MANDATES

EDITED BY

CAMPBELL BONNER
UNIVERSITY OF MICHIGAN

ANN ARBOR
UNIVERSITY OF MICHIGAN PRESS
1934

Printed and bound by CPI Group (UK) Ltd, Croydon, CR0 4YY

Set up and electrotyped. Published 1934.

Norwood Press
J. S. Cushing Co. — Berwick & Smith Co.
Norwood, Mass., U.S.A.

Paperback ISBN: 978-0-472-75041-2

To

E. H. B.

PREFACE

In offering this long-delayed volume to the public I am acutely aware that I have sinned against the sound maxim that he gives twice who gives quickly. There are students of Hermas who would have been more grateful if the text had appeared promptly, even with many more imperfections than it now presents. But it is not easy for a conscientious worker to allow a book to go forth until he has reduced its errors to a minimum. Knowing that he cannot expect to convince his readers at every point, he can at least try never to mislead them. How hard it has been, in the case of this papyrus, to attain even that modest aim will be appreciated by those who follow closely the indications of the printed pages.

Another cause of delay was the necessity — for such it seemed to me — of exhibiting as clearly as possible the relation of the readings of the codex to those found in the other sources. This might have been left to others; but I could not bring myself to resign a part of the task which was sure to be of great interest, and which was in a manner incumbent upon the first editor of the papyrus. But that work involved many side lines of inquiry, not all of which can be traced in the introduction and notes. It is needless to explain or to apologize for other responsibilities and distractions that have retarded the work on this book. They are well understood by all who know the life of an American university professor.

For such freedom from obvious mistakes as the book can claim, credit belongs in large measure to the close observation and accurate scholarship of Mr. H. C. Youtie, Research Associate in Papyrology in the University of Michigan. He has checked doubtful readings, has read the later proofs and made many valuable suggestions, and has placed at my disposal the results of several special investigations. Had his services been available from the beginning of the work I should have been obliged to disregard his modesty and place his name on the title-page as an equal collaborator.

I owe a great debt to the late Professor Cuthbert H. Turner, who generously provided me with a copy of the text of the Old Latin version as he had provisionally established it from a new study of the manuscripts, and allowed me to cite it in the notes; it should be remembered that his latest views of the text may have changed in some details after he gave me the tentative copy. His friendly interest in my work led him to answer various inquiries with the utmost patience, despite the many calls upon his time and strength. It is a pleasure to recall that I was able to thank him in person for his kindness and to confirm a friendship begun in correspondence. If the text of the Michigan codex enables his literary executor to settle any doubtful points in the Old Latin text, I shall have the satisfaction of indirectly repaying a small part of a great obligation.

Many other scholars have contributed to the progress of this work by their help and advice, and their friendliness has been the greatest compensation for my labor. Mr. H. I. Bell and his associates in the Department of Manuscripts in the British Museum saved me much preliminary labor by preparing the larger fragments for study and locating their position in the text. Before I knew of Professor Turner's undertaking I had thought it necessary to examine certain of the manuscripts of the Old Latin version for myself, and was enabled through the mediation of Sir Frederic Kenyon and the kindness of the Lambeth Palace Library to obtain photographs of the Lambeth manuscript. Professor K. Preisendanz of the Badische Landesbibliothek rendered a similar service in connection with the Carlsruhe manuscript. Professor W. Schubart did me the favor to re-examine one of the Berlin papyri for an important reading and gave me his valuable opinion about the date of the writing of the Michigan codex. At a time when he was a temporary resident of Ann Arbor, Professor Kirsopp Lake aided me in many ways by advice and criticism; and I owe various helpful suggestions to my colleagues H. A. Sanders, J. G. Winter, and W. H. Worrell, and to my former pupils, L. I. Highby and C. E. Demaray. The passage from Grotius which is placed at the beginning of the introduction was brought to my attention by J. E. Dunlap.

For the financial aid which made the publication of this work possible acknowledgments are due to the Dean and the Executive Committee of the Graduate School, to the Institute of Archaeological Research of the University of Michigan, and to the great philanthropic organization which has supported a large part of the Institute's work.

To the Editorial Committee of the *Harvard Theological Review* I am indebted for permission to use again the substance of two articles published in that journal.

A word of special thanks is due to Dr. W. W. Bishop, Librarian of the

University, for providing a place for our papyrological work, for his untiring efforts to provide the necessary books, and for his good offices with other libraries in America and foreign countries.

This volume, like others of the series, has profited greatly by the taste and good judgment of its supervising editor, Dr. E. S. McCartney.

To one other, to whom the date of this foreword is not without meaning, and to whom this book is dedicated, I owe the supreme gratitude that is due to steadfast faith and constant encouragement.

C. B.

ANN ARBOR,
September 29, 1933

CONTENTS

ILLUSTRATIONS

INTRODUCTION

INTRODUCTION

Dixeram ei collegisse me fragmenta Christianorum primi secundique saeculi diligenter. In iis erant et illa ex Epistola Clementis, quae nunc publici est iuris, et alia ex Barnabae Epistola, quam nunc nactus sum prope totam; dixeramque ei quod et tibi dictum volo, magno me ardere desiderio habendi e Graecia Pastorem Hermae, adeo praedicatum iam ab Irenaei temporibus librum. Fragmenta eius quae sunt apud Graecos cum ea quam Latinam habemus versione non male congruere video. Sed ex ipsis Graecis eius saeculi locutionibus multa daretur observare usui futura.

— From Grotius' letter to Peiresc, May 22, 1637

HUGO GROTIUS' hope that the Shepherd of Hermas might be brought to the hands of scholars in its original language was destined to go unfulfilled for more than two centuries after the death of the great jurist; and the satisfaction with which the Greek Hermas was finally welcomed was somewhat abated when the recovered texts were subjected to close scrutiny. The Sinai manuscript contains little more than one fourth of the work, and is not free from serious faults; and the manuscript of Mount Athos, a late and ill-written book, not only lacks some eight chapters at the end, but also falls short in many ways of that accuracy and trustworthiness which are essential for the reconstruction of an ancient work. When compared with the Sinai manuscript, it shows signs of a revision intended to bring its language into closer agreement with the conventional style of the church writers. On the other hand, the translations, especially the Latin versions, show that the Athos text omits a number of sentences and paragraphs, chiefly because of the similarity of their endings to something that precedes. It also presents many readings less acceptable than those which the early translators found in their copies.

It is now too late to expect the discovery of a good and complete manuscript of the Shepherd of Hermas. But hope for new light upon the character and the relative value of the existing sources was encouraged when the village-mounds of Egypt began to yield to the excavator their mutilated but precious treasures of both pagan and Christian literature. The first papyrus fragment of the Shepherd was published in 1891. Since then, from time to time, several other fragments on papyrus and two on vellum have been discovered and published, until now ten manuscripts are represented by these remains.[1] Among them the University of Michigan codex occupies the first place because of its extent. It appears also to be among the oldest of the Hermas papyri hitherto discovered, and its text is certainly one of the best. In this last point the older Berlin fragment (P. Berol. 5513) is its only rival; but the two manuscripts differ so greatly in extent, and overlap in so small a portion of the text, that a comparison of their readings leads to no conclusive results.

HISTORY OF THE MANUSCRIPT

The codex of Hermas was acquired during the year 1922 in two unequal portions. The larger, containing the better preserved leaves, belonged to a lot of papyri purchased jointly by the British Museum and the University of Michigan, which was represented in this transaction by the late Professor Francis W. Kelsey. The leaves of Hermas were bought from a well-known dealer in Cairo, who said, as he was doubtless told by the native from whom he obtained them, that they came from Batn-el-Harit, the ancient Theadelphia. The papyri were divided at the British Museum, and the leaves of Hermas, which were identified at the time of the division as belonging to that author, fell to the share of the University.

Shortly after this another lot of smaller pieces and fragments of papyri was bought for the two coöperating institutions by Dr. D. L. Askren, of Medinet-el-Fayum. When these were examined at the Museum, it was seen at once that some of the pieces were fragments of the Hermas manuscript, and they also were assigned to the University of Michigan. Dr. Askren obtained these fragments from a native of Assiut, a circumstance which might suggest that they came from that part of Egypt, were it not for the well-known migratory habits of Egyptian laborers. As is usual with papyri that are bought, not taken from the ground under the eye of a scientific excavator, it is impossible to be sure where the find was actually made.

The experts of the Department of Manuscripts in the British Museum identified the work and found the places to which all the larger pieces belonged. After the arrival of the manuscript in Ann Arbor the work of placing some small fragments, joining the pieces, and tentatively reconstructing the leaves, was done by me in the Library of the University of Michigan. The pieces were kept in

[1] Eleven, if we count P. Oxy. 5, in which a quotation from Mand. 11 occurs. The Coptic fragments are not included.

folders until repeated readings had settled their position beyond reasonable doubt. They were then mounted between panes of thin glass, labelled, and deposited in the Manuscript Room of the Library with the inventory number 917.

Under this number twenty-six separate mounts are comprised. Of these, Nos. 1 to 6 inclusive contain single leaves. No. 7–8 contains in one mount a small part of each of two separate leaves. Nos. 9 to 14 are sheets or double leaves containing four pages each; in all these cases the two leaves forming the sheet are still attached at the middle. Nos. 15 to 25 are single leaves again, and No. 26 contains four very small unplaced fragments, and two others which may not have belonged to the Hermas manuscript. The unplaced fragments show only two or three letters each, and it will probably never be possible to locate them precisely.

The labels of the mounts are also marked with numbers corresponding to the pages of the manuscript in its present state, that is, without taking account of the leaves lost at the beginning or of two that have disappeared between preserved portions. A table of the mounts and the pages that they contain is given below for the convenience of students who may wish to consult the original pieces.

Mount No.	Pages	Mount No.	Pages
1	1–2	15	29–30
2	3–4	16	31–32
3	5–6	17	45–46
4	7–8	18	47–48
5	9–10	19	49–50
6	11–12	20	51–52
7–8	13–14, 15–16	21	53–54
9	17–18, 43–44	22	55–56
10	19–20, 41–42	23	57–58
11	21–22, 39–40	24	59–60
12	23–24, 37–38	25	61–62
13	25–26, 35–36	26	unplaced and doubtful
14	27–28, 33–34		

CONDITION, EXTENT, AND GENERAL APPEARANCE OF THE MANUSCRIPT

The sheets or double leaves mentioned above (mounts 9 to 14) belonged to the middle of the book, and hence several of their pages are almost uninjured. But one side of every sheet, in most cases the left as it would lie with the book open at the middle, has suffered considerably, so that even in this part of the book some pages are sadly frayed and lacerated. Of the single leaves — half sheets torn from one another at the middle — a few are well preserved, but most of them have considerable portions broken away; and some are reduced to mere fragments of the size of the palm of the hand or even smaller.

The papyrus used was of fine quality, thin and well polished, and it still retains something of its original toughness and pliability. The tendency to crack off in small strips, so marked in some papyri, gives little trouble in handling this manuscript. The difficulties were of another kind. The jagged rents in the material, as well as the tunnellings of larvae, left many irregular projections and thin shreds which were found to have recognizable traces of letters upon very small surfaces. It was necessary to unfold and straighten out such tattered bits, and to estimate with great care the extent of the lost portions of the text; and in view of the discrepancies between the Athos manuscript and the versions, it was often a delicate matter to decide what text was represented by these sparse and dubious indications. I cannot hope that I have chosen rightly in every case; but I have followed the traces faithfully and have submitted all doubtful places to the eyes of other readers. In a few places a later inspector of the manuscript will not find all that I read, for some projecting fibers were broken off in handling. Not all of these could be properly replaced, and one or two were lost. Sometimes the edges of the leaf have been little harmed, but parts of the surface have been so damaged by the scouring action of sand that only a few faint and doubtful vestiges of the writing remain. There are also places where the upper layer of the papyrus has flaked off and taken with it every trace of the text.[1]

The extreme measurements of the double leaves are at present 24.3 cm. in height and 22.2 in breadth. Since all the margins have been broken away to a greater or less extent, the original size is somewhat uncertain; 25 by 22.5 or 23 cm. is a reasonable estimate. Thus the

[1] For the benefit of other readers of papyri it may not be amiss to say that I have found it much easier to determine dubious vestiges of the sort just mentioned if a binocular microscope of low magnifying power be used. Some of our group of readers, who are blessed with very acute vision, at first saw little to be gained by the use of so elaborate an instrument, but repeated experiments have convinced us all of its value. We have used a binocular magnifier with 5× and 10× power. The type that has proved to be most serviceable is mounted upon a jointed arm, which is attached to an upright clamped to the edge of the table. With this arrangement large pieces of papyrus can be moved about under the magnifier without the inconvenience of striking them against the foot of its support. The binocular arrangement relieves the strain upon the eyes which a single lens usually causes, and the enlargement, though unnecessary where the writing is well preserved, enables one to identify beyond doubt many broken bits of letters which would otherwise have to be marked doubtful.

book, when closed, was a tall volume, a little more than twice as high as it was wide. In its proportions it resembled the Washington papyrus codex of the Minor Prophets (published by Sanders in Vol. XXI of *University of Michigan Studies, Humanistic Series*); but that manuscript was a little taller in proportion to its breadth. The magical codices of London (P. Brit. Mus. 46) and Paris (Bibl. Nat. suppl. gr. 574) are examples of books which were still taller in proportion to their breadth. An extreme example of this form is now reported by Sir F. G. Kenyon (*Gnomon*, VIII, 48). A codex of Daniel in the Chester Beatty collection seems to have been almost three times as high as it was wide, the dimensions being estimated at 35 by 12.5 cm. when the book was complete.

The columns of writing vary from 19 to 20 cm. in height and are usually 8 or 9 cm. wide, though some are no more than 7 cm. The space between the two columns on a sheet, which varies from 2 to 3 cm., is rather narrow in view of the circumstance that the book appears, as will be shown later, to have consisted of one very large quire, each successive sheet lying inside the preceding ones.

The scribe's practice was not very regular either in the number of lines allowed for a page or in the number of letters making a line. The commonest page-length is 30 lines; but the number runs as low as 28 and as high as 34, and there are several pages of 31 or 32 lines. The variation in the length of the lines is even greater. Not taking into account several lines which have not been filled out completely, we find that there are lines with as few as 14 letters and as many as 24. The breadth of the columns and the distance between them are not much affected by the lessening of the number of letters in the line; the hand is simply more spreading. The variation in the length of the line considerably increases the difficulty of reconstructing the text when the right margin is broken away. I have been guided by the length of the lines near the passage in question rather than by their general average.

The extent of the book and the manner in which it was put together are learned from the page-numbers and from the direction of the fibers of the leaves. The pages were numbered in the middle of the upper margin by a hand different from that which wrote the text, and certainly later, as will be shown farther on. A few of the numerals have been perfectly preserved, and more or less legible traces of others can be detected. In this edition they are printed above the text of the pages where they occur. With the aid of these numerals, and by allowing for the gaps in the text, it has been possible to determine the numbers of all the pages that have survived. The first of them was 55, the last 120. A leaf containing pp. 61–62 (Similitude 5, 2, 3–8) and another containing pp. 117–118 (Sim. 9, 3, 4 — 4, 4) have been lost. These numbers were as in modern books — the right-hand pages have odd numbers, the left-hand even. At least this is true for the greater part of the extant leaves; an exception which occurs will be considered later.

In discussing the other aid to the reconstruction of the book, namely, the direction of the fibers, it seems advisable to take a hint from Sir Herbert Thompson (in his edition of *The Gospel of St. John according to the Earliest Coptic Manuscript*, 1924). Recognizing that an ambiguity might result from the application of the terms recto and verso to a papyrus codex, he uses H to represent the face of a papyrus leaf which presents fibers running in a horizontal direction and V for the face on which they run vertically. Now all the middle sheets of the Hermas codex, where the leaves are still joined together, show that when the book was closed the V side of each sheet was out, the H side in. This is true also of the midmost sheet of all, in which the two leaves have been torn apart, but in such a manner that the last letter of the last line of the left-hand page (30, counting only those that survive; it ends in Sim. 7, 3) is now on the right-hand piece, thus proving their original unity. (This sheet is contained in Mounts 15 and 16 of the table given above.) On this central sheet H faced H. Up to it the order was VH, VH, after it HV, HV. Further, when the outer single leaves were examined, it was found that the same arrangement applied to all the sheets that they represent — VH up to the middle sheet, then HV. All the extant part of the book, therefore, must have belonged to a single quire, which in order to contain the 62 pages must have had 17 sheets; for, as noted above, two leaves (four pages) are lost within the compass of our portion.

We must next consider the probable extent of the book in its original form. The middle pages of the surviving portion have lost their numerals, but they must at one time have been numbered 86 and 87, for the numerals 88 and 89 are actually preserved on the next two pages. Since the first surviving page (which should have been numbered 55) begins near the end of Sim. 2, 8, it is possible, by using a plain printed text without footnotes, to determine within fairly close limits the position of page 1. From this calculation it appears that the first numbered page must have begun in Mandate 4, probably about the end of the first chapter or early in the second. I do not think that any allowance for error could carry the beginning of the numbered pages farther back than the opening of Mand. 4. But since it is impossible to believe that the book began at that point, it is clear that the first numbered page was not the first page of the entire manuscript; therefore some leaves must have been lost from the beginning of the codex before the pages were numbered. It is probable that the book began with Vision 5, which serves as an introduction to the Mandates and properly belongs to that division of the work. If it did, eleven or twelve pages of the manuscript would have sufficed to contain the part lost before the pages were numbered.

The middle left-hand page of the surviving portion of the manuscript ends, as has been noted above, in Sim. 7, 3, near the end of the section. Now this is almost exactly the middle point of that part of Hermas which is comprehended between the beginning of Vis. 5 and the end of the whole work. Thus the middle point of our quire is probably the middle point of the whole manuscript, a circumstance which makes it likely that the whole manuscript consisted of one very large gathering of double leaves. In such a book any losses which may occur at the beginning are likely to be exactly equalled at the end, for the second half of an outer sheet would scarcely remain in place after the first had been torn away. On this supposition the injured book would have contained, at the time when the pages were numbered, just as many leaves after the middle as before it, and we may calculate that its last numbered page ended somewhere in Sim. 9, 30, since that is about as far from the end of the whole work as page 1 was from the beginning of Vis. 5.

To sum up: at the time of the numbering of the pages, the book probably consisted of a single gathering of 43 sheets, or 172 pages. It had originally contained 6 more sheets, and it is probable that still another was added, outside of them all. This served as a cover to protect the written leaves, and its inner right-hand half would afford a little more room for the writing if it were needed.

It may, perhaps, be suggested that instead of a huge gathering of 49 or 50 sheets, there were three quires of 16, 18, and 16 sheets. On the assumption that the manuscript began with Vis. 5 this would still allow the middle of the surviving portion to be the middle of the whole manuscript. But there is strong evidence, though of a negative kind, against the possibility that the book was made up of several quires, even large ones. If three such quires had been fastened together by horizontal stitches, the perforations should appear opposite one another in the inner margins of the better preserved leaves; but this is not the case. On the other hand, one might suppose that the quires were secured by vertical stitching to a substantial backing or binding; but then some trace of this binding might be expected to survive, which again is not the case. The sheets were certainly stitched, for a small bit of the twine used was found with one of the sheets near the middle, and the stitching was vertical. I submitted the inner sheets to the trained eye of Mr. W. C. Hollands, of the University's printing and binding establishment, and in his judgment there is now evidence of three stitches, since three perforations, irregularly enlarged by wear, appear in the fold of the sheets; and there must have been a fourth, the uppermost, which has disappeared in consequence of the gradual growth of a tear beginning at the top of the fold.

Against the supposition that the book might have been made in 3 large quires is the further circumstance that codices which consist of several quires seem never to have had them so large as to comprise 16 or 18 sheets. The evidence of early parchment manuscripts shows that a quire of 6 sheets was the largest used, and quires of 3, 4, or 5 sheets were more common; see, for example, Sanders's discussion of this subject in his *Old Testament Manuscripts in the Freer Collection*, p. 111 (*University of Michigan Studies, Humanistic Series*, Vol. VIII).

Considerable evidence has accumulated to show that early papyrus books often consisted of surprisingly large single gatherings. Thus P. Oxy. 208, a double leaf from the Gospel of St. John, belonged to a book made up of 25 such sheets in one quire. The Minor Prophets in the Freer Collection (published by Sanders in Vol. XXI of *University of Michigan Studies*) consisted of a quire of 24 sheets. Carl Schmidt's Coptic manuscript of I Clement had 21 sheets and 2 single leaves. The Coptic Gnostic manuscript in the Egyptian Museum in Berlin must have had 36 sheets, and the manuscript of the Proverbs of Solomon in the Staatsbibliothek in Berlin had 41.[1] Still larger single quires are now reported by Kenyon (*The Chester Beatty Biblical Papyri*, General Introd., pp. 7–8). The Beatty codex of Isaiah consisted of a single quire of 112 leaves, and the codex of the Pauline Epistles in the same collection formed a single quire of 104 leaves.

[1] What is here reported about the last two manuscripts, which are still unpublished, I owe to the kindness of Professor Schmidt, who sent this information in a letter to my colleague, Professor Sanders.

The Michigan codex of Hermas is therefore only one, though almost the largest, of several known single-quire books.[1]

It is probable that books made in one large gathering were found to have certain disadvantages; but today we are likely to exaggerate them because we know how inconvenient a modern paper book made thus would be. I have handled a dummy made in the exact measurements of the Hermas codex, with 50 sheets of paper of the thickness of the papyrus loosely sewn together in the same way; and its clumsiness and inconvenience are obvious. It will not remain closed because the tension on the middle of the outer sheets pulls the stiff paper up from the horizontal. But a quire of thin papyrus, soft and almost silk-like in pliability, would be less liable to this fault. Its chief disadvantage would be a slight tendency to bulge near the fold. The behavior of the papyrus would be much more like the soft cotton papers used in China and Japan than like the hard and stiff papers of Europe and America. Nor do I think that one would be greatly incommoded by the bulk of the quire in reading towards the inner margins. Even with so narrow a space as 3 cm. left between the columns, little of it would be taken up by the thickness of the other leaves. It is true that since some part of the width of each outer sheet would be taken up by covering those within it, the front edge of the closed book would be wedge-like, with the thin edge formed by the innermost leaves. It was possible to do away with this objection by gradually diminishing the width of the inner sheets, and Schubart thinks that such measures were sometimes taken, since a gradation in the width of the sheets has been observed in the Pierpont Morgan codex of the *Iliad*.[2] It does not seem very likely that the tedious task of grading down the width of papyrus sheets of a standard size would have commended itself to these early makers of books. Perhaps it was the irregularity of the front edge, as much as anything else, that led to the abandonment of the large gathering in favor of smaller quires of regular size.

[1] The subject of these large single-quire books has been discussed by H. I. Bell, *Early Codices from Egypt*, in *The Library*, N.S., X, 308 f.; by W. Schubart, *Einführung in die Papyruskunde*, p. 55, and *Das Buch bei den Griechen und Römern*², p. 129; by Sir Herbert Thompson, *The Gospel of St. John according to the Earliest Coptic Manuscript*, p. xii; and by H. A. Sanders, *The Minor Prophets*, pp. 7–9.

[2] See Wilamowitz and Plaumann, *Iliaspapyrus P. Morgan*, in *Sitzungsber. der preuss. Akad.*, 1912, p. 1203; Schubart, *Das Buch bei den Griechen und Römern*², p. 129. Sir Herbert Thompson (*l.c.*) surmises, with some reserves, that the leaves of the Coptic Gospel of St. John were thus graded. As to the Hermas codex, it could not be expected that the few inner sheets that are still joined together would reveal this gradation, even if it existed.

Whatever inconveniences were attached to the single-quire book would have been increased by the use of a binding, and it is doubtful whether there was any cover for the written leaves except an extra sheet added over all. The reader of that period may have handled small single-quire books, and perhaps even fairly large ones, as we do a weekly periodical, that is, turning back all the leaves except the one he was actually reading. Such a procedure may easily have been suggested by the way of using a set of wax tablets strung together at their edges.

Various observers have remarked that in writing a single-quire codex the scribe would have to proceed with some care in order to make sure that he was taking enough sheets to come out right at the end of his task. His first page he would write on the right-hand half of the V face of a sheet, then turning it over he would write the second page on the left-hand half of the H face. Then laying the sheet aside, he would take another and write his third and fourth pages in the same manner on the second sheet. Thus he would proceed, using only one half of each sheet — the left as the book would lie open — until he had reached a point which he had previously computed (by counting the columns of a roll or the pages of a codex) to be the middle point, or (as a precaution) one page past the middle, of what he was copying. Then instead of taking a new sheet, he would proceed from his last even-numbered page, i.e., the left half of the H face of the sheet, directly to the right H half of the same sheet, so that H would face H there only; then turn it over and fill the fourth space on that sheet, and so go on to the next outer half-written sheet, using for the latter half of the book the right-hand H face for odd-numbered pages, and the left-hand V face for even-numbered pages. But, when the middle point was reached, unless the scribe was skilful and extremely careful to keep his writing uniform in size and spacing, he might be in danger of spreading the second half of his material over more papyrus than was available on the blank halves of his partly written sheets. If he did so, he would be obliged either to paste in some half sheets at the end or else to use only the right-hand half of some whole sheets, which would then present blank pages at the beginning of the book. To avoid this, a prudent copyist would usually proceed a moderate distance beyond the middle point of the book before he reversed his procedure and began to write HV instead of VH. He would probably have a leaf or two blank at the end of his book with this more cautious method.

To return to the codex of Hermas, it is necessary to comment briefly upon that inconsistency in the page numbering to which I referred above. While the later and larger part of the manuscript is numbered in the same way as modern books, the earliest numerals that are preserved point to another method. One leaf, which in order to harmonize with the later pages should be pp. 59–60, bears the numeral ξ on the right-hand page and ξα on the over-leaf, or left-hand page. This must be an error of some sort; and errors in page numbering are common enough. Two explanations are possible. The first would assume that the writer who numbered the pages started with the right-hand page as 1, made a blunder somewhere before page 60, then somewhere after that point made a second (evidence of which is lost with the destruction of the upper margins), and so came back to the original system. Or it may be that when he began to number the manuscript, not only were several leaves gone, but the first page of the first surviving leaf had been so injured by handling that the writing was illegible; he therefore disregarded this page. In that case his page 1 would have been the first left-hand page of the mutilated codex, and a single error after page 60 would have brought him to the other plan of numbering.

Before leaving this part of the subject, I must revert to the question of the extent of the manuscript. It has been shown to have included the Mandates and the Similitudes, and doubtless what is now called Vision 5 introduced the whole. But the Visions proper (1–4) formed no part of the book. The importance of this fact could not escape anybody who is acquainted with the diverse theories about the composition of the work, and Professor Kirsopp Lake called attention to it in a note in *The Harvard Theological Review*, XVII, 279. This is not the place to consider the views which various students have put forward as to the dates and the relations of different parts of the work; a convenient brief survey of the monographs and shorter papers dealing with the subject will be found in W. J. Wilson's article, "The Career of the Prophet Hermas," in *The Harvard Theological Review*, XX, 33. A considerable number of scholars seem to agree in an opinion which was well stated by P. Baumgärtner in his prize essay *Die Einheit des Hermas-Buchs* (Freiburg i. B., 1889), namely, that the whole book which has come down to us under the name of Hermas is indeed the work of one author, but that it falls naturally into two parts, which may have been composed at different times. These two parts are, first, Vis. 1–4, and second, Vis. 5 to the end, including all the Mandates and Similitudes, to which Vis. 5 serves as an introduction. It is true that all three of the traditional divisions of the work (Visions,

Mandates, Similitudes) were known at an early date, for they are cited by Clement and Origen, who give the title *Shepherd* to the whole, although it seems to have belonged originally and properly only to the second part (i.e., Vis. 5, Mand., Sim.).[1] With Athanasius the case is different. He appears to have no knowledge of the Visions, gives the name *Shepherd* to the part that he does know, namely, the Mandates and Similitudes, and clearly indicates that he considers Mand. 1 to be its beginning. This circumstance does not, in my judgment, oblige us to think that the prelude, Vis. 5, was not in his copy; for in referring to the beginning of the work he would naturally touch upon the important ethical precepts of Mand. 1 rather than upon the narrative of the brief introduction.

There is more than a hint of the twofold and unequal division of the work in the manuscripts themselves. Only the Athos manuscript uses the heading ὅρασις ε̄ and nothing more for the so-called Fifth Vision. The Old Latin version has VISIO QUINTA INITIUM PASTORIS, the Palatine version has INCIPIUNT PASTORIS MANDATA DUODECIM. The Sinaiticus uses the heading ἀποκάλυψις ε̄, which, despite the numeral, seems to recognize a difference between Vis. 5 and the foregoing ones (called ὁράσεις). In the Michigan codex we now have a book, carefully written by a good scribe, which never contained the Visions. It thus confirms the supposition, already probable enough, that the Mandates and Similitudes with their introduction (Vis. 5) circulated in Egypt as a work complete in itself.

In connection with this matter, it may be significant that the smaller fragments of Hermas discovered up to this time are chiefly from the Mandates and Similitudes. Of ten manuscripts that are represented by these fragments, only one, P. Amh. 190 (now in the Morgan Library, New York), has portions of the Visions actually preserved, though the page numbering of two others, P. Oxy. 1172 and 1599, indicates that the codices to which they belonged must have contained the Visions if they were made up of the works of Hermas only. The possibility that they contained selections from various sacred writings cannot, of course, be entirely excluded.

PALAEOGRAPHY, PUNCTUATION, AND ABBREVIATIONS

The whole text of the manuscript is written in one hand, a fairly large, well-formed, moderately sloping uncial of the type which palae-

[1] For the testimonies of the Church Fathers see the edition of Hermas by von Gebhardt and Harnack, Prolegomena, pp. liii–lx.

ographers have somewhat vaguely called oval, because the curves of such letters as epsilon, theta, and sigma are elliptical or oval rather than circular. The writer was evidently an accomplished scribe, but it may be that his skill was acquired in professional letter writing rather than in the copying of books. Certainly his work is even and regular, and lapses into a cursive style only in a few cases when alpha is made without lifting the pen, and is connected with a following iota. I have found no specimen of literary writing that very closely resembles this hand, though it has points of contact with several sloping uncials which competent judges have attributed to the third century; and I can see no decadent tendency in the writing of the Hermas which would justify one in placing it in the fourth century, where a good many coarser and less elegant examples of the sloping uncial may be found.

Schubart shows in his *Palaeographie* (p. 132) that the sloping uncial is a development from his "strenger Stil," that is, the severer type of upright hand current in the second century, and that, in spite of its inclination from the vertical, it continues some of the characteristics of that style. Further, it is certain that the sloping style began some time before the end of the second century. The Michigan Dioscurides, which is an example of the small sloping hand, was probably written before 190 A.D.,[1] and Hunt has placed P. Oxy. 1788 in this period. Among other sloping uncials to which approximate dates may be assigned, two tendencies should be noted. One is represented by P. Oxy. 223 (*Iliad* 5), which almost certainly belongs to the beginning of the third century, for it is on the verso of a document of about 186 A.D., and also by the Berlin *Life of Aesop* (P. Berol. 11628, cf. Schubart's *Palaeographie*, Abb. 89). These are of the "square type," with very broad η, μ, ν, and π, rather sharply angular α and δ, small ο and flat ω placed rather high. The second tendency is seen in P. Berol. 10560 (Hesiod, *Catal.*, not exactly datable but probably early in the third century), and in a less extreme form in P. Brit. Mus. 126 (*Iliad* 2–4, in *Classical Texts*, Plate 6). Here the slant is very great, the long pointed angles of α and δ are exaggerated, and there is a general effect of vertical compression.

From both of these types the hand of the Hermas codex differs considerably, and the difference looks like a slight reaction from the tendencies of the beginning of the third century. While the square letters are still fairly broad, they are less so than in the "square" type, and on the other hand the slant is less extreme and the angles less

[1] See *Transactions of the American Philological Association*, 53, 144 f.

sharp than in the type represented by the Berlin Hesiod. It differs from both types in its freer use of curves, which removes it still further from the severe style; yet it resembles them in using a relatively small omicron and a flat omega, which has only a slight wave in the base and occasionally none at all. Both omicron and omega are set slightly above the base line. Attention may be called to the deeply notched mu and to the beta in which the lower loop is closed by a straight line that is often carried on to the right beyond the descending curve. The scribe often uses a slight hook or starting stroke in making both horizontal and vertical strokes. Other features of the hand may be studied with the aid of the plates.

Whether the change marked by the hand of the Hermas codex be viewed as a reaction or not, it is probable that a considerable period was needed to develop it, and in the absence of definite evidence one could not venture to suggest a date before 250 for it. But it is certain that similar hands were well established in the third quarter of the third century, for a letter written by Timaeus to Heroninus (P. Flor. 259) strongly resembles the handwriting of the Hermas manuscript, although the letter-writer was less careful and regular, and drops into a cursive in the last sentence. The letter is not dated, but since all the Heroninus correspondence seems to fall between the years 253 and 268, its time is fixed approximately.[1] Of course, hands of this sort may have continued in use for some decades, and all that one can say with confidence about the Hermas manuscript is that it was written in the latter half of the third century.[2]

At p. 29, 18, the word *ποιμένα* has been struck out with a horizontal line, and ἄγγελον written above it. Though some letters of both words have been destroyed there is no doubt that the correction is the work of the original scribe. The other sources vary as to this reading, so that it is of some interest. It would seem that the scribe worked with two copies at hand, or else a supervisor who had two or more texts before him directed this change while the scribe was still at work. Something of the same kind has happened at p. 38, 1 and p. 39, 24,

[1] I had noted the letter of Timaeus some time ago as an interesting parallel, and its significant resemblance to the Hermas hand was independently observed by Professor Schubart, to whom I sent a specimen photograph, in a letter written in November, 1929.

[2] From this point on, both in the introduction and in the notes, I have usually referred to readings and special peculiarities of the Michigan papyrus by the pages and lines of the manuscript itself. The extant pages are numbered from 1 on, no account being taken of the leaves lost before the extant portion begins or within its limits. But when there is occasion to refer to a longer passage, and when the reference is not directly concerned with the readings of the papyrus, I follow the ordinary method of reference, i.e. to number, chapter, and section of the Similitudes.

where short slanting lines are used to cancel something that had been written. These cancellings may also be the work of the first hand.

A second hand, probably that of the regular corrector, supplied omitted clauses at p. 34, 24 and p. 41, 3, in the former case wrongly. It is a shaky irregular hand, less sloping in general than that of the first scribe. To this corrector we should probably attribute two deletions (p. 6, 8 and p. 46, 21) made by the conventional dots placed above the cancelled letters, and a minor correction on p. 38, 12; and it is possible that three marginal glosses (pp. 18, 21, and 22 of the papyrus) were written by him also.

After the papyrus had been used a long time and the writing had been dimmed by rubbing here and there, some user of the manuscript retraced a number of letters on certain pages, particularly pp. 40–41; attention is called to the places in the footnotes. This person also wrote a more upright hand than that of the original scribe. Furthermore, some of his letters are so much like those of the "corrector" mentioned in the previous paragraph that one almost suspects that the corrector and the retracer were one and the same person. But a strong argument against their identity is found in such a situation as that described at p. 18, 6 (Sim. 6, 1, 2). Here, above the pronoun *αὐτόν*, the original scribe made a peculiar mark, the purpose of which was to call attention to a note in the margin. Small as the mark is, its general appearance agrees so closely with the first hand that it can scarcely have been written by anybody else. This must mean that the scribe worked from a copy which also had this mark, and probably a note at a corresponding place in the margin. But in our papyrus the gloss itself was written by the second hand. Hence one would expect the corrector to have done his work soon after the scribe had finished the text. On the other hand, the retracer must have come after the manuscript had undergone a long period of hard use; for striking evidence of this see the note on p. 39, 31. After all, the resemblance between the corrector's work and the retraced letters may be due chiefly to the fact that neither writer was practised in book-hands, and hence both show a certain awkwardness which makes their work look alike. I have therefore provisionally distinguished the corrector as the second and the retracer as the third hand. Still another writer or possibly two others may be responsible for the insignificant marginal annotations on pp. 20 and 25; and so far as can be judged from the few numerals that are preserved, the hand that numbered the pages is different from all the others.

The ink used in writing the original text and the passages supplied by the corrector is a good black, which has faded little, though it is often dimmed by abrasion. Some of the marginal notations, especially those last mentioned, are duller, and so also are some of the retraced letters; but the differences are not marked, and may be due to other causes than the quality of the inks.

Of the usual theological abbreviations, θ̅ς̅, θ̅υ̅, θ̅ω̅, θ̅ν̅ and κ̅ς̅, κ̅υ̅, κ̅ω̅, κ̅ν̅, κ̅ε̅ are common. The line above the letters is omitted only by an occasional oversight. π̅ν̅α̅ occurs for both *πνεῦμα* and *πνεύματα*, π̅ν̅ς̅ is found for the genitive (p. 55, 4), and the abbreviated dative certainly occurred, although it happens that the places where it should have stood were destroyed by damage to the papyrus. υ̅ι̅ς̅ is found on p. 39, 17, υ̅ι̅ν̅ on p. 15, 12. The word is written out in full on p. 7, 20 and p. 10, 23; but this is in the body of the parable, before the divinity of the Son has been explained. The shortness of the neighboring lines makes it likely that π̅ρ̅ς̅ rather than *πατρός* stood in the now lost margin of p. 14, 13.

There are several cases where a final *ν* at the end of the line is represented by a short stroke above the preceding vowel.

The high point is the only punctuation. At the ends of the Similitudes and in two other places where there is an important pause (p. 46, 3 and p. 50, 3) there is a sign which may perhaps be called a rather elaborate paragraphos; it is scarcely a coronis. It consists of a slightly sloping down-stroke which then turns to the right in a straight or lightly curved line extending under two or three letters of the text. It is slightly magnified and embellished in the typographical representation used in the printed text. Where this sign is used, the remainder of the line in which the paragraph ends is left blank. Some less important pauses are marked by a short space, from two to five letters, without any other sign. There is such a space at the end of p. 44.

The headings of the Similitudes are in some cases well preserved, in others almost destroyed. They occupy but a line each, with a little more interlinear space than usual above and below. That these headings were intended to refer to the Similitude over which they were placed, and were not subscribed titles, seems to be shown by the use of *ἄλλη παραβολή* in Sim. 4; and *ἄλλη παραβολὴ* ε̄ above Sim. 5 shows that the Similitudes were numbered as in our modern editions. The Hamburg fragment published by Schmidt and Schubart in *Sitzungsberichte der preussischen Akademie*, 1909, has the fifth Similitude numbered as the sixth, and the Coptic fragments published by Leipoldt (*ibid.*, 1903) show that our third Similitude was there numbered fourth. The Ethiopic translation has the same system, calling the eighth Similitude the ninth. Where the false, or at any rate different, division began is not known. But the titles in the Michigan codex show the error of Schmidt and Schubart's conclusion (*l.c.*, p. 1078), that the whole Egyptian tradition followed the higher numbering.

There is no certain case of written accent in the papyrus; attention will be called at the proper place in the notes to a very doubtful instance of the circumflex. The rough breathing (⊢) occurs frequently, but not regularly, with forms of the relative pronoun ὅς and also with εἷς and ἕξ. The utter irregularity of the scribe's habit is illustrated by such cases as p. 54, 6, where εἷς has the rough breathing, but not ἕκαστος, which follows immediately after it. Initial iota usually has two dots above it, and they appear somewhat less frequently over initial upsilon. The scribe writes υϊον and ϋιω in 5, 2, 11. The double dot occasionally stands over iota in the middle of a word, as in συνϊε (p. 12, 26) and αναβεβηκυϊαν (p. 58, 8). Elision occurs frequently, but is frequently neglected, as is the case in the Athos manuscript also.[1] Our scribe even writes οὐδὲ ἕν in two cases where A has οὐδέν (p. 3, 23–24, p. 4, 4). On p. 46, 15 M seems to agree with A in writing οὐδὲ εἷς. The apostrophe is used to mark an elision only twice — p. 52, 3, and p. 61, 14.

Iota adscript does not occur.

Before consonants nu movable is written more frequently than it is omitted; in fact a hasty count shows that it is present more than twice as many times as it is lacking. Before vowels it is very rarely omitted, as on p. 30, 14, and p. 37, 32. οὕτως regularly keeps its ς before vowels, according to the usual practice; the ς is dropped five times before a consonant, in agreement with A, but is kept in four cases where A drops it (p. 10, 5; p. 12, 19; p. 25, 16; p. 27, 28).

In dividing words at the ends of lines the scribe generally follows the same rule as that which is laid down in modern grammars, namely, that any combination of consonants which may begin a word is placed with the following vowel or diphthong. So scrupulous is he in this regard that we have divisions like οὐ|κ οἴδατε (p. 5, 2), πα|ρ᾽ αὐτοῦ (p. 11,

[1] In the following pages it has been found convenient to introduce the symbols for manuscripts and versions which will be used in the notes, as follows: A, the manuscript of Mount Athos; ℵ, the Sinaiticus; M, the Michigan papyrus codex; L^1, the old Latin version, L^2, the Palatine version, LL, the agreement of the two; E, the Ethiopic version; C, the Coptic version.

30). His feeling for the separate existence of the prepositions explains *συν|ίων* (p. 1, 11), *ἐκ|λεξάμενος* and *ἐξ|ελθόντος* (p. 6, 12 and 27), and *σύν|εσιν* (p. 59, 20). He goes contrary to the usual rule in dividing *ἐσ|τιν* once (p. 22, 31), *ἀπενεχ|θῆναι* (p. 61, 22), and *ῥάβ|δος* (in different cases) wherever the word occurs at the end of a line. The form *ζώ|οντος* is peculiar; see the note on p. 20, 7.

Crasis occurs several times, as in *κἄν*, *κἀκεῖ*, *κἀκεῖνοι*, *κἀγώ*, but without any mark to call attention to it.

SPELLING AND GRAMMATICAL FORMS

The orthography of the papyrus is in general very good. The only point in which it frequently departs from the usual standard of the grammars is in the matter of the long iota, for which the scribe writes *ει* so regularly as to suggest deliberate method. Thus we find *γείνομαι*, *γεινώσκω*, *λείαν*, *τειμωρῶ* consistently. But iota alone appears in *ἱμάτιον*, *ἱματισμός*. Examples of *ει* for short *ι* are not numerous, but we find *εἰδέα* (p. 19, 23; p. 21, 16), *λειπ-* in the second aorist of *λείπω* (p. 40, 12 and 16; p. 51, 8), and variation in the second aorist passive stem of *θλίβω*; cf. p. 30, 28 with p. 31, 27 f. The use of *ι* for *ει* is rare; *ἀνδρίως* (p. 15, 5), *ἱστήκει* (p. 33, 10), *ἐπιχείρι* (p. 59, 19), *ἶδον* (p. 61, 19). In *πηχιαῖα* (p. 33, 16) *ι* stands for *υ*.

There is no confusion between *ε* and *αι*. *δερόμενα* (p. 22, 11), which A spells with *αι*, is the better form. The scribe usually distinguishes *ο* and *ω*, but *ἑόρακα* occurs once (p. 33, 20) against three cases of the form in *ω*. In the comparative *ἐλαφρώτερον* (p. 32, 13) *ω* appears where *ο* is the rule. The new Liddell and Scott lexicon cites *ἐλαφρώτερον ἄλγος* from Maximus, 173.

In compounds *ν* is not changed to *γ* before the velar consonants (cf. p. 6, 1; p. 7, 18; p. 8, 5; p. 9, 31; p. 51, 8) or dropped before *σ* (p. 17, 24; p. 51, 21); but it becomes *μ* before the labials in three out of four instances (p. 9, 23; p. 22, 5; p. 59, 28; cf. p. 48, 6).

The manuscript presents, in both forms and constructions, many of the peculiarities which characterize the popular speech of the period. Since, as appears from the foregoing paragraphs, its scribe cannot have been a careless workman, it is probable that many of these features proceed from the author himself; and this would agree with the naïve, unschooled style of his work. These vulgarisms are all the more interesting because many of them are not to be found in the Athous; hence it is clear that the language of Hermas was deliberately corrected at some later period in order to bring it into closer agreement with the usual language of ecclesiastical writings. There is reason to think that a new and thorough study of the language of Hermas would be worth while, especially since the discovery of the papyrus fragments has added materially to our understanding of its character. Such a study has been undertaken by Mr. C. E. Demaray, of Whitman College, and is now nearly completed.

Attention is called in the notes to many of these peculiarities, and references are given to illustrate and explain them; but in view of the approaching completion of Mr. Demaray's study, it would scarcely be worth while to enter here upon a long discussion of the language of Hermas. The purpose of the observations which follow is merely to exhibit some of the more striking points in which the language of M agrees with that of the non-literary papyri and other specimens of popular speech.

The syllabic augment is once omitted in a compound, ἀποτελέσθη (p. 62, 11), and the temporal augment is neglected in ἐνέχθησαν (p. 36, 15). Such forms as εὑρέθησαν (p. 36, 8) are of course to be expected at this time.

In the third person plural of the perfect indicative active, -καν for -κασι occurs several times (p. 31, 5; p. 40, 18–19) along with the older form. In the third person of the imperfect δίδωμι and its compounds use the ending -ουν, although -οσαν occurs once (p. 44, 8–9); but -οσαν does not extend itself to the imperfects and second aorists of other verbs, as sometimes happens in both inscriptions and papyri. The forms ἐδίδει and διδῶν occur on p. 22, 15 and p. 39, 27; but compare δίδωσι (p. 11, 27) and ἐπεδίδου (p. 33, 15). ἀπέθοντο occurs on p. 43, 19. Our scribe uses συνίω rather than συνίημι; compare p. 1, 10 and 12, and p. 12, 26.

In the present system of ἵστημι, the papyrus has the infinitive middle ἱστάνεσθαι (p. 34, 18), but a few lines farther on in the same passage we find ἐστάνοντο in the imperfect middle (p. 34, 22 and 26; p. 35, 1). In the second instance of the imperfect P. Berol. 6789 reads ἱστάνοντο; in the other two cases it gives no evidence because of gaps in the papyrus. So far as I know, ἐστάνοντο is not attested except in the Michigan papyrus. There is evidence elsewhere for the imperfect active ἵστανε in compounds (συνίστανε, Polyb. iv. 8, 2 and καθίστανε, Diod. Sic. xv, 33), and for a form ἔστανε (in a late Attic inscription, Kaibel, *Epigrammata Graeca*, 970, 1). This ἔστανε is probably an imperfect, not an aorist as some have considered it (Kaibel, *l.c.*, and van Herwerden, *Lexicon Suppletorium*, *s.v.* σταίνω). It is perhaps doubtful whether ἐστάνοντο should receive the smooth breathing, after the analogy of the aorist ἔστησα, or whether the analogy of ἱστάνεσθαι would be strong enough to suggest the rough breathing despite the neglect of iota. The former alternative seems to me more likely. It may be that the initial syllable of ἱστάνω was so lightly pronounced that the ordinary speaker was unconscious of a difference between ἱστάνω and στάνω; it would then be as natural for him to write ἐστάνοντο as ἱστάνοντο.

Rarer peculiarities of the common language are to be seen in πρόβασι for προβάτοις (p. 19, 25), ἠκουκώς (p. 11, 10), παθοῦνται as present (p. 53, 18), ἡμίσους ξηρούς for ἡμιξήρους (p. 42, 25).

Late forms of less interest are λήμψονται (regularly), πεφυλακότες (p. 41, 11), μεμαραμμέναι (p. 57, 1), ἀναπαῆναι (p. 62, 18). ἦν for the subjunctive ᾖ occurs at p. 11, 12 and p. 13, 10.

There is much confusion and irregularity in the use of the subjunctive and the future indicative, but nothing that is not well known to students of New Testament grammar. The use of ὅτι as direct interrogative is worth noting (p. 45, 11), and there are indications of a demonstrative use of αὐτός, as on p. 50, 29.

There are not a few cases in which the papyrus follows the classical norms more closely than A does; εὐστάθει stands in p. 22, 16 where A has the late form εὐσταθοῦσαν, and in the notes attention is called to several places in which M has a more normal construction than A.

THE TEXT

The extent of the Michigan codex, taken together with its early date, makes the character of its text a matter of considerable interest; for while the previously published papyrus fragments were obviously of value for the textual study of Hermas, they were so small in proportion to the whole work that they could scarcely justify a cautious student in drawing from them any far-reaching conclusions. One naturally expects much from a manuscript written not more than one hundred and fifty years after the author's death, and containing, even when allowance is made for its numerous lacunae, nearly a fourth of his work. On the other hand, we have learned that the contributions of the papyri are in general not of a kind to upset prevailing views about ancient texts.

The text of the Michigan codex is undoubtedly good in the main. It is true that it has been corrected in only a few places and bears none of the marks of learned editing; but its comparative freedom from gross errors in spelling shows that the scribe was a man of some education. Besides its good orthography its chief excellencies are three. First, the manuscript has preserved most of the sentences that the Athous has omitted in Similitudes 2–8, thus presenting us with a genuine Greek text for a number of passages which previous editors had been obliged to reconstruct from the Latin and Ethiopic versions. Secondly, M differs from A in a great number of readings, and is so clearly right in many of its variants that all of them, except manifest blunders, deserve attention. Since in many of the places where it differs from A, M has the support of one or both of the Latin versions, the discovery of this relation does much to increase the esteem in which they were held, and it may embolden editors of Hermas to use them somewhat more freely in establishing the text of those parts of the work where neither M nor ℵ is available. Finally, it is a noteworthy fact that M, like ℵ and some of the older papyrus fragments, gives a number of vulgar forms in place of which A offers correct ones. The agreement of the older sources in this tendency leads one to believe that A represents a revised text, one that has been accommodated, at least in some obvious details, to the more grammatical language which was used by educated men in the Church. The vulgar tendency of M is to be observed also in some matters of syntax, although A also is by no means free from similar faults. Finally, A is more regular than M in the use of connectives; this seems to show that its text was "improved" in rhetorical style as well as in grammatical forms and syntax. On the whole, M and the other early witnesses bring out much more than A the naïve and popular character of the book.

The really important question about M is its relation not only to A but also to the texts used by the other witnesses — the two Latin versions, the Sahidic, the Ethiopic, the other papyrus and vellum fragments, and the quotations in Antiochus and pseudo-Athanasius. In making these comparisons I have used tables showing the agreements of M with the other sources, which were prepared for me by Mr. H. C. Youtie. These tables confirm, in the main, the impressions which I had formed and jotted down while writing the notes.

The statistics are of course to be used with a certain caution; for doubts cannot fail to arise when the translations are pressed into service, as they must be, since the Greek manuscripts are few and faulty. The differences between the Greek and Latin idioms are wide enough to make the task of retranslation a delicate one. Its perils are clearly seen when one compares the modern reconstructions of the sentences that A lacks with the actual Greek words now supplied by M. It is not easy to be sure just what Greek words are represented by L^1 and L^2; and to decide accurately upon the relations of the two Latin versions to the Greek sources — M, A, the smaller fragments, and the quotations in the Church writers — is a decidedly difficult matter. It has been my aim to refrain from citing the versions whenever the reader could entertain a serious doubt about the Greek text upon which they are based, or at least to call attention to all uncertain cases; but I cannot hope to have avoided all mistakes of judgment. The field of error is especially wide when the Latin idiom involves a change of construction, and in the matter of sentence connection both agreements and differences may be due merely to the translator's notions of style.

The uncertainty which attends the use of the Latin versions is greatly increased when one deals with the unrelated idioms of the Coptic and Ethiopic versions. With regard to the Ethiopic especially I must beg indulgence; for I have had to depend upon d'Abbadie's Latin translation of his Ethiopic text, with occasional help from Professor W. H. Worrell. A special difficulty consists in the fact that the Abyssinian translator has very often abbreviated or paraphrased his original copy, so that his version has to be used more sparingly than the Latin ones.

With these reservations we may now consider some figures. The cases considered are passages, all falling within the portion covered by M, in which at least one of the sources used presents a reading that is clearly different from the others. There are 977 instances all together. M could be used in 959 of these, A in 964, L^1 in 678, L^2 in 633, E in 556. The following percentages of agreement are to be noted, first by pairs:

MA	26.5	AL^1	30	LL	68
ML^1	50	AL^2	41	L^1E	53
ML^2	49	AE	52	L^2E	53
ME	47				

In larger groups the following percentages are obtained:

MLL	35	MAE	20.4	AL^2E	26
ALL	27	ML^1E	27	MALL	8
LLE	38	ML^2E	26	MLLE	18.6
MAL^1	14.5	AL^1E	26	ALLE	17.4
MAL^2	14.7				

The impression derived from these figures is a fairly consistent one. In spite of the fact that the versions could be used in only about two thirds of the cases, M is nearer to all of them than to the Greek text of A. It is most closely akin to the Latin translations, and it is especially worthy of note that the slight difference between the agreements of M with L^1 and with L^2 scarcely justifies us in attributing a general superiority to the older Latin version — always provided that the evidence of M is a satisfactory criterion. Even E, in spite of the translator's vagaries, is oftener found on the side of M than A is. A's closest relation is with E, a point which has often been observed; next most common is its association with L^2. The agreement of M with both Latin versions is quite high; and considering that each added factor lessens the probability of general agreement, the concurrence of MLL in more than one third of the possible cases tells heavily against A. In preparing the notes, I was struck by the combination AL^2E in many interesting readings; but the complete tabulation shows that it is a fraction less frequent than AL^1E.

Thus far the position of M with reference to the other sources seems strikingly analogous to that of ℵ in the parts where that manuscript is preserved. The situation is thus stated by Harmer:[1] "A comparison of the early chapters where the Greek of the Sinaitic MS exists shows us that ℵ generally agrees with L^1L^2 against AE, the close connexion of this latter pair of authorities being noticeable throughout."

The position of the Sahidic version (C) has been reserved for a separate paragraph because the fragments are of such slight extent that only 66 readings could be considered. Any conclusions which may be drawn from them will naturally be received with caution. The following are the percentages of agreement: MC 54.8, AC 37.5, L^1C 49.2, L^2C 50.7, EC 62.5. After all allowances are made, it seems probable that the version was an excellent one, and that it would be very valuable for the constitution of the text had more of it been spared. The close relation of C to E is only to be expected, since the makers of both versions would naturally use copies of the Greek text of the sort current in Egypt. One may fairly safely assign to the Coptic version a position equal or nearly equal to that of the Latin versions and superior to the Ethiopic. Its loss is all the more to be deplored.

The passages in which Antiochus copies Hermas are too few (within the limits of the papyrus) to allow any general conclusions, and it must suffice to refer to the notes on Sim. 5, 3. From pseudo-Athanasius 124 readings were considered, with the following percentages of agree-

[1] *The Apostolic Fathers:* revised texts with short introductions and English translations by J. B. Lightfoot, edited and completed by J. R. Harmer (Macmillan, London, 1912), p. 296.

ment: M Ath^2 19, A Ath^2 48, L^1Ath^2 38, L^2Ath^2 40, E Ath^2 49. The last figure may be somewhat deceptive, since E could not be used as frequently as the Latin versions. But there can be no doubt that the copy from which the quotations in Ath^2 were drawn was closer to A and E than to any other sources; hence there is reason to think that even at that time the text of Hermas had undergone some of the modifications which remove the Athos manuscript so far from the papyrus fragments and the Sinaiticus.

Thus far the method which we have followed, comparing M with each of the other sources and noting the frequency of the agreements, would naturally suggest that this papyrus has a right, by virtue of its age and general excellence, to be taken as a standard of comparison. But of course no such inference can be justified without further examination. An extensive papyrus may prove to have little or no textual value, as, for example, is the case with the Morgan codex of the *Iliad;* and the numerous instances in which papyrus fragments evidently belong to personal copies, carelessly executed and perhaps ignorantly changed, warn us to proceed cautiously. M seems to stand towards the other sources in much the same relation that ℵ does, and this similarity encourages us to set a high value upon the papyrus; but it is possible that if M and ℵ covered the same part of the work important differences would show themselves. To a small extent the text of M can be compared with contemporaneous or nearly contemporaneous Greek sources, namely, the other papyrus fragments; and we shall now examine the results of this comparison, keeping in mind the caution that percentages calculated upon so small a total number of readings are less significant than the figures which we have heretofore considered. With the older Berlin papyrus (5513) M has a percentage of agreement of 66 against A's 31; but many of the cases are mere matters of orthography, and the agreements of M P. Berol. against A in readings that are worthy of note are only slightly more numerous than the agreements of MA against P. Berol. On the other hand, A is supported by P. Berol. against M in only one clear case.

The situation is similar in P. Oxy. 1172. M agrees with this fragment also more closely than A does, and has in common with it (and L^2E) the reading ἀγαθόν at the end of Sim. 2, where P. Berol. and L^1 omit the word. In editing P. Oxy. 1172 Professor Hunt rightly emphasized its near kinship to the old Berlin fragment; and in spite of some variance, it is clear that these two texts belong to one tradition. Certainly the agreement between the two is closer than the relation of either to M, and since P. Berol. 5513 is older than M, one might incline to give it, with its fellow, P. Oxy. 1172, the highest place among extant sources. Yet the readings in which M differs from them do not mark it as an inferior text, and it is safer to regard it as *par inter pares*.

P. Oxy. 1599, apparently of the early fourth century, is not a very good text, since it has some corrupt readings and carelessly omits certain passages. It agrees with M about as often as with A. P. Berol. 6789, attributed by the editors to the sixth century, actually seems nearer to A than to M in the more important cases where variation occurs. The vellum leaf in Hamburg (fourth or fifth century), like P. Oxy. 1599, is scarcely nearer to M than to A. One of its readings, involving the irregular use of the genitive absolute in place of the more grammatical nominative (Sim. 6, 1), is noted by the editors as original, because they thought it improbable that a copyist would make such a change of his own accord, especially a change which is in the careless manner of Hermas himself. Yet M agrees with A in using the normal nominative participle. If we could assume that a scribe's changes would always take the direction of greater attention to grammatical accuracy, the evidence of M in this passage would oblige us to suppose that even in the third century the process of improving the language and style of Hermas had begun — which is not in itself unlikely. But in the face of the quite unsystematic variations with which all our sources confront us, it may be doubted whether such changes as a scribe would make were always from irregular to regular forms or constructions and never the reverse.

Of the Amherst fragments (P. Amh. 190, sixth century), only one, fragment (e), coincides with M, and there is so little text in common that no conclusions of value can be drawn. Nor can anything significant about the value of M be learned from P. Oxy. 1828 (a vellum leaf, probably of the third century), which was recognized as part of Hermas and republished by Mercati (*Biblica,* VI, 336–338). With it the list of fragments which coincide with parts of M comes to an end.

It appears, then, that as regards helping us to a just estimate of M, some of the papyrus fragments give negative results. But let us return to P. Berol. 5513 and P. Oxy. 1172, which are closely related and present a text different from A in many points and certainly better. M overlaps these fragments for only a short space; but, although it cannot be grouped with P. Berol. P. Oxy., it resembles those manuscripts enough to justify us in regarding it, like them, as a popular text of the type current in the third century. Such texts may have been slightly amended in matters of grammar, but they have not been extensively revised by copyists who had in their minds the example of the learned and conventional ecclesiastical style.

In spite of the fact that the Athos manuscript has been modified considerably in the manner just mentioned, there can be no doubt that it alone has preserved the right reading in a goodly number of cases. Furthermore, it has here and there an irregular construction where M has a regular one. A is, therefore, probably derived from a fairly good ancestor of the popular type. Its worst faults are (1) omissions, often due to homoioteleuton, which may have occurred at any stage of its descent, and (2) the tendency to improve the text in various ways, such as by inserting connectives, adopting a more conventional order of words, and occasionally substituting one word for another of similar meaning (e.g. *βεβηλώσωσι* in Sim. 8, 6, 2, where M, and probably the versions, read *βλασφημήσωσιν*).

Some further light is shed upon the history of the A text by three interesting passages in which the text of M has been corrected. Their connection with the question was observed by Mr. H. C. Youtie. The following discussion is based, sometimes even verbally, upon the memoranda which he has generously placed at my disposal.

1. P. 6, 8–9, the first hand of M wrote ἀνήκουσαν τῇ νηστείᾳ, but the words were afterwards deleted. They stand in A, and are translated in all the versions, here including the Coptic.

2. P. 29, 18. ποιμένα ALL: ἄγγελον ME. The first hand of M wrote ποιμένα but cancelled it and wrote ἄγγελον above.

3. P. 38, 1. πειράσωμεν καὶ . . . παραχέειν A, *temptemus et irrigemus* E. The scribe of M wrote πειράσωμεν καὶ . . . παραχέω, but cancelled the syllable μεν. *Temptabo et suffundam* LL.

All the readings thus rejected by M are found in A, which has strong support for the first two. Allowance for casual error may perhaps be made in the last two cases, but scarcely in the first. On the whole it seems likely that the manuscript from which M was copied was more closely related to the primitive A text than was a second manuscript from which M was corrected in a few places. If the scribe himself worked with this second manuscript at his elbow, he may have adopted from it still other readings without betraying his procedure by the change of mind which these examples indicate. Just how far his use of it went is impossible to say.

Another guarantee for the antiquity of a text of the A type is given by the support which the versions lend it in important readings where it varies from M. As early, therefore, as the time when the Old Latin translation was made, and as early as the time when M was written, a text of the A type must have been current; but, if this view be correct, it was a primitive A text without those attempts at refinement which have been so often mentioned, and which we may safely assume to have been due to later handling of the text.

Since the writer of M must have used two manuscripts, and may have had more for all we know, it is only natural to suppose that the makers of the versions also used more than one exemplar. We need not impute to the translators any very high conception of their tasks. They may not have set to work with any notion of "diligently comparing" the existing texts. The fact that any papyrus text was likely to have omitted some words or phrases and to have some places where the writing was illegible or torn away was enough to suggest to them the expediency of having two or more copies at hand. If one copy was more clearly written than the others, an uncritical worker would be likely to follow it in the main. If there was little difference in the legibility of the manuscripts, his first choice among them might be little more than a matter of chance. He would probably work with his first copy until he came to a torn or illegible passage, then change to another manuscript and translate from it until he encountered a fresh difficulty.

Under such circumstances it is not surprising that the various versions agree first with one and then with another of the Greek sources, and that sometimes they draw upon a source different from all the extant Greek sources, but not inferior to them. Although certain relationships seem to be clearly established, there is no regularity, no constant community of readings which would permit us to construct a satisfactory stemma. Every possible combination of the authorities, in pairs and in larger groups, is to be found; and in the case of the Palatine version the problem of the underlying text is made harder because of the virtual certainty that the translator had before him the already existing Old Latin version. This opinion is now generally held and need not be discussed at length; but a striking example may be cited. In Sim. 8, 7, 2 M reads *οὗτοι δίψυχοί εἰσι καὶ κατάλαλοι*, A *οὗτοι καὶ δίψυχοι καὶ κατάλαλοί εἰσι*. Here L^1 has *hi . . . et dubii sunt et maledici*, but adds immediately afterwards *de absentibus detrahentes*, which is merely a further explanation of *maledici*, and represents nothing in the Greek text. L^2 has omitted the first part of the sentence, a mistake due to its resemblance to the foregoing section (1), and proceeds, after the closing words of 1, *nec vivi nec mortui sunt*, with *de absentibus enim detrahebant*, thus keeping only the words with which L¹ glossed *καταλαλοι*. Such a situation can be explained only by the assumption of deliberate borrowing from the older version.

From what has been said thus far, it is sufficiently clear that an editor of Hermas is not richly endowed with resources for constituting a text. The merits of ℵ and M justify him in using them as bases for the parts which they cover, but even there they are by no means always to be preferred to A. Other papyrus fragments contribute readings of importance, and since the texts used by the various translators are not to be identified with any Greek texts now extant, it is necessary to consider the versions at every point, all the more because here and there one of them has preserved a text which is better than any other.

In short, the procedure must be eclectic — a word of fear, it may be, to textual critics of the older school, but no longer an offense to those who have studied the papyrus fragments of extant classical authors and considered such papers as (to go no farther) those in which Professor Hunt and the late Professor Grenfell have discussed the relations of the papyri to the textual study of the Greek writers.[1]

In the case of Hermas there is all the more reason to adopt an eclectic procedure, because it is doubtful whether there ever was an authoritative text after the writer's autograph copy had perished. Absolute fidelity in copying such a writer probably did not seem to those who came after him to be an imperative duty; and the decided probability that the first copies were private ones made by ordinary persons, not by trained scribes, makes it still more natural that some laxity should result. With those authors whose works required accurate transmission in order to preserve essentials of their form or contents — their verse, their rhetorical cadences, their exposition of historical events or philosophic arguments — the case was very different. But when it was a question of a homely work dealing through allegories and precepts with the problems and duties of the Christian life, what reason have we to think that an early copyist would have felt himself bound to follow the exact turn of the author's expression? One may imagine such a scribe, even an imperfectly educated one, thinking to himself, as he wrote down the artless words of Hermas,

[1] A. S. Hunt in *The Journal of Egyption Archaeology*, I (1914), 81–92; B. P. Grenfell, *Journal of Hellenic Studies*, XXXIX (1919), 16–36. In a valuable paper in *Revue des Études grecques*, XLII (1929), 255–287, P. Collomp has protested against a certain careless use of the word eclecticism with reference to the papyri, and has done much to clarify our ideas of the various possible relations of papyrus texts to those which have come down to us in mediaeval manuscripts.

"Our pious brother has left us a work which is well fitted to build up the Christian virtues; but his language and style fall far below the elegance which now marks the doctors of the Church. Surely to improve the connection of these awkward sentences, to put the right word for a wrong one, to amend a vulgar form here and there, is only a service to the book and to the memory of him who wrote it." Certain it is that, whether with conscious purpose or not, divers scribes introduced many slight changes, rarely, if ever, seriously modifying the thought and purpose of the author. How far a similar procedure, prompted by similar motives, may account for variant readings in those writings which became permanent parts of the canon of Scripture is an interesting question, but one which does not concern us here.

THE PLAN OF THIS EDITION

In printing the text, the actual appearance of the papyrus has been reproduced as far as possible. The words have been separated, but the text has been divided into lines as in the manuscript, and the abbreviations, which are of the kind employed in ecclesiastical writings, have been retained. Breathings, apostrophes, marks of punctuation, and other signs are shown when, and only when, they appear in the papyrus. Second thoughts suggest that fidelity to the actual appearance of the papyrus has been carried farther than was desirable in one respect, namely, the typographical imitation of a few interlinear corrections and marginal glosses; but it was not practicable to change these details after the pages had been set up. The notes should make the situation clear in every case.

Gaps in the writing are filled, as a rule, from the text of Gebhardt and Harnack; but there are numerous exceptions. For the leaves still preserved in the convent of Saint Gregory on Mount Athos, Lake's photographic facsimile has been used instead of the readings reported by Gebhardt and Harnack from the copy made by Simonides; and in several places the discovery of new fragments since the publication of their work has recommended readings different from theirs. In other cases still, the choice of a reading to fill a lacuna has been determined by the available space or by the neighboring context. The scribe's habits with regard to spelling and abbreviation have also been taken into account.

Consistency in the matter of doubtful letters is not easy to maintain. When a characteristic part of a broken letter can be read, the letter is printed as if it were perfect. This is also done when a trace, although capable of forming a part of various letters, is consistent with a letter required by the context; for when the neighboring letters leave no doubt as to what must have been written, it is useless to disfigure the page with signs that only call attention to the damaged condition of the writing without suggesting a different reading. In this text a dot under a letter indicates one of two things: either the remaining trace is very small or, as sometimes happens, capable of being interpreted as a casual stain or ink spot; or else another letter could be read and give a tolerable text.

The pages of the papyrus are numbered in order without taking account of losses, and these numbers, with the numbers of the lines, appear in the left-hand margin of the printed text. In the right-hand margin are the numbers of the Similitudes and their chapters and sections. Such numerals as have survived from the ancient numbering of the pages are printed above the point where the page of the papyrus begins.

The notes are meant to serve several purposes. First, and most important, to make the actual state of the papyrus clear, and in case of doubt, to explain why one reading rather than another has been printed. Secondly, to show the relation of the papyrus text to that known from the other sources, and to draw such conclusions as the facts seemed to warrant regarding the position of this manuscript in the tradition. Thirdly, to call attention to orthographic and grammatical peculiarities and illustrate them by examples drawn from other sources. Certain passages have been treated more diffusely than may seem appropriate to the character of footnotes. It is hoped, however, that the material offered will not be useless. Students of Hermas in other countries than this may find the complete information about difficult passages especially serviceable because the papyrus is not easily accessible to them.

LIST OF WORKS CITED IN THE NOTES

I. Hermas

A. The Greek Text (Except Fragments)

Gebhardt, O. von, Harnack, A., and Zahn, T., Patrum apostolicorum opera, editio post Dresselianam alteram tertia. Fasc. III: Hermae Pastor graece, addita versione latina recentiore e codice Palatino. Recensuerunt et illustraverunt O. de Gebhardt et Adolphus Harnack. Lipsiae, 1877.

Cited as G.-H. Several emendations recorded in this edition are mentioned without reference to the place of their original publication.

—— Patrum apostolicorum opera, editio quinta minor. Lipsiae, 1906.

Hollenberg, W., Hermae Pastorem emendavit, indicem verborum addidit G. H. Saarbrücken, 1868.

Lake, Kirsopp, Facsimiles of the Athos Fragments of the Shepherd of Hermas. Oxford, 1907.

—— Codex Sinaiticus Petropolitanus. The New Testament, the Epistle of Barnabas, and the Shepherd of Hermas, preserved in the Imperial Library in St. Petersburg, now reproduced in facsimile from photographs by Helen and Kirsopp Lake. With a description and introduction to the history of the codex by Kirsopp Lake. Oxford, 1911.

—— The Apostolic Fathers, with an English translation by Kirsopp Lake. Vol. II, the Shepherd of Hermas, etc. London and New York (Loeb Classical Library), 1917.

Lightfoot, J. B., The Apostolic Fathers. Revised texts with short introductions and English translations, by the late J. B. Lightfoot . . . edited and completed by J. R. Harmer. London, 1912.

B. FRAGMENTS OF THE GREEK TEXT ON PAPYRUS OR VELLUM

Bonner, Campbell, A Papyrus Codex of the Shepherd of Hermas. The Harvard Theological Review, XVIII (1925), 115–127.

Diels, H., and Harnack, A., Über einem Berliner Papyrus des Pastor Hermae. Sitzungsberichte der preussischen Akademie der Wissenschaften zu Berlin, 1891, erster Halbband, 427–431. P. 5513, Sim. 2, 7–10 and 4, 2–5.

Grenfell, B. P., and Hunt, A. S., The Amherst Papyri, II. London, 1901. No. 190. Sim. 9, 2, 1–5.

—— The Oxyrhynchus Papyri, XIII. London, 1919. No. 1599. Sim. 8, 6, 4 — 8, 3.

—— The Oxyrhynchus Papyri, XV. London, 1922. No. 1828. Vellum. Sim. 6, 5, 3 and 5.

Hunt, A. S., The Oxyrhynchus Papyri, IX. London, 1912. No. 1172. Sim. 2, 4–10.

Mercati, S. G., Passo del Pastore di Erma riconosciuto nel pap. Oxy. 1828. Biblica, VI (1925), 336–338.

Schmidt, C., and Schubart, W., Fragment des Pastor Hermae aus der Hamburger Stadtbibliothek. Sitzungsberichte der preussischen Akademie der Wissenschaften zu Berlin, 1909, erster Halbband, 1077–1081. Vellum. Sim. 4, 6 — 5, 5.

—— Berliner Klassikertexte, VI: Altchristliche Texte. II, Der Hirt von Hermas. Berlin, 1910. No. 5513 (Sim. 2, 7–10 and 4, 2–5) and No. 6789 (Sim. 8, 1, 1–12).

C. THE LATIN VERSIONS

Dressel, A. R. M., Patrum Apostolicorum Opera . . . recensuit atque emendavit . . . Albertus Rud. Max. Dressel. Editio altera aucta supplementis ad Barnabae epistolam et Hermae Pastorem ex Tischendorfiana codicis Sinaitici editione haustis. Lipsiae, 1863. Both versions.

Funk, F. X., Zur Versio Palatina des Pastor Hermä. Zeitschrift für die österreichischen Gymnasien, XXXVI (1885), Heft 4, 245–249.

Gebhardt, O. von, and Harnack, A., as above. The Palatine version is given in full, facing the Greek text. The Old Latin version is cited in the critical apparatus, and given in full where the Greek is lost.

Hilgenfeld, A., Hermae Pastor. Veterem Latinam interpretationem e codicibus edidit Adolphus Hilgenfeld. Lipsiae, 1873.

[Turner, C. H., Typescript of a tentative text of the Old Latin version, established on the basis of a new study of the manuscripts by the late Professor Cuthbert H. Turner; given by him to the editor for comparison with the text of the Michigan papyrus codex. Covers only Sim. 2, 8 — 9, 5, 1.]

D. THE COPTIC VERSION (FRAGMENTS APPARENTLY BELONGING TO ONE MANUSCRIPT)

Delaporte, Louis. Le Pasteur d'Hermas. Fragments de la version copte-sahidique. Revue de l'Orient chrétien, X (1905), 424–433. Sim. 2, 7 — 3, 3; 4 (end) — 5, 2, 1.

—— Le Pasteur d'Hermas. Nouveaux fragments sahidiques. *Ibid.*, deuxième série. I (XI, 1906), 301–311. Mand. 12, 3, 4 — 4, 4; Sim. 6, 2, 1–7; Sim. 8, 10, 3 — 11, 5.

Leipoldt, Johannes, Der Hirt des Hermas in saïdischer Übersetzung. Sitzungsberichte der preussischen Akademie der Wissenschaften zu Berlin, 1903, erster Halbband, 261–268. Mand. 12, 3, 4 — 4, 4; Sim. 2, 7 — 3, 3; Sim. 9, 5, 1 — 6, 1.

—— Ein neues saïdisches Bruchstück des Hermasbuches. Zeitschrift für ägyptische Sprache und Altertumskunde, XLVI (1909–10), 137–139. Sim. 9, 2, 7 — 4, 2.

E. THE ETHIOPIC VERSION

D'Abbadie, Antonius, Hermae Pastor. Aethiopice primum edidit et aethiopica latine vertit A. D'A. Abhandlungen für die Kunde des Morgenlandes, herausg. von der Deutschen Morgenländischen Gesellschaft, II, No. 1. Leipzig, 1860.

F. EXEGETICAL

Dibelius, Martin, Der Hirt des Hermas. Handbuch zum Neuen Testament, herausg. von Hans Lietzmann. Ergänzungsband: Die apostolischen Väter IV. Tübingen, 1923.

Zahn, Theodor. Der Hirt des Hermas. Gotha, 1868.

II. Other Ancient Authors

Antiochus Laurae Sancti Sabae monachus, Pandectes scripturae divinitus inspiratae. Migne, J.-P., Patrologiae cursus completus. Series Graeca LXXXIX. Paris, 1865.

Athanasii Alexandrini Praecepta ad Antiochum ad codices duos recensuit Guilielmus Dindorfius. Lipsiae, 1857.

S. Marci monachi et eremitae opuscula. Migne, J.-P., Patrologiae cursus completus. Series Graeca, LXV. Paris, 1864.

III. Inscriptions

Dittenberger, Wilhelm, Orientis Graeci inscriptiones selectae. Leipzig, 1903–5. 2 volumes.

—— Sylloge inscriptionum Graecarum[4]. Leipzig, 1915–24. 4 volumes.

Kaibel, Georg, Epigrammata Graeca ex lapidibus conlecta. Berlin, 1878.

IV. Grammars and Lexicons

ΑΡΚΑΔΙΟΥ ΠΕΡΙ ΤΟΝΩΝ, ed. E. H. Barker. Lipsiae, 1820.

Bauer, Walter, Griechisch-deutsches Wörterbuch zu den Schriften des Neuen Testaments und der übrigen urchristlichen Literatur. Zweite, völlig neu gearbeitete Auflage zu Erwin Preuschens Vollständigem griechisch-deutschem Handwörterbuch zu den Schriften des Neuen Testaments und der übrigen urchristlichen Literatur. Giessen, 1928.

Cadbury, H. J., Lexical Notes on Luke–Acts. I. Journal of Biblical Literature, XLIV (1925), 214–227.

Crönert, Wilhelm, Memoria Graeca Herculanensis. Lipsiae, 1903.

Debrunner, Albert, Friedrich Blass' Grammatik des neutestamentlichen Griechisch. Fifth edition. Göttingen, 1921.

Hatzidakis, G. N., Einleitung in die neugriechische Grammatik. Bibliothek indogermanischer Grammatiken, V. Leipzig, 1892.

Herwerden, Henricus van, Lexicon Graecum suppletorium et dialecticum. Editio altera. 2 volumes. Leyden, 1910.

Hilgard, Alfred, Grammatici Graeci, IV: Georgii Choerobosci Scholia, 2 pts. Leipzig, 1889, 1894.

Horn, R. C., The Subjunctive ἦν in the Papyri. Transactions and Proceedings of the American Philological Association, LIII (1922), xx.

Jannaris, A. N., An Historical Greek Grammar. London, 1897.

Johannessohn, Martin, Der Gebrauch der Präpositionen in der Septuagint. Nachrichten von der Gesellschaft der Wissenschaften zu Göttingen. Philologisch-historische Klasse, 1925, Beiheft.

Kuhring, Walter F. A., De praepositionum Graecarum in chartis Aegyptiis usu. Bonn, 1906.

Mayser, Edwin, Grammatik der griechischen Papyri aus der Ptolemäerzeit. 2 volumes. Leipzig, 1906, 1926–33.

Moulton, J. H., A Grammar of New Testament Greek. Third edition. 2 volumes. Edinburgh, 1908–19.

Moulton, J. H., and Milligan, G., The Vocabulary of the Greek Testament illustrated from the Papyri and other Non-literary Sources. 8 parts. London, 1915–29.

Preisigke, Friedrich, Wörterbuch der griechischen Papyrusurkunden, mit Einschluss der griechischen Inschriften, Aufschriften, Ostraka, Mumienschilder, usw. aus Ägypten. 3 volumes. Berlin, 1925–31.

Preuschen, Erwin, see Bauer, Walter.

Radermacher, Ludwig, Neutestamentliche Grammatik. Handbuch zum Neuen Testament, herausg. von Hans Lietzmann. I. Second edition. Tübingen, 1925.

Reinhold, Henricus, De Graecitate patrum apostolicorum librorumque apocryphorum Novi Testamenti quaestiones grammaticae. Dissertationes philologicae Halenses, XIV (1898).

Robertson, A. T., A Grammar of the New Testament in the Light of Historical Research. New York, 1914. (Fourth edition, 1923.)

SYMBOLS AND ABBREVIATIONS

A	Codex Athous. The manuscript of Mt. Athos (6 leaves still in the convent of St. Gregory, 3 in the library of the University of Leipzig).
א	Codex Sinaiticus (Leningrad).
M	The Michigan papyrus codex.
L^1	The Old Latin version.
L^2	The Palatine Latin version.
LL	Agreement of the two Latin versions.
C	The Coptic version.
E	The Ethiopic version.
Ath^2	The text of excerpts from Hermas contained in the second (Paris. 635) of Dindorf's two manuscripts of Pseudo-Athanasius, Praecepta ad Antiochum; see "List of Works Cited."
Ant.	The text of excerpts from Hermas in Antiochus, Pandectes; see "List of Works Cited."
BGU	Berliner Griechische Urkunden.
J. H. S.	Journal of Hellenic Studies.
P. Berol.	The text of that one of the two Berlin fragments which covers the passage at which the symbol is used; for their extent see "List of Works Cited," under Schmidt and Schubart, Berliner Klassikertexte, VI.
P. Oxy.	The Oxyrhynchus Papyri, edited by Grenfell and Hunt, Volumes I–XVII. Cited by the numbers of the papyri. But, in the footnotes to the text of this volume, " POx " without a number is used for the sake of brevity to indicate the text of that one of the Oxyrhynchus fragments of Hermas which covers the passage at which the symbol is used. For the extent of the various fragments see "List of Works Cited."
Hamb.	The Hamburg vellum fragment.
G.–H.	The larger edition of Hermas in Gebhardt, Harnack and Zahn's Patrum apostolicorum opera; see "List of Works Cited."

THE SHEPHERD OF HERMAS

THE SHEPHERD OF HERMAS

P. Mich. 129
Inv. 917

p. 1 Sim. II

[σιοι χ]ορηγου[ν]τες τοις πεν̣η 8
[σι τα] δεοντα πληροφορουσι
[τας ψ]υχας α̣υ̣των γεινοντα[ι 9
[ου]ν αμφο[τερ]ο̣[ι] κοινωνοι του
[ερ]γου του δ[ικα]ιου ταυτα ουν
[ο π]οι̣ων [ου]κ [εν]κ̣αταλειφθη
[σετ]αι υπο τ̣[ου θ̅υ̅] αλλα εσται
[ενγ]ε̣[γ]ραμμε̣[νος ει]ς τας βυβλους
[των ζ]ων[των] μακαριοι οι εχον 10
[τες κα]ι συ[νιον]τ̣ες οτι απο τ̣ου
[κ̅υ̅] πλουτ̣[ιζοντα]ι ο γαρ συν
[ιω]ν τουτ[ο] δ̣υ̣νησεται δια
[κ]ονησαι τ[ι α]γαθον·

παραβ[ο]λ̣η γ̅ Sim. III

[ε]δειξε μοι δ[ε]νδρα πολ̣λα [μ]η 1
[εχ̣]ο̣ντα φυλ̣[λ]α̣ [α]λ̣λα ωσει ξ̣[η

P. 1. 1 σιοιχ fills the space better than επιχ. χορηγοῦντες PBerol A: ἐπιχορηγοῦντες POx.

4–5 τοῦ ἔργου τοῦ δικαίου MPBerol POx AL²C: *operibus bonis* L¹, *operibus iustitiae* E.

7 ὑπό MPBerol POx: ἀπό A, which Hollenberg had emended to ὑπό. ἀλλ' A.

8 The space before ε is not enough for επιγ but is more than enough for γ alone. γεγραμμένος PBerol and probably POx, ἐπιγεγραμμένος A: L¹ *scriptus* L² *inscripti*. The usage of Hermas elsewhere favors the reading of M; cf. examples of ἐγγράφω in Vis. *1*, 3, 2, Mand. *8*, 6, Sim. *5*, 3, 2, *9*, 24, 4. He uses neither ἐπιγράφω nor γράφω εἴς τι elsewhere.

9 ζώντων is the reading of all the Greek texts and of L²CE: L¹ has *vitae*.

10 παρά PBerol POx A.

11–13 A omits ὁ γὰρ . . . ἀγαθόν.

12 PBerol POx have καί before διακονῆσαι, but the versions take no account of it.

13 τι PBerol POxLL: τό C. τά, probably an error for τό, was written by the first hand of POx. — ἀγαθόν MPOx L²CE: PBerol L¹ omit.

14 ἀρχὴ ἄλλης παραβολῆς A, *III. alia similitudo* L¹, *explicit similitudo secunda, incipit III* L²: no heading in E.

15 πολλά om. L²: *bonas multas* E. — E omits μή.

16 ἀλλ' A.

[ρα] εδοκει μ[οι ειν]αι ομοια
[γα]ρ ην παν[τα λ]εγει μοι β[λε
[π]εις φησι τα [δε]νδρα ταυ[τα
[βλ]επω φημι κ̅ε̅ ομοια οντ[α
[και ξ]ηρα· αποκριθεις μοι λ[ε
[γει τ]αυτα τα δενδρα α βλε
[π]εις οι κατοικουντες εισιν
[ε]ν τω αιωνι τ[ο]υτω δια τι 2
φημι ουν κ̅ε̅ ωσει ξηρα και
[ο]μοια εστιν· οτι φησιν ου
τε ο[ι] δικαιοι φα[ι]νονται ου
[τ]ε οι αμαρτωλοι [α]λλα ομο[ι]οι
[ε]ισιν ο γαρ αιω[ν ο]υ[τ]ος δικαι
[ο]ις χειμων εστιν και ου φαι

p. 2

νονται μετα των αμ[αρτω
λων κατοικουντες [ωσπερ 3
γαρ τω χειμωνι τα [δ]εν[δρα
αποβεβληκοτα τα φυλ[λα
ομοια εσ[τ]ιν και ου φα[ινε
ται τα ξη[ρ]α π[οι]α εστι[ν η τα
ζωντα [ουτ]ως εν τω α[ιωνι
τουτω ο[υ φα]ινον[ται ουτε
οι δικαιοι [ου]τε οι α[μαρτω
λοι·

18 καὶ λέγει ALL: C omits καί (with M).

19 φησί MLL: om. A.

20 *similes aridae* L^1 (v. l. *quod similes sunt aridis*).

21 *et dixit mihi* L^2, *et respondit et dixit mihi* E.

23 πάντες οἱ κατοικοῦντες C.

25 οὖν φημί A.

26 εἰσι (after ξηρά) A.

28 After ἁμαρτωλοί A and L^2 read ἐν τῷ αἰῶνι τούτῳ, and something of the sort underlies the version of L^1, *similes sunt huic seculo.* The words are omitted by C and E; but the Ethiopic translator has abbreviated this similitude to such an extent that his testimony is of uncertain value.

29 τοῖς δικαίοις A.

P. 2. 3 ἐν τῷ χειμῶνι A.

5 εἰσι and φαίνονται A.

6 εἰσιν A.

7 οὕτως καί LLC.

10 All other authorities (ALLCE) add ἀλλὰ πάντες ὅμοιοί εἰσιν.

αλλη παραβολη [Sim. IV
εδειξε μοι παλιν δενδ[ρα 1
πολλα α μεν βλαστωντ[α
α δε ξηρα λεγει μοι βλεπ[εις
φησι τα δενδρα ταυτα [βλε
πω φημι κ̅ε̅ α μεν βλασ[των
τα α δε ξηρα ταυτα φη[σι 2
τα δενδ[ρ]α τα βλαστω[ντα
ο[ι] δικα[ι]οι εισιν οι μελ[λον
τες κατ[ο]ικει[ν] εις τον [αιω
να τον ερχομενον ο [γαρ αι
ων ο ερχομενος θερ[ει]α
εστιν τ[ο]ις δικαιο⟨ι⟩ς τοις [δε
αμαρτωλοις χειμων οτ[αν
ουν επιλαμψη το ελεος
του κ̅υ̅ τοτε φανεροι ε[σ]ον
ται οι δουλευοντες [τω] θ̅ω̅
και πασι φανεροποιηθησο[ν
ται ωσπερ γαρ τη θερεια 3
ενος εκαστου δενδρου
οι καρποι φανερουνται [και

p. 3

επιγεινω[σκονται] ποιοι
τ[ι]νες εστιν ουτ[ως κ]αι των

11 It is uncertain whether a numeral followed παραβολή or not. ἀρχὴ ἄλλης παραβολῆς A, *IIII. alia similitudo* L[1], *explicit similitudo III, incipit similitudo IIII* L[2]: no heading in E.

14 καὶ λέγει ALLE.

16–17 τὰ μὲν . . . τὰ δέ A; cf. 13–14.

22 θερεία MPBerol LLE (*aestas*): θρόνος (error for θέρος) A.

26 φανερωθήσονται A: *declarabuntur* LL, *dignoscentur* E.

27 The last two letters are very doubtful. Of the two remaining traces the first seems to be the end of the extended horizontal stroke of θ, which in this papyrus often crosses the right side of the oval; the second is the beginning of ω. κω is not, however, impossible. ALL have θεῷ, E κυρίῳ.

28 πάντες φανερωθήσονται A. The versions support M's reading πᾶσι: L[1] *omnibus perspicui erunt* (with a variant *omnes*), L[2] *omnibus palam fient*, E *omnes cognoscent eos*. The Berlin papyrus, which here offers only the first few letters of a column, gives no evidence as to the variants in 26–28. φανεροποιεῖν is not found elsewhere in Hermas; it occurs, however, in 1 Clem. 60, 1.

29 τῷ θέρει A.

P. 3. 1–3 ποταποί εἰσιν A. Although the lacuna in l. 1 of M is long enough to

[δ]ικαιων οι καρποι φανεροι
[εσο]ντα[ι] και γνωσθησονται
παντ[ες ε]υθαλεις οντες εν τω
αιωνι [εκει]νω τα δε εθνη και 4
οι αμαρ[τωλο]ι ἁ ειδες τα δεν
δρα τα ξη[ρα τοιο]υτοι ευρε
θησονται ξηρ[οι] και ακαρποι
εν εκεινω τω αιω[νι κα]ι ως ξη
ρα ξυλα κατακαυθ[ησ]ονται
και αφανεροι εσονται οτι η

accommodate as many as nine letters, there is little doubt that the restoration above is right. ποῖοι is almost certain. ὁποῖοι would help to fill out the superfluous space, but this pronoun occurs but once in Hermas (Mand. *11*, 15), while ποῖος is found twelve times without including this passage.

L[2] has *qualis unusquisque est*, which rests upon a text similar to that of M, the translator taking τινες distributively. L[1] reads *declaratur et paret*, omitting the dependent relative clause. E translates ἐπιγινώσκονται (not φανεροῦνται) and omits the dependent clause. The Berlin papyrus also omits φανεροῦνται καί. It could have accommodated either ποῖοί τινες or ποταποί, but only the first π remains. — οὕτω A.

5 The papyrus gives no sign that anything has been lost here. Some critics, however, following certain indications in the Latin versions, have assumed that a few words have dropped out; so G.-H. L[2] has *omnesque parebunt laetantes, qui minimi erant, in seculo isto*, whence Harmer supplies, after πάντες, οἱ ἐλάχιστοι ὄντες. L[1] *et parebunt omnes hilares et gaudentes in illo saeculo restituentur*. A has πάντες οἱ and repeats εὐθαλεῖς ὄντες. καὶ ἐν PBerol.

7 M confirms ἅ of A against οἷα, the conjecture of Hilgenfeld and M. Schmidt, which Harmer adopted. E seems to agree with M: LL *sicut*.

10–11 The reading ξηρὰ ξύλα is supported by LLE, and ξηρά may have stood in PBerol also, since in that text the line is unusually short without it. The agreement of the versions in ξηρά was overlooked by G.-H. A omits ξηρά.

12 φανεροὶ ἔσονται ὅτι A, *et palam fient quoniam* L[1], *et manifestabuntur quoniam* L[2].

M is without support in its reading ἀφάνεροι. If ἀφάνεροι ἔσονται can be regarded as a slovenly equivalent for ἀφανεῖς γενήσονται or ἀφανισθήσονται, one is strongly tempted to accept the unsupported ἀφάνεροι as the right reading; for annihilation is the consequence of the burning, and the ὅτι clause would be causal. On the other hand, the word ἀφάνερος is very rare. It does not appear in the new Liddell and Scott Lexicon, and I have seen it only in Marcus Eremita (Migne, Vol. 65, p. 913 A) where it signifies *dark, obscure*. An example of ἀφανέρως quoted by Stephanus from Suidas has been rightly emended to φανερῶς.

If φανεροί of A is right — and it has the support of the Latin versions — the sense seems weak. "And shall be manifest" is an anticlimax. Perhaps, if the sense be carried on into the following words, φανεροὶ ἔσονται ὅτι κτλ. may be compared to such passages as Xen. *Cyrop. 2*, 2, 12 (φανεροὶ γιγνόμενοι ὅτι ποιοῦσιν) and *5*, 3, 2 (φανεροὶ εἶναι ὅτι πειρώμεθα), where the ὅτι clause takes the place of a supplementary participle; but in the Hermas passage the subject changes. It will be noted that, like ὅτι, *quoniam* of the Latin versions may be either *because* or *that*.

πραξις αυτων πονηρα εγε
[ν]ετο εν τη ζωη αυτων· οι
μ̣ε̣ν̣ γαρ αμαρτωλοι καησον
[τ]αι οτι ημαρτον και ου μετε
[ν]ο̣ησαν̣ τα δε εθνη καησον
[τ]αι οτι ο̣υκ εγνωσαν τον κτι
[σαν]τα αυτ̣ο̣υς· συ ουν εν σε 5
αυτω [καρπο]φ̣[ορ]ει ϊνα εν εκ[ει
νη τ̣η̣ [θερεια γν]ω̣σθ[η
σου ο κ̣[αρπος απεχου δε απο
πολλων [π]ρ̣αξ[εων και ουδε
εν δια[μ]α̣ρ̣της ο[ι γαρ τα πολ
λα πρα[σσο]ν̣τες πολ[λα και α
μαρτα[νο]υ[σ]ιν περισ[πωμε
νοι πε[ρι] τας πραγματ̣[ειας αυ
των μ[η]δε̣ δουλευ[οντες τω
κ̅ω̅ αυ[τω]ν̣· πως ουν [φησι δυ 6
νατα[ι ο] τ̣οιουτος αιτ[ησασθαι

Dibelius considers φανεροὶ ἔσονται an intolerable repetition, and would read φανερὸν ἔσται, connecting this with the following ὅτι clause. He cites L[1] *palam fiet* as support for this suggestion; but *fient* is the better reading, according to Professor Turner.

The Ethiopic translator seems to have omitted from καί (l. 12) to αὐτῶν, and to have attached ἁμαρτωλοί (l. 15) to κατακαυθήσονται (l. 11).

13 γέγονεν A.

15 καυθήσονται A and so also in 17. PBerol may have had καήσονται in the former instance because there its line begins with η. The whole word is lost in the second instance.

19–20 καρποφόρησον A, omitting ἐν σεαυτῷ, cf. L[1] *fac fructum bonum.* M has the support of L[2], *tu igitur intra te fer fructum* (cf. E *fac tibi fructum*) and probably PBerol. Schmidt and Schubart restored ἐν σοί to fill out a short line, but ἐν σεαυτῷ is better, making l. 50 of PBerol exactly equal in length to l. 51.

21 ἐν τῷ θέρει ἐκείνῳ A; cf. p. 2, 22 and 29. Possibly γνωσθήσεται should be restored both here and in PBerol; otherwise the lines are too short. For the future, cf. Blass-Debrunner, § 369.

22 τῶν πολλῶν A. I have omitted τῶν (with PBerol) on account of the unusual length of the line. It is probable that τά should be omitted in 24, where A reads it.

24 οὐ[δέποτε] οὐδὲν διαμάρτῃς A. PBerol [δια]μαρτήσεις, which had been suggested by M. Schmidt; the negative is lost, but the text seems to have been as long as that of A. The sense seems to demand a statement (cf. L[1] *nihil delinques*) rather than a prohibition (L[2] *nihil peccaveris*), and the futural subjunctive is well attested; cf. Moulton, *Gram.* pp. 185 and 240, Jannaris, App. iv, 8. In Sim. *5*, 7, 3 A reads πῶς σωθῇ, M πῶς σωθήσεται; but the situation is reversed in Sim. *4*, 7, *q.v.*

27 πράξεις A.

28 μηδέ MLL: καὶ μηδέν A.

29 ἐ[αυτῶν] A: om. LLE.

30 ὁ τοιοῦτος δύναταί τι αἰτήσασθαι A.

[τι] π[αρα του] κ̅υ̅ [κ]αι λα[βειν μη
[δουλευων τ]ω κ̅[ω̅] οι δ[ουλευον

p. 4

τες α[υτω ε]κε[ιν]οι λημψον
ται τα αιτηματα αυτων
οι δε μη δουλευοντες τ[ω
κ̅ω̅ ουδε ε̅ν̅ λημψοντ[αι
εαν δε μιαν τις π[ραξιν ε]ρ 7
γασηται δυνατ[αι κ]αι τω κ̅ω̅
δουλευσα[ι ου γα]ρ μη δια
φθαρη η [δια]νοια αυτου
απο [του] κ̅υ̅ αλλα δουλευ
σει [αυτ]ω εχων καθαραν
την διανοιαν αυτου ταυ 8
τα ουν εαν ποιησης δυ
νηση καρποφορησαι εις
τον αιωνα τον ερχομενον
και ος εαν ταυ[τ]α ποιηση
καρποφορησει

αλλη παραβολη ε̅ Sim. V, 1

νηστευων και καθημε[νος 1

31 τι is demanded by the space.

32 M and A agree in omitting γάρ. It had been added by various editors following Hollenberg. *qui enim serviunt* L¹, *servientes autem* L².

P. 4. 1 λήψονται A.

3–4 οἱ δὲ . . . λήμψονται om. L¹.

4 A has ἐκεῖνοι after κυρίῳ: om. MHamb L². L² omits τῷ κυρίῳ also. — οὐδέν AHamb. — λήμψονται MHamb: λήψονται A.

6 καί MAL²: om. Hamb L¹E. — *poterit* LL.

7 οὐ γὰρ διαφθαρήσεται AHamb (but in Hamb γάρ stood in a lost margin and γὰρ μή is possible): *non alienatur* L¹, *non alienabitur* L². The Ethiopic condenses the similitude from this point on.

9–11 ἀπὸ . . . αὐτοῦ om. Hamb (homoioteleuton).

10 τὴν διάνοιαν αὐτοῦ καθαράν A.

12 δυνήσῃ MLL: δύνασαι A. The ending is lost in Hamb. E appears to have had a present tense in its original.

15 ὃς ἄν MAHamb: *omnes qui* (ὅσοι ἄν?) L¹, *omnes quicunque* L².

17 ἀρχὴ ἄλλης παραβολῆς A, παραβολὴ ε̅ Hamb, *similitudo quinta* LL: no heading in E.

18–19 νηστεύοντός μου καὶ καθημένου εἰς

[ε]ι[ς ο]ρ̣[ο]ς τι και [ευ]χ̣αριστων
[τω κ̅ω̅ πε]ρι πα[ντω]ν ων
[εποιησε]ν μ[ετ εμο]υ βλε
[πω τον π]οιμ[ε]να [π]αρακα
[θημεν]ον μοι λε[γ]ο̣ντα
[μοι τοι]αυτα τι ω̣ρθινος
[ωδε ε]ληλυθας οτι φημι
[κ̅ε̅ στα]τιωνα εχω τι φη 2
[σιν εσ]τιν στατιων· νη
[στευω] φημι κ̅ε̅· ν[η]στεια
[δε φησ]ιν τι εστ[ιν αυ]τη
[ην ν]ηστ[ε]υετ[ε ως ει]ω[θειν

p. 5

ξ

φημι κ̅ε̅ ουτω νηστευω· ο[υ 3
κ οιδατε φησιν νηστευει[ν
τω θ̅ω̅ ουδε εστιν νηστεια
αυτη η ανωφελης ην νη
στευετε αυτω· δια τι φημι

ὄρος τι εὐχαριστῶν Hamb. The loose use of the gen. abs. is found elsewhere in Hermas (*e.g.* Vis. *I*, I, 3), and editors consider it a proof of the originality of the text of the Hamburg fragment; so Schmidt and Schubart (*Sitzungsber. Berl. Akad.* 1909, p. 1079) and Dibelius in his notes on this passage and on Vis. *I*, I, 3.

20 πάντων MHambL[1]CE : τούτων AL[2].

21 ἐποίησεν Hamb, ἐποίησε A. μετ' ἐμοῦ MAHambL[1] (*mecum*) : *mihi* L[2]CE.

23 καὶ λέγοντα AHamb; the Latin and Ethiopic versions also have the conjunction, but the Coptic omits it.

24 μοι MLLCE : om. AHamb. In spite of the loss of the left-hand margin the restoration above is certain. μοι is needed to fill the space, and ταῦτα is for the same reason less satisfactory than τοιαῦτα. M has no support for τοιαῦτα. C had ταῦτα, and L[1] has *ac dicentem* with a variant *et haec dicentem*, which should be preferred. Hamb AL[2]E omit the object pronoun.

The ω of ωρθινος is almost certain. ὀρθρινός AHamb.

25 ὧδε (AHamb) is local, as always in Hermas. *Tam mane huc* LL; but C and E have no word for *so*.

26 τί, φησίν, ἐστίν MA (ἐστι) : τί ἐστιν, φησίν Hamb.

27 νηστεύω AHamb L[2]E : *ieiunium* L[1].

30 ἣν νηστεύετε MAHambE : om. LL. There is a gap in the Coptic text. — εἰώθειν AHamb LL : εἴωθα CE.

P. 5. 3 θεῷ MHambLLC : κυρίῳ AE. By a slip, Delaporte has translated the Coptic *domino* and Dibelius has been misled by this error. — ἡ νηστεία A, corrected by Harnack.

3–4 *Neque hoc est ieiunium utile* C.

5 διὰ τί τοῦτο, φημί, κύριε, λέγεις Hamb.

κε τουτο λεγεις· λεγω φησιν
οτι ουκ εστιν αυτη νηστεια
ην δοκειτε νηστευειν·
αλλ εγω σε διδαξω τι εστιν
νηστεια δεκτη και πληρης
τω κω· ναι φημι κε μακα
ριον με ποιησεις εαν γνω
την νηστειαν την δεκτη
τω [θ]ω· ακουε φησιν ο θς 4
[ου βο]υλεται τοιαυτην νη
[στεια]ν ματαιαν ουτω γαρ
[νηστ]ευων τ[ω] θω ουδε[ν ερ
[γαζη τ]η δ[ικαιοσυνη νη

(The remainder of the page is lost.)

p. 6

ξα

και ενκρατευση απο παν 5
[τ]ος πονηρου πραγματ[ος
ζηση τω θω· ταυτα δε
εαν εργαση μεγαλην νη

6 λέγω σοι AC: σοι is omitted by MHamb L^1 (*dico enim*). L^2 omits both words. E paraphrases, but its testimony favors σοι.

8 *quod ieiunatis* C, *quod ieiunas* E.

10 δεκτὴ καὶ πλήρης MAHambC: *plenum acceptumque* LL.

11–14 ναὶ . . . θω om. A (homoiot.) L^1E: Hamb L^2C agree with M in giving the fuller text. L^2C introduce this sentence with *et dixi ei*, which, as Dibelius points out, is due to misreading καί for ναί.

14 τῷ θεῷ Hamb: *domino* L^2C.

17 τῷ θεῷ MAHambC: om. LL.

18 ἐργάζῃ HambLLE: ἐργάσῃ AC.

After line 18 there is a ragged and badly abraded projection of the papyrus extending downward from the middle for a distance of several lines. A few traces of letters are discernible, but their position is not such that they can be certainly identified and related to the text. Such as they are, they suggest that in the lost passage the text differed slightly from that of A, at least in the arrangement of words.

P. 6. The numerals ξα seem to have been written by the same hand that wrote ξ at the head of p. 5; but this ξ is a little more cursive.

3 καὶ ταῦτα ἐάν A.

στειαν τελεις και δε
κτην τω κ̅ω̅· ακουε την 2, 1
παραβολην ην μελλω σοι
λεγειν [[ανηκουσαν τη
νηστεια]]· ειχεν τις αγρον 2
και δουλους πολλους εις
μερος τι του αγρου εφυ
τευσεν αμπελωνα εκ
λεξαμενος ουν δουλον
τινα πιστοτατον και ε[υ
αρεστον αυτω αποδ̣[ημησων
προσεκαλ̣ε[σ]ατο α[υτον και
λεγει αυτω λαβε [τον αμ
[πελωνα τουτον ον εφυ]
[τευσα και χαρακωσον]
[αυτον εως ερχομαι και]
[ετερον δε μη ποιησης]
[τω αμπελωνι και ταυ]
[την μου την εντολην]

5 There is a short and very faint line above the iota of τελεῖς, which might be taken for an accent. — ποιεῖς A, ποιήσεις (probably) C: *consummabis* LL. — C omits καί, L^2 both καί and μεγάλην (l. 4).

6 κυρίῳ ML^1C: θεῷ AL^2.

8–9 The bracketed words were deleted by a dot above each letter; they are read in ALLCE.

10 A has καί in place of εἰς, and it is likely that this was the text of the original of L^1 (*quandam partem eius fundi vineam posuit*) and E (*eius partem unam obsevit vineis*). L^2, however, has *et in partem eius vineam posuisset*.

12–13 καὶ ἐκλεξάμενος AE (*et elegit*). The construction is so changed in LL that the exact form of the original cannot be determined.

14 πιστότατον MLL: πιστόν AE.

15 *probatissimum* L^2. — A omits αὐτῷ. ἀποδημήσων has been restored from the indications of the Latin and Ethiopic versions. L^2 reads *cui peregre afuturus adsignavit vineam*, E *et cum iter facturus esset vocavit eum*, etc. The manuscripts of L^1 read *a futuris deinde peregre profectus elegit*. Professor Turner takes *afuturus deinde elegit* to be the original form of this clause; *profectus* may be a doublet, as Dibelius notes. It is possible that the Greek copy used by the translator had the order ἀποδημήσων οὖν δοῦλον . . . ἐκλεξάμενος προσεκαλέσατο. — The reading of A, ἔντιμον (a word not found elsewhere in Hermas) may be a corruption of ἐκδημήσων through an intermediate stage ἐκδημῶν.

17 After this line the papyrus has been torn away at both sides so that only a narrow and badly injured projection remains. I find nothing legible in ll. 18–23.

φυλαξον κ]αι ελε[υθερος
εση παρ εμοι ε]ξηλ[θε δε
ο δεσποτης] του [δουλου
εις την αποδημ]ιαν [εξ 3
ελθοντος δε α]υ[του ελα

(This page has lost two lines.
After it, a whole leaf is wanting.)

p. 7

ξ]δ
ο οικοδεσποτης] αυτου κ[αι 9
[επεμψεν αυτω] εδεσμ[ατα
[εκ του δειπ]ν[ο]υ πολλα · λα
[βων δε ο δου]λος τα εδεσμα
[τα τα πεμφ]θε[ν]τα αυτω απ[ο
[του δεσποτο]υ αυτου τα αρ
[κουντα αυτ]ω [ελα]βε τα δε λοι
[πα τοις συνδουλ]οις αυτου
[διεδωκεν οι δε συνδο]υλ[ο]ι αυτου 10
[λαβοντες τα] ε[δεσμ]ατ[α] εχ[α
[ρησαν και ηρξαντ]ο και [ε]υχε
[σθαι υπερ αυτου ινα μ]ειζονα χ[α
[ριν ευρη παρα τ]ω δεσποτη
[οτι ουτως εχρησα]το αυτοις ·

24–28 Since the legible parts of these lines are confined to a narrow vertical strip, the letters legible in 24 are almost exactly above those legible in 25 and so on down. But it is impossible to arrange the ordinary text in such a manner as to conform exactly to the indications of the papyrus. The text of the papyrus must have differed from that of A, at least in the matter of word-order, and I have therefore left off the usual bracket at the left.

P. 7. On a torn projection of the papyrus at the top of the page there is a trace which is probably part of δ (ξ is less likely). If δ is rightly restored, the error in the numbering of the pages (see Introduction, p. 13) continued at least to this point.

1 *paterfamilias* LL, *herus* E: om. A.

2–3 ἐκ τοῦ δείπνου ἐδέσματα πολλά A.

5 παρά A.

6 A omits αὐτοῦ.

7 [ελα]βε: the injured letter before ε is almost certainly β, not ρ. ἦρε A and probably the versions (*sustulit*, *sustulisset* LL, *sumpsit* E). — τὰ λοιπὰ δέ A.

11 A omits the second καί and the versions ignore it.

12 χάριν μείζονα A.

[ταυτα παντα τα γ]ε[γ]ονατα 11
[ο δεσποτης αυτο]υ ηκουσεν
[και παλιν λ]ε̣ι̣α̣ν̣ εχαρη επι
[τη πραξει α]υτου συνκαλε
[σας παλιν π]αντας τους φιλ[ους
[ο δεσποτ]ης και τον υἱον
[αυτου απ]ηγγειλεν αυτοις
[την πραξι]ν του δουλου ην
[επραξεν] επι τοις εδεσμα
σ̣ι̣ν̣ ο̣ι[ς ελα]βεν· ο[ι δ]ε ετι μαλ
λον συνευδοκησ[αν] γενε
σθαι τον δουλον συνκληρο
ν̣ομον τω ϋιω αυτου· λεγω 3, 1
αυτω κ̅ε̅ εγω ταυτας τας
παραβολας ου γεινωσκω
ουδε δυναμαι νοησαι αυ
τας [εα]ν μη μοι επιλυσης
α̣υ̣[τας] π̣αντα σοι επιλυσω 2

p. 8

φησιν κ̣[αι οσα αν λαλησω
μετα σο̣υ [δειξω σοι τας
εντολας [του κ̅υ̅ φυλασ

15 γεγονότα A. For the change ο > α, cf. Mayser, p. 61.

18–19 συγκαλεσάμενος πάλιν τοὺς φίλους A. The versions omit πάντας, E omits πάλιν also. It is possible that M read συγκαλεσάμενος and omitted πάλιν; but I have preferred the text above because, since Hermas does not use this verb elsewhere, we have no reason to assume that he would have preferred the middle. The usage of the N. T. writers is divided, though the middle is more frequent in similar contexts.

22 τοῦ δούλου MLL, αὐτοῦ A and perhaps E, which translates freely.

24 A has αὐτοῦ after ἐδέσμασιν, without support. — LL (*miserat*) seem to have read ἔπεμψεν in place of ἔλαβεν; *acceperat* E.

25 After συνευδόκησαν G.-H. added αὐτῷ because an object occurs in the versions (*patri familias* L¹ *ei* E). The agreement of M with A makes this unnecessary.

28 αὐτῷ MLLE: om. A. — σάς A alone.

30 A omits αὐτάς, and the versions do not take it into account; but in such a sentence that is not significant.

32 The letters αυ at the beginning of the line are almost certain. Just before πάντα there are traces which do not much resemble sigma. Perhaps we should read αὐτὰς ἅπαντα for which there seems to be room enough.

P. 8. 3–7 τοῦ κ̅υ̅ . . . ἐντολάς om. A (homoiot.). — 4–7 καὶ ἔσῃ . . . αὐτοῦ om. E.

σε και εσ[η] ε̣[υαρεστος αυ
τω και ενγ[ραφηση εις αριθμον
των τηρου[ντων τας εν
τολας αυτου [εαν δε τι αγα 3
θου ποιη[σης εκτος της
ε̣ν̣τ̣ο̣[λη]ς̣ τ̣[ου θ̅υ̅ σεαυτω
περιπ[οιηση δοξαν περισσο
τεραν [και εση ενδο
ξοτερο̣[ς παρα τω θ̅ω̅ ου ε
μελ[λες ειναι εαν ουν φυλασ
σ̣ω̣[ν τας εντολας του θ̅υ̅
προσθη̣[ς και τας λειτουρ
γιας ταυτ[ας χαρηση εαν
τηρησης αυ[τας κατα την
εμην εντολη[ν λεγω αυ 4
τω κ̅ε̅ ο εαν [μοι εντειλη
φυλαξω αυτο [οιδα γαρ
οτι συ μετ εμ̣[ου ει εσομαι
φησι μετα σο[υ οτι τοιαυ
την [π]ροθυμι[αν] εχ̣ε̣ι̣ς̣ [τ]η̣ς
αγ[αθο]ποι[ησεως κ]α̣ι̣ μετα
παντων δε εσομαι οσοι εαν
φησι την αυτην προθυ
μιαν εχωσιν· η νησ̣τεια 5
φησιν αυτη τηρουμενω̅

4 The scribe may have written ἔσι. The space after σ is scarcely broad enough for η, and a small dot which I seem to detect above the line may belong to the lost iota.

5 This line has 24 letters without τόν, so the article seems to have been omitted; but we have εἰς τὸν ἀριθμόν in Sim. *9*, 24, 4.

6 τῶν τηρούντων ML[1]: *qui custodierunt* L[2].

7 δέ LLE: γέ A. — ἀγαθοῦ ML[2] (*aliquid boni*): ἀγαθόν A, om. E. L[1] has *aliquod bonum* with a variant *aliquid boni.*

25–27 A reads μετὰ πάντων δὲ ἔσομαι, φησίν, ὅσοι ταύτην τὴν προθυμίαν ἔχουσιν. The use of the subjunctive in the Latin versions (*quicumque . . . habuerint*) seems to support the reading of M.

26 τὴν αὐτὴν προθυμίαν ML[1] (*idem propositum*): ταύτην τήν A, *tale propositum* (*i.e.* τοιαύτην) L[2]. E has omitted this with much of the context.

28 αὕτη, φησί A. — In several other passages of this papyrus final ν in a word which ends a line is indicated by a short stroke above the last vowel.

των εντολων του κ̅υ̅ λει
αν καλη εστιν ουτως ουν̣
φυλαξεις την ν̣η̣στεια[ν

p. 9

[πρωτον παντων φυλαξαι] 6
[απο παντος ρημ]ατος πο
[νηρου και πασης επ]ιθυμιας
[πονη]ρ̣α̣[ς και καθα]ρισον σου
[την] κ̣α̣ρ̣[διαν απο] παντων
[των] ματ[αιωμα]των του αιω
[νος] το[υτου ε]α̣ν̣ ταυτα φυ
[λαξ]η̣ς̣ ε[στ]α̣[ι] α̣[υτ]η̣ η νηστεια
[τελ]ε̣ια· ουτω δ̣[ε] ποιησεις 7
[συ]ν̣τελε[σ]α̣ς̣ τ[α] προγεγραμ
[μ]ε̣να εν ε̣κ̣[εινη] τη ημερα
[η ν]ηστευε̣ις [μηδ]εν γευση
[ε]ι̣ μ̣[η] αρ[τ]ον κ[αι υδ]ω̣ρ και εκ
[τω]ν̣ εδεσμ[α]τ̣[ω]ν σου ω̃ν
[εμε]λ̣λ̣ε[ς] τ̣ρωγειν συνοψι
[σα]ς̣ την ποσο[τη]τα της δα
[πα]νης εκειν[ης] της ημερας

30 The reading of A at this point is οὕτως οὖν φυλάξεις τὴν νηστείαν ταύτην ἣν μέλλεις τηρεῖν· πρῶτον πάντων φύλαξαι κτλ. Now the papyrus has lost nothing at the bottom of this page, and page 9 has not lost more than one line at the top. It appears, therefore, that M omitted the words ταύτην ἣν μέλλεις τηρεῖν, agreeing with L[1] (*sic igitur servabis illud: primum omnium*, etc.). L[2] omits from οὕτως οὖν through τηρεῖν.

P. 9. 8 ἔσται σοι αὕτη A and probably E (*perfectum erit ieiunium tuum*): MLL omit the personal pronoun.

9 τελεία MA, *perfectum* E, *iustum* LL, ἀληθινή Antiochus.

10 προγεγραμμένα M, confirming a conjecture of G.-H., who cite Vis. *4*, 3, 6. γεγραμμένα A: *quae supra scripta sunt* L[1], *quae audisti* L[2].

15 συνοψίσας MA, *computata quantitate* L[1], *computa pretium* L[2], συμψηφίσας Ath[2] p. 31. Compare the situation in Vis. *3*, 1, 4 συνώψισα A, συνεψήφισα ℵ, where L[1] has *extimavi* (Hilgenfeld's text); L[2] paraphrases.

In these passages the editors have preferred συμψηφίσας and συνεψήφισα. They were doubtless led to this decision by the authority of the Sinaiticus in Vis. *3*, 1, 4; and not understanding the special meaning which συνοψίζω has in both places, they wrongly considered that the testimony of the Latin versions favored συμψηφίζω. But it is an easy step from the ordinary

[η]ς ε[μ]ελλ[ες ποι]ε[ι]ν αποθε
[μενος δωσεις] α[υ]το χηρα
[η ορφ]ανω η υστερουμενω
[και ου]τω ταπεινοφρονη
[σεις ι]να εκ τ[ης] ταπεινοφρο
συ[νης] σου ο ε[ι]ληφως εμ
πλη[σ]η [τ]ην [ε]α[υ]του ψυχην
και [ευξη]ται περι σου

meaning of σύνοψις, a *comprehensive view*, to *computation*, *estimate*; and since συνοψίζω could be reasonably interpreted in this way, it might well have been preferred as the harder reading. We should adopt συνοψίζω in both passages, not only because of the testimony of M, but also because both συνοψίζω and σύνοψις occur several times in papyrus documents with a meaning either identical with or very close to the sense demanded in Hermas. The passages are collected in the articles on these words in Preisigke's *Wörterbuch*; but I think that in formulating his definitions Preisigke adheres too closely to the earlier meaning of *view*, *inspect*; *estimate* will serve in most, if not all, of the cases.

This development of the meaning of συνοψίζω may be Egyptian. The language of the great inscription of Khargeh (Dittenberger, *Orient. Graec. Inscr. Sel.* 669, 55) ἡ λεγομένη κατὰ σύνοψιν ἀπαίτησις, may be taken to indicate that it was not quite familiar in ordinary Greek. If such be the case it may lend strength to Zahn's conjecture that Hermas was Egyptian by birth (see the note of G.-H. on Vis. *1 ad init.*).

If the view here taken of the present passage be correct, Vis. *3*, 1, 4 stands out as a noteworthy case in which the late Athos MS has been more faithful to the original text than the venerable Sinaiticus.

18 ποιεῖν MALL: ἐσθίειν Ath[2] Ant. But Ath[2] has τῆς δαπάνης τοῦ ἀρίστου οὗ ἔμελλες ἐσθίειν, and ἐσθίειν may have been a result of his inserting ἄριστον into the context. — ἀποθέμενος is omitted by A and E, but was read by L[1] *sepones et dabis*. L[2] *et inde* (ἀπὸ τούτων ?) *da*.

25 εὔξηται A Ath[2] Ant; cf. L[1] *et pro te adeat dominum oratio eius*, L[2] *et pro hoc opere vadet ad dominum oratio tua*.

The reading of the first part of this line is extremely doubtful because of the abrasion of the papyrus. καί must be right, but it appears to have been broadly written. The lacuna which follows seems too broad for ευξη alone. Comparing the Latin versions one might think of καὶ εὐχὴ ἔρχηται (αἱ προσευχαί σου . . . ἀνέβησαν . . . ἔμπροσθεν τοῦ θεοῦ, Acts 10, 4); but the phrase is awkward, and the Latin versions may be expanded from a single verb. Other possibilities are καὶ προσεύξηται (cf. Vis. *1*, 1, 9) and καὶ ἐντεύξηται (Mand. *10*, 2, 5). So far as one can judge by comparison with the lines above and below, l. 25 should have about 19 letters.

περί M; ὑπέρ AAth[2]. The text of Antiochus printed by Migne (Vol. 89, p. 1456) has ὑπέρ, but at least one copy reads περί. In the University of Michigan Library there is a small manuscript (No. 155), probably of the thirteenth century, containing several writings on asceticism, most of which have not yet been identified. But it contains Homilies 7, 8, and 9 (in part) of Antiochus, and reads περὶ ἑαυτοῦ in our passage. This same manuscript has χήρᾳ καὶ ὀρφανῷ above where Migne's text reads χήρᾳ ἢ πτωχῷ.

περί is often used in the O. T. for Attic ὑπέρ, especially with εὔχομαι; cf. Johannessohn, *Der Gebrauch der Präpositionen in der Septuaginta* (Gött. Nachr. 1925, p. 222). It is also found in the N. T.; cf. Moulton and Milligan, *Vocabulary*, p. 504. To the examples there cited from papyri add P.Oxy. IX, 1216, another case of εὔχομαι περί.

[πρ]ο̣[ς τον] κ̣̅ν̣̅ · εαν ουν ου 8
[τω τελεση]ς̣ την νη
[στειαν] ως σ[ο]ι εντελ
λ̣ο̣μ̣α̣ι̣ ε̣σ̣ται η θυσια σου
[δε]κ̣τ̣η παρα τ̣[ω θ]ω̅ και εν
[γραφο]ς εσται [η] νηστεια

p. 10

[αυτη και η λειτουργια ου]
τως [εργ]αζ[ομενη καλη
και ι[λα]ρα εστ[ι και ευ
προσ[δε]κτος [τω κ̅ω̅ ταυ 9
τα ουτως τηρησ[εις συ
μετα των τεκνω[ν σου
και ολου του οικου [σου
τηρησας δε αυτα μ̣[ακα
ριος εση και οσοι εα[ν ακου
σαντες αυτα τηρη[σ]ωσι
μακαρι[οι] εσονται [κα]ι̣ ο[σα
εαν αιτησωντα[ι] π̣α̣ρ̣α̣
του κ̅υ̅ λημψοντα[ι] ε̣[δ̣]ε̣[η 4, 1
θην αυτου πολλ[α ι]ν̣[α μοι
δηλωση την παρα[βολην
του αγρου και του δε[σπο
του και του αμπ[ε]λ̣ω̣[νος
και του δουλου τ̣[ου χαρα
κωσαντος τον α[μπελωνα
και τω[ν] χαρακω[ν και των
βοτανων των εκτε⸢⸤τιλ̣

27 ἐὰν οὖν οὑτῶ ML[1] (*si sic igitur*): ἐὰν οὕτω A, ἐὰν οὖν Ath[2], *et sic* (for *et si sic*) L[2], *hoc igitur* E.

28 ἐντέλλομαι ML[1] (*praecipio*): ἐνετειλάμην AAth[2] L[2] (*mandavi*).

30 θεῷ AAnt: κυρίῳ Ath[2] LLE.

P. 10. 3 ἐστί: the end of the word is supplied from A and L[1]; L[2] has *erit*.

5 οὕτω A.

9 ἄν A.

12 ἄν A. — ἀκούσονται A: *quicquid petierint* L[1], *petent* L[2].

13 λήψονται A. — The versions begin the new sentence with a conjunction (*et* L[1]E, *itaque* L[2]).

14 LLE omit πολλά.

μενων εκ του αμ[π]ε̣[λω
νος και του υἱου κα[ι] των̣
φιλων και των συμβου
λων συνηκα γαρ οτι πα
ραβολη εστιν ταυτα παν
τα· ο δε αποκριθεις μοι 2
λεγει αυθαδης ει λειαν
εις το επερωταν ουκ ο
φειλεις φησιν επερω

p. 11

[ταν ο]υ[δε]ν̣ ολως εαν γαρ
[σοι δ]εη δ[ηλ]ωθηναι δηλω
[θησε]ται [λε]γω αυτω κ̅ε̅ οσ[α
[εαν] μοι δε̣[ι]ξης και μη δη
[λ]ω[σ]η̣ς̣ ματην εσομαι εω
[ρακ]ως αυτα και μη νοων
[οτι] εστιν ωσαυτως κα̣[ι
[εαν] μ̣οι παραβολας λαλ[η]σ[ης
[και μ̣]η επιλυσης μοι εις μα
[την] εσομ[αι] ηκουκως π̣α
[ρα σο]υ ο δε παλιν λεγει μοι 3
[ος α]ν δουλος ην φησιν του
[θ̅υ̅ κα]ι εχη τον κ̅ν̅ αυτου

24 καί was probably carelessly inserted by the scribe of M; it is omitted by A and LL (*amicis quos in consilio adhibuerat*).

26 παραβολή τις A without support. — LL omit πάντα.

28 λέγει M and probably LL (*ait*): εἶπεν AE (*dixit*).

P. 11. 4 The space suggests ἐάν rather than ἄν; cf. p. 10, 9 and 12. ἄν A.

5 The first omega was found on a small fibre which has since become detached and been lost.

6 A agrees with M here, but it is probable that the original of the Latin versions omitted καί; *si non intellexero* L[1], *quia non intelligo* L[2].

7 ὅτι is supplied because of the space: τί A.

9 μοι αὐτάς A.

10 ἠκουκώς: compare ἠκουκέναι P.Oxy. 237 (col. 7, l. 23): ἀκηκοώς A. — A adds τι, cf. LL *frustra audiero eas*.

11 ὁ δὲ πάλιν ἀπεκρίθη μοι λέγων A, *respondit mihi rursus dicens* L[1], *et dixit mihi* L[2]E.

12 ὃς ἄν, φησί, δοῦλος ᾖ A. — For the subjunctive form ἦν, see R. C. Horn, *Proc. Am. Philol. Assoc.* 1922 (Vol. 53, p. xx).

13 ἑαυτοῦ A: LL omit, but in l. 14 L[1] reads *in praecordiis suis*.

[εν τη κ]ạρδια αιτειται παρ αυ
[του σ]υνεσιν και λαμβανει
[και] π̣ασαν παρ̣αβολην επι
[λυει] και γνωστα αυτω [γει
[νον]ṭαι [μ]ετ[α] του $\overline{κυ}$ τα [α
[πορο]υμενα δι[α] παραβολων
[οσοι] δε φησιν [β]ληχροι ει
[σιν κ]αι αργοι προς την εν
[τευξι]ν εκεινοι διστα
[ζουσ]ιν αιτεισθαι παρα
[του] $\overline{κυ}$ ο δε $\overline{κς}$ πολυσπλαγ 4
χ̣ν̣ος εστιν [κ]α̣ι πασιν
τοις αιτουμενο[ι]ς παρ αυ
[τ]ου αδιστακτως διδω
σ̣ι συ δε ενδεδυναμω

15 αὐτῳ A, emended by G.–H.

18 ἀπορούμενα cannot be regarded as certain, for the margin is torn away after τά, and it is possible that the line ended there. One naturally thinks of λαλούμενα: Barnabas (11, 11) has λαλουμένων and Hermas (Sim. *6*, 1, 4) has λελάληται. A, however, reads λεγόμενα, not λαλούμενα. Hermas uses the middle ἀποροῦμαι (Sim. *8*, 3, 1), but not the passive. The latter is well known in philosophical language (Plat. *Soph.* 243 B, Arist. *Pol.* 1281a 38) and seems to explain the reading of L[1] *quae quaestiones ferunt*; but in that case L[1] would seem to have disregarded διὰ παραβολῶν. L[2] *verba domini quae dicuntur in similitudinibus* agrees with A.

μετά, M's reading, appears to be an error for τὰ ῥήματα (ALL).

20 ALL omit φησίν.

24 πολυεύσπλαγχνος A. M has πολύσπλαγχνος in Sim. *5*, 7, 4 also and πολυσπλαγχνίαν in Sim. *8*, 6, 1. Throughout the work the scribe of A has either written πολυευ — or has used a phrase, like πολλὴ εὐσπλαγχνία. The testimony of ℵ is in favor of πολύσπλαγχνος, πολυσπλαγχνία (Vis. *1*, 3, 2, *2*, 2, 8, *4*, 2, 3), and now that we have the additional testimony of M, those forms should be adopted as representing the language of Hermas.

27 ἀδιαλείπτως A, *sine intermissione* LL. Notwithstanding the important testimony of the Latin versions and the fact that Hermas has the phrase ἀδιαλείπτως προσηυχόμην in Sim. *9*, 11, 7, there is reason to think that M has preserved the original text here. Though ἀδιαλείπτως offers a contrast to βληχροὶ καὶ ἀργοί (20–21), ἀδιστάκτως presents an equally effective contrast to διστάζουσιν (22); and Mand. *9*, 2–6 argues strongly for ἀδιστάκτως. Further, if the original reading had been ἀδιαλείπτως, nothing but an arbitrary change without reference to palaeographical similarity could explain the occurrence of ἀδιστάκτως in M. On the other hand an original ἀδιστάκτως might easily be corrupted into, or misread as, ἀδιαστάτως (used by Philo in the sense of *uninterruptedly*), which would explain the Latin translation. The change to ἀδιαλείπτως in A would be brought about at a later date by the influence of such a passage as 1 Thess. 5, 17 (ἀδιαλείπτως προσεύχεσθε) or by Hermas' own use of the word, as cited above.

μενος ϋπο του ενδοξου
αγγελου και ειληφως πα

p. 12

ρ αυτου το[ιαυ]την [εντευ
ξιν και μη [ω]ν αργ[ος δια
τι ουκ αιτη παρα το[υ $\overline{κυ}$
συνεσιν και λαμβαν[εις
παρ αυτου· λεγω αυ[τω $\overline{κε}$ 5
εγω εχω⟨ν⟩ σε μετ εμα[υτου
αναγκην εχω π[αρα σου
αιτεισθαι και σε [επερω
ταν συ γαρ μ[ο]ι δε[ικνυ
εις παντα και λ[αλεις
μετ εμου [ε]ι δε α[τερ σου
εβλεπον ταυτα [η ηκου
ον ηρωτων α[ν τον $\overline{κν}$
ϊνα μοι δηλωθη ε[ιπον 5, 1
σο[ι] φησι κα[ι] αρτι ο[τι
π[α]ν[ο]υ[ρ]γος ει κ[α]ι [αυθα
δης επ[ε]ρωτω[ν τας επι
λυσεις [τ]ων παραβ[ολων
επει δε [ου]τως πα[ραμο
νος ει συ επιλυσ[ω σοι
την παραβολη[ν του
αγρου και των λο[ι]π[ων
των ακολουθουντ[ων
ϊνα γν[ω]στα πασι π[οι]η

29 ἐνδόξου: ἁγίου A, *venerabili* LL, which probably represents ἐνδόξου, although that word is usually rendered *honestus*, *praeclarus*, *dignitosus*. ἅγιος is regularly *sanctus*. Cf. Sim. 7, 1, 9, 1, 3.

P. 12. 6 M has omitted the ν of ἔχων by accident. —μεθ' ἑαυτοῦ A.

7 σε αἰτεῖσθαι A.

11 *nam si* LL.

12 ἔβλεπον ἢ ἤκουον αὐτά A (*ea* LL). L[2] omits ἢ ἤκουον.

19 ἐπειδὴ δὲ οὕτω A.

20 A omits σύ.

23 τῶν ἀκολούθων πάντων A. For ll. 21–23 L[1] has only *hanc quam desideras similitudinem*, L[2] *hanc quam desideras similitudinem agri et omnium*.

σης αυτα· ακουε νυν
φησι και συνϊε αυτα
ο αγρος ο κοσμος ουτος 2
εστιν ο δε κ̅ς̅ του αγρου
ο κτισας τα παντα και

p. 13

(Eighteen or nineteen lines are lost.)

[κτισθεντες η] δε αποδη[μια
[του δεσποτου ο] χρονος ο πε
[ρισσευων εις] την παρου
[σιαν αυ]του λεγω αυτω 4
[κ̅ε̅ μεγ]αλως και θαυμαστως
[παντ]α εστιν και ενδοξως
[εχει] μη ουν φημι κ̅ε̅ εγω
[ταυτα η]δυναμην νοησαι
[ουδε ετε]ρος ανθρωπος
[καν] λειαν συνετος ην
[τις ου] δ[υ]ναται νοησαι
[αυτα] ετι φημι κ̅ε̅ δηλω
[σον μοι] ο [μ]ελλω σε επερω
[ταν λ]εγε φησιν ει τι βου 5

p. 14

(Fifteen lines are lost.)

ρει[ν εκαστους και αυ **6,** 2

P. 13. 6 A has a second πάντα after ἐνδόξως; the Latin versions do not translate it, but this proves little or nothing.

7 κύριε MLL: om. A.

8 ἠδυνάμην ταῦτα νοῆσαι A.

9 The Latin and Ethiopic versions seem to have read ἄνθρωπος, like M: τῶν ἀνθρώπων A.

10 ἦν is subjunctive as above, p. 11, l. 12: ᾖ A.

11 δύναται MA: *poterit* L[1], *poterat* L[2], *intellexisset* E (for ἐδύνατο νοῆσαι?).

P. 14. 1 I have supplied ἑκάστους instead of αὐτούς (A) because the Latin versions read *ad conservandos singulos*, and because there is a doubtful trace which might be κ in the third or fourth letter-space of the damaged papyrus after ρει. With αὐτούς l. 1 would be four letters shorter than l. 2. The Ethiopic seems to have read αὐτούς.

τος τας [αμαρτιας αυτων
εκαθ̣αρ[ισε πολλα κοπι
ασας κα[ι πολλους κοπους
ανηντληκως [ουδεις
γαρ αμπελων δ[υναται
σκαφηναι ανευ [κοπου
η μοχθου αυτος [ουν κα 3
θαρι[σ]ας τας αμα[ρτιας
του λαου εδειξε[ν αυτοις
τας τριβους τη[ς ζωης
δους αυτοις τον [νομον
ον ελαβεν παρα [του $\overline{\pi\rho\varsigma}$
αυτου βλεπεις ο[υν φη 4
σιν οτι αυτος $\overline{\kappa\varsigma}$ [εστι

p. 15

(Seventeen lines are lost.)

[μενην ουν αυ]τη[ν] καλω[ς 6
[και αγνως και σ]υ[ν]κοπια
[σασαν τω $\overline{\pi\nu\iota}$ κ]αι συνερ
[γησασαν εν πα]ντι πραγμα
[τι ισχυρως και] ανδριως
[αναστραφε]ισαν [μ]ετα του
[$\overline{\pi\nu\varsigma}$ ειλατο] κ̣ο̣ι̣ν̣[ω]ν̣[ο]ν ηρε
[σε γαρ] η̣ π̣ορ[ει]α τ[ης] σαρκος
[ταυτης οτι] ουκ εμιανθη
[επι της] γης εχουσα το
[$\overline{\pi\nu\alpha}$ το] αγιον συμβουλον 7

2 αὐτῶν LLE : ἡμῶν A.

5 ἠντληκώς A.

5–7 οὐδεὶς . . . σκαφῆναι: M confirms Anger's emendation of A, which is corrupt here, reading οὐδεὶς γὰρ δύναται σκαφῆσαι.

7 ἄτερ A.

14 βλέπεις κτλ. This sentence is omitted by A and E. The Latin versions read *vides inquit*, omitting οὖν; but (according to Hilgenfeld) some MSS of L[1] read *igitur* for *inquit*. All those used by Professor Turner give *inquit*.

P. 15. 7 A adds τοῦ ἁγίου, and so also LL. κοινωνόν is very uncertain. The papyrus is much injured, and the traces do not agree well with the usual text.

8 ἤρεσε γάρ without dative MA: *placuit enim deo* L[1], *domino* L[2]E.

[ουν ελα]β[ε] τον $\overline{υιν}$ και
[τους αγ]γελου[ς] τους ενδο
[ξους ινα] και η σαρξ ἄυτη

p. 16

(Seventeen lines are lost.)

καθα[ρ]αν [και αμιαντον 7, 1
ϊνα τ[ο $\overline{πνα}$ το κατοικη
σαν εν ạ[υτη μαρτυρηση
αυτη κ[αι δικαιωθη σου
η σαρξ β[λε]π̣[ε μηποτε 2
σου ẹπι̣ τ̣ην [καρδιαν
αναβ̣η την σα[ρκα ταυ
τη[ν] φθαρτη[ν ειναι
και παραχρηση [αυτη
εν μιασμω τιν[ι εαν μια
νης την σαρκα [σου
μιαινεις και το [$\overline{πνα}$ το
αγιον καν μιαν̣[ης την
σαρκα σο[υ] ο̣υ̣ [ζηση ει δε 3

p. 17

τ̣ι̣ς φημ̣[ι γεγο]νεν αγνοια
προτερ̣[α πριν α]κουσθηναι

P. 16. 2 κατοικῆσαν is supported by L[1] (*qui inhabitaverit*) and E (*qui super te habitavit*). κατοικοῦν AL[2] (*qui inhabitat*).

6 ἀναβῇ ἐπὶ τὴν καρδιαν σου A.

7 τὴν σάρκα σου ταύτην A: L[1] does not translate σου.

10 Since the lines of this fragment are 18 letters long or less, M must have agreed with A in omitting γάρ. L[1] has *enim*, L[2] *quod si* (ἐὰν δέ ?).

12 μιανεῖς A, *maculabis* LL.

13 ἐὰν δέ A.

14 τὴν σάρκα A (omitting σου? The report of G.–H. is not quite clear on this point): *corpus tuum* L[1] (v. l. *spiritum sanctum*) L[2]. The Ethiopic version presents this chapter in so condensed a form that its testimony is of little or no value. Editors emend to τὸ πνεῦμα or τὸ πνεῦμα τὸ ἅγιον, which is unnecessary, as Dibelius rightly remarks.

P. 17. 1 AL[2]E add κύριε after φημί: om. L[1], with M, which has not room for $\overline{κε}$ in the lacuna. — M here supports the text of A, against Dibelius's εἰ δέ τι γέγονεν ἐν ἀγνοίᾳ πρότερον.

2 ἀκουσθῶσι A. Hermas uses πρίν in three other places, and always with the infinitive: Vis. *3*, 1, 3, Sim. *9*, 16, 3, *9*, 26, 6.

τα ρηματ[α τ]αυ̣τ̣α πως σω
θησεται ο αν[θρ]ωπος ο μια
νας την σαρκα εαυτου
περι των [πρ]ο̣τερων φη
σιν αγνοη[μα]των τω θ̅ω̅
μονω δυ[νατο]ν ϊασιν δου
ναι̣ αυτ[ου γαρ πα]σα εστιν
η εξου[σια αλ]λα τα νυν 4
φυλα̣[σσε και ο κ̅ς̅] παντως πολυ
σπλα̣[γχνος ω]ν̣ [α]υ̣[τα] ιασετα[ι
α̣ν̣ [την σαρκα] λ̣ο̣[ιπον] μη [μια
νης μ̣[ηδ]ε̣ [τ]ο̣ π̣[ν]α̣ αμφο
τερα γα̣[ρ κοινα] εστ[ι]ν και
ατερ αλ[ληλω]ν μιανθηναι
ου [δυ]νατ[αι αμ]φ[ο]τερα ο[υ]ν
καθ[αρα φυ]λα̣σ̣[σ̣ε] και ζ[η
ση τ̣[ω θω]
. . Sim. VI, 1
[καθη]μ̣ε̣ν̣ος [ε]ν̣ [τ]ω οικω 1
μου κ̣α̣ι δοξαζων τον κ̅ν̅
περι παντων ω[ν] εωρα
κειν κα̣[ι] συνζη̣[τω]ν πε
ρι των εντολων οτι κα

4 σωθῇ A; see note on Sim. *4*, 5.

5 αὑτοῦ A.

9 αὐτοῦ γάρ ἐστι πᾶσα A. — There is scarcely space for even six letters in the lacuna; possibly αὐτῳ was M's reading.

10 A omits ἡ.

10–12 ἀλλὰ . . . ἰάσεται om. A. L[1] has *et cum sit dominus omnipotens misericors*, where *omnipotens* seems to be due to the translator's taking πάντως, or some corruption of that word, as an abbreviation for παντοκράτωρ. L[2] *et misericors dominus fortasse* etc. For πάντως in the sense of "perhaps," see Cadbury's remarks in *Journ. Bibl. Lit.* XLIV, 223–227. — It is possible that M did not have ο κ̅ς̅, but left the subject to be supplied from the foregoing sentences; for l. 11 seems to have been only two or three letters longer than l. 10. Either the writing of l. 11 was crowded, which the first part of the line does not indicate, or else ο κ̅ς̅ was omitted.

13 ἐὰν τὸ λοιπὸν μὴ μιανῃς σου τὴν σάρκα A. — Rather than place an epsilon at the end of l. 12, which is already long, I have assumed that M had in this case the less common ἄν instead of ἐάν.

20 The dots mark the place of an illegible letter and the stroke which is commonly placed over numerals. ἀρχή A, *similitudo sexta* L[1], *explicit similitudo quinta, incipit similitudo VI* L[2]: no heading in E.

λαι και δυναται και ϊλαραι
και ενδοξοι και δυναμε
ναι σωσαι ψυχη[ν] ανθρω
που ελεγον δε εν εμαυτω
τα[υτα]· μα[κ]αρ[ιος ε]σομαι εαν

p. 18

εν ταις ε[ντολαι]ς ταυτα[ις
πορευθω [και ος ε]αν πορε[υ
σηται εν αυ[ται]ς μακαρι
ος εσται· εω[ς] ταυτα εν 2
εμαυτω λαλω βλεπω
ο ποιμ]ην αυτο͂ν εξ[αιφ]νης παρα
καθημεν[ον] μο[ι] και λεγον
τα ταυτ[α τι δι]ψυχεις πε
ρι των εν[τολω]ν ὧν σοι
εντεταλμαι [κα]λαι εισιν
ολως μηδεν δ[ιψ]υχησης
[αλλ ενδ]υσ[αι τη]ν πιστιν
του [κ̅υ̅ και εν αυ]τ[α]ις πο
ρευσ[η ε]γω [γαρ σε] δυναμω
σω εν αυτα[ις α]υται αι εν 3
τολα[ι] συμφ[οροι] εισιν τοις

26–27 *honesta ac* (*et*) *laeta* LL. A agrees with the order of M.

29 L^1 has *dicebam autem*, in spite of the fact that all the preceding portion of this section is in dependent construction (*cum sederem*, etc.)—a striking agreement with the corresponding peculiarity of M. AL^2E omit δέ.

30 ταῦτα MLL (*haec*): om. AE.

P. 18. 1 A omits ἐν. The practice of Hermas as regards the use and the omission of ἐν in such phrases seems to have varied; see the note of G.-H. on Mand. *12*, 4, 6.

2 ὃς ἄν A. The space in M seems to demand ἐάν.—A reads ταύταις πορευθῇ (without ἐν).

3 μακάριος ἔσται MAL^2: *vivet deo* L^1.

4 ὡς A.

5 ἐλάλουν βλέπω A: *loquor* and *video* LL (but *loquerer*, *vidi* as a v. l. in L^1), *cogitabam*, *vidi* E.

6 ἐξαίφνης MAL^2E: om. L^1.—The mark over αὐτόν, which is intended to call attention to a gloss, seems to have been made by the first hand, but the gloss itself is by the diorthotes. A mark of similar form is used in the Sinaiticus, *e.g.* Vis. *2*, 3, 4, where the facsimile shows it plainly.

7 *et ait mihi* L^2, *et dixit mihi* E.

10 ἐνετειλάμην A.

11 μηδέν MLL (*nihil*): μή A.

14 ἐνδυναμώσω A.

μελ[λο]υσι μ[ετα]νο[ει]ν εαν
γαρ μ[η] πορε[υθωσ]ιν εν αυ
ταις [ει]ς μ[ατην] εστιν
η μ[ετ]αν[οι]α [αυτων] οι ουν 4
μετα[ν]οουν[τες α]ποβαλε
τε τα[ς] π[ο]νηρι[α]ς τ[ο]υ αιω
νος [τ]ουτου τας εκτρι
βου[σ]ας υμας ενδυσα
με[νοι] πασαν α[ρ]ετην
δικαιοσυνης δυνησε
σθε τηρησαι τας εντο
λας ταυτας και μηκετι
προστιθετε ταις αμαρ
τιαις υμων μηδεν ουν
π[ρ]οστιθεντες πολυ κο

p. 19

ψετ[ε] τω[ν προτ]ερων υμων
αμαρτι[ων πορ]ευεσθε ουν
ταις εντ[ολ]αι[ς] μου και ζη
σετε τω θω ταυτα παρ εμου
λελαληται υμειν· μετα το 5
ταυτα λαλη[σα]ι αυτον μετ ε

19–20 L^1 omits εἰς μάτην . . . αὐτῶν, and in consequence of this loss *non* corresponding to μή of l. 18 has disappeared from all but one of the manuscripts (the Bodleian), and γάρ is ignored by all.

21 ἀποβάλλετε A.

23–24 τὰς ἐκτριβούσας ὑμᾶς MAL^2: om. L^1E.

25 There is no room for δέ after ἐνδυσάμενοι: δέ ALL. — *virtutem et aequitatem* L^1.

29 προστιθέναι A; but cf. L^1 *nec post hoc adiciatis*, L^2 *ut non postea aliquid adiciatis*. E, which condenses and paraphrases, has *neque amplius peccetis*.

30 μηδὲν οὖν . . . ἁμαρτιῶν (p. 19, l. 2) om. A.

P. 19. 1 There is no doubt about the reading of M here. The letters κο at the end of page 18 are clear, and while ψε in this line is partly broken away, the traces are unmistakable. L^1 has *nihil igitur adicientes plurimum ex prioribus recidetis* (from *recīdo*), L^2 *nihil igitur adicientes exceditis a prioribus peccatis vestris*. Following L^2 editors have reconstructed the latter part of the sentence ἀποστήσεσθε ἀπὸ τῶν προτέρων ἁμαρτιῶν ὑμῶν; but *exceditis* of L^2 may be regarded as an error for either *excīdetis* or *excĭdetis*; cf. note on p. 20 l. 20.

3 A adds ταύταις after μου: om. LL.

4 ζήσεσθε A. — *domino* E. — A adds πάντα after ταῦτα: om. LL.

5 καὶ μετά AL^2: L^1 omits καί.

μου λεγει μ[οι α]γωμεν εις
αγρον και [δειξ]ω σοι τους
ποιμεν[ας τ]ων προβατων
αγωμεν φημι κε· ηλθομεν
εις τι πεδιον και δεικνυ
ει μοι π[οιμ]ενα νε[α]νισκον
ενδεδυ[με]ν[ον συνθ]ε[σι]ν
ϊματιων τω χ[ρ]ω[μ]ατι κρο
κωδη εβοσκε δ[ε] προβατα 6
πολλα λει[α]ν και τ[α] προβατα
τα[υτ]α ωσε[ι] τρυ[φ]ωντα ην
κα[ι λ]ει[α]ν σπατα[λ]ωντα
και [ιλαρα] ην σκιρ[τ]ωντα
ωδε κ[α]ι εκει και αυτος ο ποι
μην ϊλαρο[ς] ην ε[πι] τω ποι
μνιω αυτου κ[αι αυ]τη η
ειδεα του πο[ιμενο]ς λει
αν ϊλαρα ην κα[ι] ε[ν] τοις
προβασι περιε[τρε]χεν·
λεγει μοι βλεπ[εις] φησιν 2, 1
τον πο[ι]μενα τουτον· βλε
πω φημι κε· ουτος φησιν
εστιν αγγελος τρυφης
και απατης ουτος ουν
εκστρεφει τας ψυχας
των δουλων του θυ των

10 καὶ ἤλθομεν AL[1]E: L[2] omits καί.

11 δείκνυσι Ath[2].

15 ἔβοσκε δέ MAL[1]E: βόσκοντα Ath[2] L[2].

20 ὧδε κἀκεῖ Ath[2], ὧδε κἀκεῖσε A, *huc et illuc* LL, *hic et illic* E.

21 πάνυ ἱλαρός Ath[2], cf. L[1] (*vehementer*) L[2] (*magnam percipiebat voluptatem*): A omits πάνυ. Hermas does not use it elsewhere; perhaps LL had λίαν, cf. 24.

23–24 ἱλαρὰ ἦν λίαν A.

25 προβάτοις A. πρόβασι is cited by Arcadius (p. 138, 5) and Hesychius *s.v.*

After 25 Ath[2] has καὶ ἄλλα πρόβατα εἶδον σπαταλῶντα καὶ τρυφῶντα ἐν τόπῳ ἑνί, οὐ μέντοι σκιρτῶντα, for which there is no equivalent in any of the other authorities; yet it seems to be required by ch. 2, 4 and 6, as various editors observed.

26 λέγει μοι MLL: καὶ λέγει μοι AAth[2]E. — φησίν ML[2]: om. AAth[2]L[1]E.

29–30 A places the ἐστίν after ἀπάτης.

30 οὗτος οὖν MLL: AAth[2]E omit οὖν.

31 ἐκτρίβει AAth[2] and probably LL (*corrumpit*), for the Latin translators ren-

p. 20

κενων [και κα]ταστρεφε[ι
αυτους α̣[πο τ]η̣ς αληθει̣
ας απατων [α]υτους ται[ς
επιθυμιαις ταις πονη
ραις εν αις απολλυνται
επιλανθ[αν]ονται γαρ τας 2
εντολας [το]υ θ̅υ̅ του ζω
οντος κ[αι πορ]ευονται
ταις απατ[αις κ]αι τρυφαις
ταις̣ ματ[αι]α[ι]ς και απολ
λυνται απο τ[ου] αγγελου
του[τ]ου εις θ̣[αν]ατον·
τιν[α] δ̣ε ε[ις κα]ταφθοραν·
λεγω αυτ[ω] κ[ε] ου γεινω 3
σκω εγω τι ει[ς] θανατον
και τ[ι] εις κα[τα]φθοραν
εστ[ι]ν̣· α̣[κ]ουε φη[σι]ν̣ οσα
ειδ[ες] προ[ο]βατα λ̣[εια]ν ϊλ̣α̣
ρα κα[ι] σκι̣[ρ]τ̣[ωντα ο]υτο̣ι
εισι[ν] οι αφεσταμενοι

der compounds of *στρέφω* by compounds of *verto*. The reading of M is an error due to the influence of the following *καταστρέφει*.

P. 20. 1 *τῶν κενῶν* MA: om. Ath^{2}LLE, followed by G.-H. and Dibelius.

5 M here confirms the restoration by G.-H. of *ἀπόλλυνται* from Ath^{2}LL (C also had this text): *ἀπλοῦνται* A, whence Tischendorf and Hilgenfeld derived *ἀπολοῦνται*.

6 *ἐπιλανθάνονται* MALLC: *ἐπιλανθανόμενοι* Ath^2. — *τῶν ἐντολῶν* AAth^2. For the accusative in M, see Robertson, *Grammar* p. 509, citing Philipp. 3, 13, Hebr. 13, 2 (ℵ), and P.Oxy. 744, ll. 11–12.

7 *ζῶντος* AAth^2. *ζώω* is an Epic and Ionic form of the verb; but *ζώοντος* in M seems to be due partly to the scribe's uncertainty how to divide the word, and partly to the analogy of verbs like *λύω*. *ντ* is occasionally carried over to a following vowel in the papyri (Crönert, *Mem. Graeca Hercul.* p. 15). — After *ζώοντος* there is a point in the papyrus, but it is probably an accidental spot.

9–10 *ἀπάταις* (without article) *καὶ τρυφαῖς ματαίαις* A, *ταῖς ματαίαις τρυφαῖς καὶ ἀπάταις τοῦ βίου τούτου* Ath^2. — *ὑπό* A.

12–13 *τινὰ μὲν εἰς θάνατον, τινὰ δὲ εἰς καταφθοράν* AL^{1}E: L^2 omits the first clause (whereas M has omitted only *τινὰ μέν*), *εἰς θάνατον καὶ καταφθοράν* Ath^2, abbreviating.

15 A places *ἐστιν* after the first *τί* and so Ath^2. — The Coptic version implies an original reading *τί εστι τινὰ εἰς θάνατον καὶ τινὰ εἰς καταφθοράν*. Cf. also E *nescio . . . quis in mortem, quis in perniciem eat*.

17 *ὅσα* MLL (*quaecumque*): *ἃ* AAth^2 CE.

18 *λείαν* (*valde* LL): om. AAth^{2}CE.

20 M is supported by L^1 (*discesserunt*)

απ[ο του θ̅]υ̅ εις̣ τελος και
παρ[αδεδω]κοτες εαυ
του[ς] τ̣[αις] επιθυμιαις
το[υ] α[ι]ωνος τουτου εν
το[υτο]ις ουν μετανοια
ζωη[ς] ουκ εστιν οτι
προσεθηκαν κατα̣ ονο
μα του κ̅υ̅ βλασφημιαν
πα νεϊ ν̣ των τοιουτων ουν ο θα
νατος· α δε ε̣ιδες μη σκιρ 4
τωντα αλλα εν ενι τοπω

p. 21

β̣[οσκομενα ουτ]οι εισιν πα
ραδεδ[ωκο]τες μεν εαυτους
ταις τρ[υφα]ι̣ς̣ και απαταις
εις δε τον κ̅ν̅ ουκ εβλασφη
μησαν ουτοι ουν κατεφθαρ
μενοι εισιν̣ [α]π̣ο της αλη
θειας εν τ[ουτ]ο[ι]ς ουν ελ
π̣[ις] εστιν̣ μ̣[ετ]ανοιας εν ῃ

L[2] (*exciderunt*), and apparently C: ἀπεσπασμένοι AAth[2].

23 A has omitted (by homoioteleuton) the words ταῖς ἐπιθυμίαις . . . ἑαυτούς (p. 21, l. 2), and editors have reconstructed the passage from Ath[2] and the versions.

26–28 ὅτι καὶ τὸ ὄνομα τοῦ θεοῦ δι' αὐτοὺς βλασφημεῖται Ath[2]; cf. E *quia blasphemaverunt nomen dei.* The Latin versions expand the passage but agree in the main with M: L[1] *quoniam quidem adiecerunt ad reliqua delicta sua quod etiam nomen dei nefandis insecuti sunt verbis*, L[2] *adiecerant enim ad alia delicta sua etiam aliud maius, ut domini nomen nefandis insequerentur blasphemiis.*

29 *huiusmodi homines morti sunt destinati* L[1], *huiusmodi ergo*, etc. L[2]: *hi in morte sunt* E. The text of Ath[2], which is mutilated here, is printed by Dindorf τῶν τοιούτων [ἡ ζωὴ θάν]ατός ἐστιν; but οὖν ὁ would suit as well as ἡ ζωή, and the only variation from M would then be the insignificant addition of ἐστίν.

30 I can make nothing of the gloss in the margin.

31 *sed uno loco* LL, *et in uno loco* E; cf. Ath[2] καὶ ἐν τόπῳ (a corruption of καὶ ἐν ἑνὶ τόπῳ ?).

P. 21. 1 εἴσιν οἱ π. Ath[2], *hi sunt qui* LL, *ii sunt qui* E.

2–3 ἑαυτοὺς ταῖς τρυφαῖς καὶ ἀπάταις MALLC: τῇ τρυφῇ καὶ ἀπάτῃ ἑαυτούς Ath[2], *semet voluptati* E.

4 οὐδὲν ἐβλασφήμησαν ALL: μὴ βλασφημήσαντες Ath[2], *non blasphemaverunt* E.

7 AAth[2] omit οὖν: *ideoque . . . habent spem* LL, *sed iis est poenitentia* E.

δυναντ[αι] ζ[η]σα[ι] η κατα
φθορα ουν [ελπι]δα εχει ανα
νεωσεω[ς] τινα ο δε θανα
τος απωλεια[ν] εχει [α]ιωνιον·
παλιν π[ροεβημε]ν μει 5
κρον κα[ι] δε[ι]κ[νυε]ι μοι
ποιμενα μεγαν [ωσ]ει αγρι
ον τη ειδ[ε]α περικειμενον
δε[ρμ]α α[ιγ]ειο[ν] λε[υ]κον και
πηραν τιν[α] ειχ[εν] επι
τον [ωμον] κ[α]ι ρ[αβ]δον
σκληρ[α]ν λειαν οζ[ο]υς εχου πετ[
σαν κα[ι] μαστι[γα με]γαλην
και το βλεμμ[α ειχ]εν πε
ριπικρον ω[στε φοβ]ηθη
ναι αυτον τ[οιουτο] ειχε
το βλε[μ]μα ο[υτος ο] ποι 6
μην παρελαμβ[αν]ε τα
προβατα παρα του ποι
μενος του νεανισκου
εκεινα [τ]α σπαταλωντα

11 The α of τινα is mutilated, but the trace is unmistakable; cf. L[1] *spem aliquam*, L[2] *aliquam spem*. τινος A, ἕως τινός (where ἕως is a dittography) Ath[2].

13 προέβημεν M (προέβην would not fill the gap), with Ath[2]LLC: προέβην AE.

14 δείκνυσί μοι ἕτερον Ath[2].

15 ὡς Ath[2].

17 ἄγριον A, an error due to the presence of the word in 15.

19 τὸν μώμον (error for ὦμον) Ath[2], *in humero* LLC: τῶν ὤμων AE. Cf. Vis. 5, 1, where the plural τῶν ὤμων is read by ℵE, τὸν ὦμον by ALL.—For the loose use of the accusative with ἐπί where no motion is implied, see Robertson, *Grammar*, p. 602.

20 καὶ ὄζους ἔχουσαν AAth[2] (ῥόζους), *et in manu virgam nodosam et (ac) vehementer duram* LL.—I can make nothing of the marginal gloss.

21 Ath[2] omits καὶ μάστιγα μεγάλην.

23 Ath[2] πικρόν, L[1] *amarum et saevum*, L[2] *amarum saevumque*, E *et saevus aspectus eius et terribilis facies eius*.

24 A adds με after φοβηθῆναι, and so also Ath[2]; cf. E *et timui eum*. But L[1] (*ut possit terreri* [v. l. *horrere*] *aliquis*) and L[2] (*ut etiam posset horreri*) seem to support M.—The space is hardly sufficient for τοιοῦτον, and the ν may be omitted even before a vowel; cf. Mayser, p. 309.

24–25 Ath[2] and L[2] omit τοιοῦτον εἶχε τὸ βλέμμα.

25 οὗτος ML[2]: οὗτος οὖν AAth[2] L[1] (the last omits ὁ ποιμήν), *et hic pastor* E.

27 ἀπό AAth[2].

28 Ath[2] inserts τοῦ πρώτου after ποιμένος.

και τρυφωντα μη σκιρ
τωντα δ[ε] και ενεβαλλεν
αυτα εις τινα τοπον κρη

p. 22

μνωδη και τριβολωδη
ωστε α[π]ο τ[ων] ακανθω[ν
και τρι[β]ολ[ω]ν μη δυνα
σθαι [ε]κπλεξαι τα προβ[α
τα αλλα εμπλεκεσθαι
αυτα [εις τα]ς ακανθας
]το και [τριβο]λους αυτου 7
]γον ουν ε[μπ]επλ[ε]γμ[ε]να
εβοσκ[ον]το τ[ας] ακανθα[ς
και τρ[ιβο]λους και λειαν
εταλαιπωρ[ο]υν δερο
μενα [υπ α]υ[το]υ· και ωδε
και [εκε]ι πε[ρι]ηλαυνεν
αυτ[α κ]αι [ο]λω[ς] αναπαυ
σιν [α]υτοις ο[υ]κ εδιδει

31 ἔβαλεν A, ἔβαλλεν Ath^2.

P. 22. 1 The complete text is preserved in Ath^2 (κρημνώδη καὶ ἀκανθώδη καὶ τριβολώδη), L^1 (*praecipitem . . . et spinosum tribulisque confertum*), C and E; cf. L^2 (*praecipitem . . . ac spinosum dolisque repletum*). A omits καὶ τριβολώδη, M καὶ ἀκανθώδη.

5 ἀλλ' AAth^2.

6 αὐτά is omitted by AAth^2. — ταῖς ἀκάνθαις καὶ τριβόλοις Ath^2.

7–8 Again I can make nothing of the marginal writing. Something preceded το; and τον is perhaps as likely as γον. — ταῦτα οὖν A: *sed implicata* (*implicita*) *ibi* LL. Ath^{2}CE omit the sentence.

9 ἐν ταῖς ἀκάνθαις καὶ τριβόλοις A. The Latin versions support the reading of M; cf. L^1 *pascerentur spinas et tribulos*.

11 δαιρόμενα AAth^2.

13 κἀκεῖσε A, κἀκεῖ Ath^2, *huc et illuc* L^{2}E, om. L^1.

14 ὅλως MAth^{2}E (*ne minime quidem requiem iis concedens*); cf. L^2 (*nec ullam eis requiem dabat*): om. AL^1.

15 ἐδίδου AAth^2. For the form ἐδίδει, see Crönert, *Mem. Graeca Hercul.*, p. 250, n. 2a. — After ἐδίδου Ath^2 adds οὐδὲ ἵσταντο. It would seem that the Latin versions had this clause in their originals; for L^1 has *nec consistendi eis locum aut tempus permittebat*, which ignores ἀνάπαυσιν αὐτοῖς οὐκ ἐδίδου, unless one prefers to assume that the version incorporates both clauses in a free translation. L^2 has *nec ullam eis requiem dabat, nec consistere eis ullo loco permittebat*. It should be further observed that neither Ath^2 nor the versions take account of the clause beginning with l. 16 (καὶ ὅλως . . . ἐκεῖνα). Is it possible that the peculiarities of their texts are due to a misunderstanding of εὐστάθει, taking it literally as *stand well*? Cf. Sim. 7, 3, where L^1 renders εὐσταθοῦντος *bene stabilitus*.

και ολως ουκ̣ [ε]υσταθει̣
τα [πρ]οβ̣[α]τα εκεινα βλ[ε 3, 1
πω[ν] α̣υ̣[τα] μαστειγ[ο]υ
με[να] κα̣[ι] τ̣αλ̣αι̣π̣ωρουν
τα [ε]λυπουμην επ αυ
το[ις οτι] ουτως εβασα
νι[ζοντ]ο̣ και ανοχην
ο[λως ουκ] ε̣ιχον· λεγω 2
τ[ω ποιμ]ενι τω μετ ε
μο[υ λαλ]ουντ[ι] κ̅ε̅ φημι
τι[ς] ε̣[σ]τ̣ι̣ν ουτος ο ποι
μην [ο]υτως ασπλαγχνος
και πικρος και ολω̣ς
μηδεν σπλαγχ̣ν̣[ι]ζο
μεν[ο]ς επι τα προβατα
ταυτα [ο]υ[τος φ]ησιν εσ
τιν αγγελος [τ]η̣ς̣ τειμω

p. 23

ρ̣ι̣α̣ς εκ δε τ[ων α]γγελ̣ω̣ν
των δι̣καιω̣ν̣ [εσ]τιν κε̣ι̣με

16 εὐσταθοῦσαν A. This is a noteworthy case in which A has a vulgar form while M has the normal and correct one. Cf. ἐδοκοῦσαν, Sim. *9*, 9, 5. Jannaris (*Hist. Greek Gram.* § 789) cites several similar forms from the LXX and one from Acts 17, 5 (v. l.). Choeroboscus credits Euripides with ἐπληροῦσαν in Hec. 574, and there are examples in inscriptions of the third and second centuries before Christ.

18 βλέπων οὖν αὐτὰ οὕτω AL[1], βλέπων οὖν αὐτὰ ἐγὼ οὕτως Ath[2]; cf. L[2] *quae cum viderem ego sic*, etc. Here, however, G.–H. suggest that *ego* may be an error for *ergo*. —μαστιζόμενα Ath[2].

19 ταλαιπωροῦντα MAth[2]: ταλαιπωρούμενα A. The active is used in Vis. *3*, 7, 1, Sim. *6*, 2, 7. There is no other case of the middle in Hermas.

24 ἀγγέλῳ Ath[2] without support.

25 λαλοῦντι MAAth[2]E: omitted in LL (*qui erat mecum*). —φημί M and some MSS of L[1]: omitted by AAth[2]L[2]E and most MSS of L[1].

27 ὁ after ποιμήν AAth[2]. —οὕτως MALL: om. Ath[2]E. The omission of ὁ by M is probably an haplography.

28–31 καὶ ὅλως . . . ταῦτα om. Ath[2].

29 μή A: the testimony of the versions is not conclusive as to this reading, since *nullo modo* (LL) and *nec unquam* (E) may be due to ὅλως μή only.

31 *hic pastor inquit* L[1], *hic inquit pastor* L[2].

32 ὁ ἄγγελος AAth[2]. The Latin versions seem to have read οὗτος, φησίν, ὁ ποιμήν ἐστιν ἐκ τῶν ἀγγέλων τῶν δικαίων.

P. 23. 1 τῶν ἀγγέλων τῶν δικαίων MAth[2]: τῶν δικαίων τῶν ἀγγέλων A.

2 τεταγμένος Ath[2].

νος δε επ[ι] τ[ης] τειμωριας
παραλαμ[β]α[νει ο]υ[ν] τους 3
αποπλανωμ[ενο]υς απο
του θ̅υ̅ και [πορευ]θεντας
ταις επιθ[υμιαις] του αιω
νος τουτου [και] τειμωρει
αυτ[ο]υς καθ[ως τ]ις [α]ξιος
εστιν δε[ιναις] τε[ιμω]ρ[ι]αι[ς
και ποικιλα[ις] ηθελον 4
φημι γνωνα[ι τα]ς π[ο]ικιλας
τειμωριας [τ]α[υτας] ποτα
παι εισιν· ακο[υε φη]σιν τας
ποικιλας βασ[ανους] και
[τ]ε[ι]μωριας βιω[τικα]ι ει
σι βασανο[ι αι μεν] ζημι
αις αι δε ὑσ[τερησ]εσιν
αι δε α{ι}σθ[ενειαις] ποι
κιλαις αι δε π[αση] ακα
ταστασια οι [δε υβριζο

5 ἀποπλανηθέντας Ath[2]LLE.

7 ταῖς ἐπιθυμίαις καὶ ἀπάταις τοῦ αἰῶνος τούτου ALL, ταῖς ἐπιθυμίαις αὐτῶν Ath[2], *in cupidine peccati huius mundi* E.

8 τιμωρεῖ MA: τιμωρεῖται Ath[2]. Hermas uses the passive elsewhere, but not the middle.

9 The Latin versions support M, *sicut meruit unusquisque (quisque) eorum;* it is not certain that they had αὐτῶν in their Greek copies. καθὼς ἄξιοί εἰσιν AAth[2]E (*quantum iis congruit*).

10 δειναῖς καὶ ποικίλαις τιμωρίαις AAth[2], *saevis variisque poenis* L[1]: *saevis variis poenis* L[2]; cf. E *castigationibus acerbissimis variis.*

12 All others read κύριε (after φημί in A). Ath[2] introduces the sentence with λέγω αὐτῷ; cf. E *et dixi ei.* — *varias has poenas* L[1], *varias poenas has* L[2], τὰς ποικίλας ταύτας τιμωρίας Ath[2]. τὰς ποικίλας βασάνους ταύτας τιμωρίας A; cf. E *qualis sit hic cruciatus castigationes variae* — a "locus mancus," as d'Abbadie remarks.

14–17 A reads as M except εἰσιν αἱ βάσανοι. — αἱ ποικίλαι τιμωρίαι καὶ βάσανοι βιωτικαί εἰσι βάσανοι Ath[2], *variae poenae atque tormenta haec sunt quae homines cottidie in vita sua patiuntur* L[1] and similarly L[2] (which, however, omits ἄκουε . . . τιμωρίας).

17 The space after εἰσι in l. 17 is longer than usual, and εἰσι[ν] may have been written. There is a trace in the bracketed portion which may belong to ι of αι or to μ.

After βάσανοι A has τιμωροῦνται γὰρ οἱ μέν, then οἱ δέ in 18, 19, and 20. τιμωροῦνται was read by LL and probably by Ath[2], who paraphrases. The omission of τιμωροῦνται γάρ in M, which seems to be an error, led the scribe to write αἱ μέν as long as the article was accompanied by datives. In 21 he returned to the right gender with οἱ δέ. LL read the masculine throughout. E omits αἱ μὲν (17) . . . δύναμιν (p. 25, 26).

μενοι υπ[ο αναξιω]ν̣ κ̣α̣ι
ετεραις πο[λλαις πρα
ξεσιν πασχ[οντες πο]λ 5
λοι γαρ ακατ[αστα]το̣υ̣ν
τες ταις βου[λαις] αυτω̣̄
επιβαλλοντα[ι πο]λλα̣
κα[ι] ουδεν αυ[το]ις ολω̣[ς
προχωρει και λεγ̣ουσιν ε̣
αυτους μη [ευο]δουσθ̣α̣ι̣
εν ταις πρ[αξεσι]ν̣ αυ[τω]ν̣

p. 24

και ο̣υκ α̣ναβαινει
επι τ[η]ν̣ καρδιαν αυ
τω[ν οτι ε]πραξαν πον[η
ρα [εργα] αλλα αιτιων
ται [τον] κ̄ῡ· οταν ουν 6
θ[λειβωσι] παση θλει
ψει [τοτ]ε εμοι παρα
[δι]δ̣[ονται] εις αγαθην
παιδ[ειαν] και ϊσχυρο
ποιουν̣τ̣α̣ι εν τη πιστ[ει
του κ̄ῡ [κ]α̣[ι] τ[α]ς̣ λοιπας
ημερ[α]ς̣ τ̣ης̣ ζωης αυ
των [δ]ο̣υ̣λε[υ]ουσιν τω

22 Ath² has ἐλαττόνων for ἀναξίων, but in this portion he is paraphrasing freely.

26 ἐν ταῖς Ath².

29 The ε at the end of the line is very doubtful; the only trace, and that an uncertain one, may be part of the horizontal stroke.

P. 24. 2 αὐτῶν ἐπὶ τὴν καρδίαν A.

4 It is possible that the Latin versions (*quae nequiter fecerunt*) did not have ἔργα; cf. Ath² τὰ πονηρὰ ἃ ἔπραξαν. The suggestion of G.–H. also merits attention, that *quae* (*qui* in some MSS of L¹) is for *quia*. — ἀλλά MA, *et* L¹, *adhuc et* L²; cf. καὶ λοιπόν Ath². Hollenberg's conjecture ἀλλ' ἔτι would explain the *adhuc* of L² and the λοιπόν of Ath². But the similarity of the sounds ἔτι, αἰτι- could lead to the erroneous insertion of the former as well as to its omission, and the text of MA should be preferred.

6 *omnem vexationem et incommodum* LL: G.–H. suggest that this may represent πάσῃ θλίψει καὶ συμφορᾷ.

θ̅ω̅ εν καθα[ρ]α καρδια
οταν ουν̣ μετανο̣η[σω
σιν τ[ο]τ̣ε̣ αναβαινει
ε̣π[ι] τ[ην] κ̣αρδιαν αυ
των̣ [τα] εργα̣ τ̣α πονη
ρα̣ [α] ε̣[πρ]α̣ξαν και το
τε δο[ξα]ζουσι τον θ̅ν̅
οτι̣ δ[ικα]ι̣ο̣ς κριτης
δι̣και̣ως ε̣π̣αθεν παν
τα ε̣[κα]στος κατα τας
πρ[αξ]εις αυτου τα δε
λοι̣π[α] δ̣ουλευσουσιν
τω κ̅ω̅ εν καθαρα καρ
δια αυτ̣ων και ευοδουν
τα[ι] εν π̣αση πραξει αυ
των λαμβανοντες παν

p. 25

τ̣α παρα του κ[υ] οσ[α αιτου]ν
[τ]α̣ι και το̣τε [δοξ]α[ζο]υ̣σ[ι]ν
[το]ν κ̅ν̅ οτι [εμοι] π[αρε]δ[ο]θ̣η
σα̣ν και ουκε̣[τι ουδεν] π̣α
σχουσι των [πονηρων
[λ]εγω αυτω κ̣[ε ετι μοι φ]η 4, 1
μι τουτο [δηλωσον τι
φησιν επιζ̣[ητεις ει α]ρ̣α̣
φημι κ̅ε̅ το̣ν [αυ]τ[ον χρο
ν̣ον βασαν̣ι̣ζ̣[ον]ται ο̣ι τρ̣[υ

14 *κυρίῳ* ALL. Ath[2] is still paraphrasing freely at this point, but the sentence *δουλεῦσαι τῷ θεῷ ἐν καθαρᾷ καρδίᾳ* seems to correspond to our passage.

15–26 *ὅταν οὖν . . . καρδίᾳ* omitted by A (homoiotel.). The Latin versions agree closely with M.

21 After *κριτής* M has omitted *ἐστι καί* by an error.

29 — p. 25, 1 *παρὰ τοῦ κυρίου πάντα* A.

P. 25. 1 In the gap near the end of the line there is room for six letters, but not more. It is therefore probable that M read *ὅσα αἰτοῦνται*; cf. L[1] *quaecumque poscunt*. A has *ὅσα ἂν αἰτῶνται*, L[2] *quaecumque petierint*.

6 ALL omit *φημί*.

8 The traces of *ρα* are very uncertain.

φωντες κ̣α̣ι̣ [α]π̣ατ̣ωμε
νοι ο̣σ̣[ο]ν̣ τ̣ρ[υφωσ]ι̣ κ̣α̣ι̣
απατωντ[αι] λ[ε]γει μ̣ο̣ι̣
τον αυτον χρ[ο]ν̣ον .[
β̣ασανιζονται . . . .[
[εδ]ει τους [ο]υ̣τ̣ως τρ̣υ 2
φ̣ωντας και [επ]ιλανθα
νομεν[ο]υς τ̣ο̣υ̣ [θ̅υ̅] ε[π]τ̣[α
πλασιω[ς] βασαν[ιζεσ]θ[αι
λεγει μοι αφ[ρων ει κ]α̣ι̣ 3
ου νοεις τ̣ης [βασανου
την δυνα[μιν] ε̣ι γ̣α̣ρ
εν[ο]ουν φημ[ι] κ̅ε̅ ουκ α̣ν̣
σε επηρωτω[ν ι]να μοι
δ̣ηλωσης· ακ̣ου[ε] φησιν
αμφοτερων [τη]ν δυ̣ν̣α

11 οἱ τρυφῶντες καὶ ἀπατώμενοι MA, *qui desciscunt a metu dei* LL.

12 The last letters are very doubtful.

14 There is room for more writing after χρόνον, perhaps καί (cf. L[1] *per idem tempus etiam cruciantur*), though the single remaining trace might belong to a φ (φησί?) as well as to the κ of καί. There is nothing corresponding to this in A or L[2].

15 The textual problem is particularly difficult at this point. There is space for at least four letters after βασανίζονται, and it is not impossible that even more might have been written if the scribe encroached upon the margin, as he did not infrequently. But just after βασανίζονται the papyrus has been so injured by worm-holes that the remaining traces, which are very slight, are completely illegible, and the right-hand margin has been so scoured by sand that the length of the line is uncertain. After βασανίζονται A has ἔδει γάρ, and this was also the reading of the Latin versions (*oportebat enim* L[1], *cum oporteat* L[2]). But both Latin versions have after βασανίζονται a sentence which does not exist in M and A: L[1] *et dixi ei: exiguum inquam cruciantur* (*ei* and *inquam* omitted from one MS), L[2] *et dixi, multum exiguum domine cruciantur*. Because of this, editors have reconstructed a Greek sentence to correspond to the Latin texts.

Undoubtedly it is possible that M and A agree in a common error, the omission of a sentence by homoioteleuton (βασανίζονται). On the other hand it is possible to regard the extra sentence of the versions as a piece of translator's padding, especially if ἀλλά or ἀλλὰ γάρ stood after βασανίζονται in M. One might also think of λέγω or λέγω αὐτῷ. λέγω without the dative is rarely used to introduce another speaker; it is found in Vis. *1*, 3, 3, and Sim. *5*, 3, 1 (A). The transition without λέγω is somewhat abrupt, and since A certainly has not λέγω, it may be the safest procedure to accept the supplementary sentence from the Latin texts and read ἀλλά in l. 15 of M. — The reading of the beginning of l. 16 was unfortunately wrongly reported in Harvard Theol. Rev. XVIII, 125.

24 σε ML[2]: om. AL[1].

μ̣ι̣[ν] της τρυφης και απα 4
[τ]ης ο χρ̣ονος ωρα εστιν
μια· της δε βασανου η
ωρ̣α τ[ρ]ιακοντα ημερων
δ̣υ̣ναμιν εχει· εαν ουν

p. 26

μιαν ημεραν τις τρ[υ
φ[η]σ̣η̣ κ̣α̣ι̣ απα̣τηθη μ[ι
α[ν δ]ε [η]μεραν βασαν[ισθη
[ολον ενι]αυτον ϊσχυει
η ημ̣ε̣[ρ]α̣ της βασανου
[οσας ουν] ημερας τρυ
[φηση τι]ς̣ τοσουτου[ς
[ενιαυ]τους βασανιζε
τ̣[αι βλεπ]εις ουν φησι[ν
οτι τη[ς] τρυφης κα[ι
απατης ο χρονος ε[λ]α
χιστος εστιν· της δε
τειμωριας και βασα
ν̣ο̣υ πολυς· επει φη 5, 1
μι κ̄ε̄ ου νενοηκα ολ̣[ως
τους χρονους της απ[α
της και τρυφης και [βα
[σα]ν̣ου δηλαυγεστε

27 After δύναμιν Ath[2] adds τῆς τρυφῆς καὶ τῆς βασάνου. — τῆς ἀπάτης Ath[2].

29 After βασάνου Ath[2] has ὧραι τριάκοντα ἡμερῶν δύναμιν ἔχουσαι.

31 In the lower margin a later hand has written κ(αι) τιμωριας, perhaps a gloss to be inserted after βασάνου.

P. 26. 1 τις τρυφήσῃ MAth[2], τρυφήσῃ τις A.

4 ὅλον ἐνιαυτὸν ἰσχύει MA, ἐνιαυτοῦ ὁλοκλήρου ἰσχὺν ἔχει Ath[2]. The versions seem to have read ἰσχύσει; L[1] *anni spatium dies cruciatus eius valebit*, L[2] similarly, but *erat* (almost certainly an error for *erit*) in place of *valebit*: E *erit*.

5 Ath[2] adds ἐκείνη, which E supports.

8 βασανισθήσεται Ath[2] E.

11–12 ὁ χρόνος ἐλάχιστος MALL, *paucos dies* E, οὐδέν Ath[2].

14 ἐπεί is supported by LL (*quoniam*) and E (*quia*): A has ἔτι, a corruption of ἐπεί, cf. p. 47, 26.

16 τοὺς χρόνους MLL, περὶ τοῦ χρόνου A and perhaps E (*quia non intellexi, doce me de diebus*, etc.).

18 τηλαυγέστερον A. δηλαυγῶς is a va-

[ρο]ν μοι δηλωσον · απο 2
κριθεις μοι λεγει η
αφρο[σ]υνη σου παρα
μονος εστιν και ου
θελει[ς] σου την καρδι
αν καθαρισα[ι] και δου
λευειν τω θ̅ω̅ βλεπε
φησιν μη ποτε ο χρο
ν[ο]ς πληρωθη και συ
[α]φρων ευρεθης · ακουε
[ο]υν φησιν καθως βου
[λε]ι ϊνα νοησης αυτα

p. 27

[ο] τρυφων κα[ι] απα[τω]μ[ε 3
νος μιαν ημεραν [και] πρ[ασ
σων ᾱ βουλεται [πολ]λη[ν
αφροσυνην ε[νδεδ]υται
και ου νοει τη[ν πραξ]ιν
ην ποιει ει[ς την αυρι]ον
επιλανθαν[εται τι πρ]ο
μιας επραξε[ν η γαρ] τρυ
φη και απατη [μνημας
ουκ εχει δια [τ]ην αφροσυ
νην ην ενδ[ε]δυτ[α]ι ·
η δε τειμωρια κα[ι] βασα

riant in Mark 8, 25, and Hesychius has δηλαυγῶς· ἄγαν φανερῶς. δ appears for τ not infrequently in the papyri (Mayser, *Gram.* p. 175), and in this case the change of spelling may have been facilitated by a mistaken etymology connecting the word with δῆλος. The Ambrosian scholiast on Theocritus 3. 29 attests δηλέφιλον for τηλέφιλον, *i.e.* δηλοῦν τὴν φιλίαν.

29 οὖν A: *nunc* L¹E, *ergo nunc* L². There is nothing in M to show whether ν or ο stood in the vacant space.

P. 27. 2 The letters νο are on a very small separate fragment.

6 αὔριον γάρ A. The versions all have a co-ordinating conjunction (*ac*, *et*), which argues against the reading of A, but does not prove that a conjunction stood in the Greek texts from which the versions were made.

7 At the end of the line it is not quite certain whether what remains is ο or the upper part of ρ.

12 ἡ βάσανος A.

νος οταν κολληθη τω
ανθρωπω μιαν ημεραν
μεχρι ενιαυτου τειμω
[ρ]ειται βασανιζεται μνη
μας γαρ μεγαλας εχει η
τειμωρια και βα[σ]αν[ος
βασανιζομενος ου[ν] κα[ι 4
τειμωρουμενος ολο[ν
τον ενιαυτον μνημο
νευει τοτε της τρυφης
και απατης και γεινω
σκει οτι δια ταυτα πα
σχει τα πονηρα πας
ουν ανθρωπος ο τρ[υ
φων και απατωμε[νο]ς
ουτως βασανισθη[σε
ται οτι εχοντες ζ[ωη]ν
εαυτους εις θανατ[ον

p. 28

π[αραδε]δ[ωκασ]ι· ποι[α]ι 5
φ[ημι] κ̅ε̅ τρυφαι ει[σ]ι
β[λαβερα]ι· πασα τρυφη
φ[ησιν] τω ανθρωπω
[ο εαν η]δεως ποιη·

15 μέχρις A. — τιμωρεῖται καὶ βασανίζεται A, and so also E (*castigatur et patitur*): LL βασανίζεται only (*torquetur*). The omission of καί in M may be only an insignificant error; but there is a possibility that we have to do with a double reading, in which the scribe meant to adopt the second word, but neglected to strike out the first. In that case M would go with the Latin versions.

18 A adds ἡ as above (l. 12). — E probably had βάσανος καὶ τιμωρία (*passionis et castigationis*): LL τιμωρία (*poena*) only.

22 τότε MLLE: ποτέ A.

24 διὰ ταῦτα MLL (*propterea*): [δι'] αὐτά A; cf. E *propter illas* (sc. *delicias et lasciviam*).

28 οὕτω A. — βασανίζεται ALLE; but Ath[2] has a future tense in the sentence ἀντὶ γὰρ τῆς τρυφῆς καὶ ἀπάτης ἑκάστης ἡμέρας ἀποτίσει βάσανον μεγάλην, ἐνιαυτὸν τῇ ἡμέρᾳ. This, however, is a condensation of a much longer passage, and its testimony is of little value.

30 εἰς θάνατον ἑαυτούς A.

P. 28. 1 Possibly π[αραδε]δ[ωκα]ν; cf. p. 31, 5.

3–5 πᾶσα, φησί, πρᾶξις τρυφή ἐστι τῷ

[και γαρ ο] οξυχολος τη
[εαυτο]υ̣ πραξει το ϊκα
[νον] π̣ο̣ι̣ων τρυφα και
[ο μοιχος κα]ι ο̣ μεθυσος
και ο καταλ̣αλ̣ο̣ς̣ κα̣[ι ο
ψ[ε]υστης και π[λ]ε̣ο̣ν
εκτης και αποστε[ρη
της [κ]α̣[ι] ο̣ τουτοις [τα
ομ[οια πα]ν̣τα ποιων̣
τη ϊδ̣ι̣α̣ νοσω το̣ [ικα
νον π[οιε]ι τρυφ̣[α ουν
εν τη π̣ραξει α̣[υτου
αυ̣[ται π]α̣σαι τρυ̣[φ]α̣[ι 6
[β]λ̣α̣β̣ε̣[ρ]αι εισ̣ι̣ν [το]ι̣ς̣
[δ]ουλο[ις τ]ου θ̅υ̅ δια
ταυτ̣[ας ο]υν τας απα
τας πασχουσ̣ι̣ν οι τει
μω[ρ]ουμεν[οι] κ̣α̣ι βασα
νι[ζ]ομενο̣[ι ει]σιν δε 7
κ[αι] τρυφαι̣ [σ]ωζουσαι
τ̣[ο]υς ανθρωπους πολ
λ̣[ο]ι ουν αγ[αθο]ν̣ εργαζο

ἀνθρώπῳ ὃ ἐὰν ἡδέως ποιῇ A, πᾶσα πρᾶξις σαρκικὴ τρυφή ἐστιν, ἐὰν ἡδέως ποιῇ αὐτήν Ath²; cf. L² *omnis actus delitiarum, quodcumque homo libenter facit*, E *omnis res quam agit homo ut ipsum delectet*. On the other hand, the reading of L¹ *omni (inquit) homini voluptas est quodcumque libenter facit* may be derived from *omnis*, etc., which would agree closely with M. In l. 4 it is not quite certain whether φ[ησιν] or ε[στιν] should be read. The shape of the trace resembles the left side of the oval of φ slightly more than the curve of ε.

6–7 τῷ ἑαυτοῦ πάθει AAth². The reading of L² *in sua opera* supports M. L¹ (*satisfaciens moribus suis*) and E (*et iracundia eius secundum voluntatem eius agit et naturam eius delectat*) are less clear.

11–12 ὁ πλεονέκτης καὶ ὁ ἀποστερητής AAth².

13 After τούτοις the surface of the papyrus has flaked off, so that it is impossible to say whether τά followed or not.

14 A omits πάντα. *simile aliquid* L¹, *similia* L²E. ὅσα τοιαῦτα in the paraphrase of Ath² may possibly be regarded as allied to the reading of M, because of the notion of number involved in ὅσα. — The ν of πάντα is doubtful, but the trace which remains does not resemble any other letter.

17 ἐπί A. Ath² has ἐν in a free paraphrase, τρυφῶσι γὰρ ἐν τῇ αὐτῶν πράξει.

18 αὗται πᾶσαι αἱ τρυφαί A: αὗται δὲ αἱ πράξεις Ath².

27 οὖν M alone: γάρ Ath²LLE. A omits the conjunction. — ἀγαθόν MAE (the

μενοι τρυφωσιν τη
ε[α]υτων η[δο]νη φερο
[μ]ενοι · α[υτη ου]ν η τρυ

p. 29

[φη] συμφορος εστιν [τοις
[δου]λοις του θ̅υ̅ και ζ[ωην
περιποιειται τ[ω] αν[θρω
πω · αι δε βλαβ[εραι τρυ
φαι αι προειρη[μεναι β]α
[σ]ανους και τε[ιμωριας
περιποιουν[ται εαν] δε
επιμεινωσι και [μη μετ]α
νοησωσιν θαν[ατον ε]αυ
[το]ις περιποιο[υν]τ[αι

Sim. VII

παραβο[λ]η
[μετ]α ημερας ολ[ιγας ειδο]ν 1
[α]υτ[ο]ν εις το π[εδιον τ]ο
[αυτο ο]που και τ[ους ποι]με
[νας ε]ωρακειν κ[α]ι λ[εγε]ι μοι
[τι επιζ]ητεις · [π]α[ρειμι
[φημι κ]ε ερωτη[σαι σε ινα
αγγ]ελ[ο]ν
[τον πο] [[ιμενα]] τον [τειμω

ν of M is all but certain) : ἀγαθά Ath² and probably LL (*opera bonitatis*).

P. 29. In the upper margin there is a trace which may be part of the numeral π.

4 A has τῷ τοιούτῳ after ἀνθρώπῳ, and so all the versions.

7 αὐτοῖς περιποιοῦνται A and perhaps E (*quae eis supervenient castigationes et afflictiones*). The dative is omitted in LL.

8 ἐπιμένωσι A, probably an error: *permanserint in illis* LL. The translations may have had ἐν αὐταῖς in their originals.

11 The papyrus is so lacerated after παραβολή that it is impossible to say whether a numeral followed or not. ἀρχή A, *similitudo septima* L¹, *explicit similitudo VI, incipit similitudo VII* L², *similitudo octava* E.

16 ἐπιζητεῖς MAL¹: L²E add *hic*. — παρ' ἐμοί A.

17 ἐρωτῆσαί σε ML¹ (*rogare te*), *rogare* L²: AE omit.

18 The scribe wrote ποιμένα, then crossed out the word with a single stroke and wrote

[ρητην] κελευση[ς] εκ του
[οικου] μου εξελθει[ν οτ]ι
λεια[ν θλ]ειβει· δει [σε φη
σιν [θλειβ]ηναι ου[τω γαρ
[προσε]τα[ξ]εν ο εν[δοξ]ος
[αγ]γε[λο]ς τα πε[ρ]ι σου [θε
[λει γαρ] σε και πειρ[α
[σθη]ναι· τι γαρ φημι [κε
εποι[ι]ησα ουτω π[ο]ν[η
ρον ινα τουτω τ[ω αγγε
[λω] παραδοθω· α[κ]ου[ε 2
φησ[ι]ν αι μεν αμ[α]ρ[τιαι

p. 30

. .

σου πολλαι αλλ ου [το
σα[υ]ται ωστε σε τω
α[γγε]λω παραδοθηνα[ι
[αλλα] ο οικος σου μεγα
[λας] αμαρτιας και αν[ο
[μιας] ηργασατο και π[α
[ρεπι]κρανθη [ο] ενδο
[ξος] αγγελος επι το[ις
[ε]ργοις αυτων και [δια

ἄγγελον above it. This is the reading of E, whereas ALL have *ποιμένα*.

21 λίαν με θλίβει ALLE.

22 A adds φησί after γάρ: om. MLLE.

25 ALLE omit καί. — The versions seem to have read an active infinitive: *temptare te* LL, *te probare* E.

28 τῷ ἀγγέλῳ τούτῳ A.

This page has some letters which were retraced, sometimes awkwardly, by a later hand after the original writing had grown dim, viz., η (19), υ (20), ε (25).

P. 30. At the top of this page there are traces which, though minute, it is possible to reconcile with the numerals πϛ.

2 A omits σε. — E omits ἀλλ' οὐ τοσαῦται.

3 τῷ ἀγγέλῳ τούτῳ ALLE.

4 ἀλλ' A. There is room for four letters in M. — μεγάλας MAE, *multa* L[1], *copiosa* L[2].

5 ἀνομιας καὶ ἁμαρτίας A. The order of the versions agrees with M: *delicta et scelera* LL, *peccata et crimina* E.

6 εἰργάσατο A. The η of M is broken, but not doubtful. Cf. PBerol 5513, col. 1, l. 8, where ἠργάσατο is read in Sim. *2*, 7 against εἰργάσατο of A. See also Crönert, *Mem. Graeca Hercul.* p. 203, n. 4, Mayser, *Gram.* p. 332.

τουτο εκελευ[σε σε
χρονον τινα θ[λειβη
ναι ινα κακεινοι [μετα
νοησωσι και κ[α]θα[ρισω
σι εαυτους απ[ο πασης
επιθ[υ]μιας τ[ου αιωνος
[το]υτου οτ[αν ουν με
ταν[ο]ησωσιν κ[αι καθα
ρισθ[ω]σιν τοτε [αποστη
σετα[ι] ο αγγελος [της τει
μωρειας· λεγω αυτω [κ̅ε̅ 3
ει εκεινοι τοιαυτα η[ρ
γασαντο ϊνα παραπ[ι
κρανθη ο αγγελος ο ε[ν
δο[ξ]ος τι εγω εποιησ[α
αλλως φησιν εκειν[οι
ου δυν[α]νται θλειβη
[ναι] εα[ν μη σ]υ η κεφαλη
[το]υ ο[ι]κ[ο]υ θλιβης σ[ου
γαρ θλ[ε]ιβομενου εξ α

p. 31

πζ

[ν]αγκης κακεινοι θλειβησον
[τα]ι ευσταθουντος δε σου
ουδεμιαν θλειψιν δυναν
ται εχειν· αλλ' ϊδου φημι 4

12 Letters have been retraced in ἵνα (να), also below, l. 14 (ε) and l. 20 (ει).

19 A agrees with M in omitting ἀπὸ σοῦ, which some editors had inserted on the authority of the Latin versions (*a te*). But E has *ab iis*.

21 εἰργάσαντο A.

23 ὁ ἔνδοξος ἄγγελος A.

25–26 οὐ δύνανται ἐκεῖνοι A.

29 Pages 30 and 31 originally formed a single sheet which was torn in such a way that the last letter of p. 30 (α) now stands on the right-hand portion, to which p. 31 belongs.

P. 31. 2 The letters ευ were retraced after the surface had been abraded by use; so also πο below, l. 14.

3 οὐδεμίαν δύνανται θλῖψιν A.

4 ἀλλ' ἰδοὺ MA: *sed ecce iam nunc* L[1], *sed iam* L[2], *ecce* E.

κ̅ε̅ μετανενοηκαν̣ ε̣ξ ολης
καρδιας̣ αυτων· των ουν
μετανοουντων φησιν δ[ο
κεις [τ]ας αμαρτιας ευθυ[ς
αφι̣ε̣σ̣θαι ου παντ[ω]ς αλ[λα
δει τον μετανοησαντα βα̣
σανισαι την εαυτου ψυχη[ν
κ̣α̣ι ταπεινοφρονησαι [εν
[α]παση τη πραξει αυτου ισχ̣[υ
[ρ]ως και θλειβηναι πολλα̣[ις
[θλ]ε̣[ι]ψεσιν και ποικιλαις και
[εαν] υ̣πενεγκη τας θλειψεις
[τας επ]ερχομενας αυτω πα[ν
[τως σ]πλαγχνισθησετα[ι
[ο τ]α παντα κτισας και δυ
ν̣[α]μωσας· και ϊασιν τι[ν]α

5 The papyrus has been perforated at the end of μετανενόηκαν, but the form is scarcely in doubt. The space would be scant for σι, and the slight traces correspond better to ν. This form is common in papyri (Mayser, *Gram.* p. 323), and is found below, p. 40, 18–19. A has — ασιν. L[1] has *agunt paenitentiam.*

6 After αὐτῶν A has οἶδα, φησί, κἀγὼ ὅτι μετανενοήκασιν ἐξ ὅλης καρδίας αὐτῶν, which M omitted by error (homoioteleuton). L[2] agrees with A, and so does L[1], except that it has *agere* (cf. *agunt* l. 5); E omits ἐξ ὅλης καρδίας αὐτῶν.

7 φησίν ML[1], om. AE. L[2] changes the construction.

8 εὐθύς MLLE: om. A.

9 A has οὐ παντελῶς, which may explain the strange rendering in E *nonne potius omnibus absolutis?* L[1] has *non proinde continuo;* L[2] combines this sentence with the foregoing in such a way that its Greek text for the words in question cannot be determined.

10 μετανοοῦντα ALLE.

13 πάσῃ A. The reading of M is scarcely in doubt. The space at the beginning of the line accommodates one letter only, hence it is impossible to transfer ἐν from the preceding line to this place. The form ἅπας seems to occur only here in Hermas, though it is found elsewhere in the Apostolic Fathers; but cf. p. 7, 32.

ἰσχυρῶς MAE: om. LL.

14–15 ἐν πάσαις θλίψεσι ποικίλαις A: *multas variasque* LLE, agreeing with M.

17–18 M and A are in agreement here if the restoration of M above is right. The Latin versions differ slightly; L[1] *cumque perpessus fuerit omnia quae institerint* (as if the original were πάντα τὰ ἐπερχόμενα), L[2] *cumque perpessus fuerit omnia.* So far as the indications of the papyrus go, M might have had πάσας instead of πάντως. But all the other authorities had πάντως, so I have kept it. The *omnia* of LL may be an insertion on the part of the translators. E read no corresponding word: *simulac afflictiones futuras perpessus est.* — πάντως is rendered *necessario* in E, *forsitan* L[1], *fortasse* L[2]. Cf. Sim. 5, 7, 4 above, with the reference to Cadbury's discussion of this word.

19 ἐνδυναμώσας A.

20 ἰσχύν A, emended to ἴασιν by Anger: *remedium* LLE.

δωσει αυτοις και τουτο 5
παντως εαν ϊδη την κα[ρ
διαν του μετανοησα[ν]τος
καθαραν απο παντος πον[η
ρου πραγματος· σοι δε συμ
φορον εστιν [κ]αι τω οικω
σου νυν θλει[β]ηναι· τι δε
πολλα λεγω· θλειβηνα[ι] σε
δει καθως προ[σ]εταξεν ο
αγγελος του $\overline{κυ}$ εκεινος ο π[α
ραδους σε εμοι και τουτο ε[υ

p. 32

πη

χαριστει τω $\overline{κω}$ οτι α[ξι
ον σε ηγησατο του πρ[ο
δηλωσαι σοι την θλειψιν
ϊνα προγνους αυτην
υπε[ν]εγκης ϊσχυρως·
λεγω αυτ[ω] $\overline{κε}$ συ μετ ε 6
μου γεινο[υ] και π[α]σαν
θλειψιν δυνησ[ο]μαι υπε
νεγκαι· εγω φησιν εσο
μαι μετα σου ερω[τ]ησω

21 A also reads *αὐτοῖς*, which editors have changed to *αὐτῷ* on the authority of L², *dabit ei*. L¹E omit the dative. Little importance can be attached to the agreement of M and A in a grammatical error of this sort, which is especially likely to occur in a general sentence. The error may go back to Hermas himself, or the scribes may have committed the same fault by a mere coincidence.

22 *πάντως* MA: *ταῦτα πάντα* (apparently) E. The Latin versions omit the word. — A omits *ἐὰν ἴδῃ τὴν καρδίαν*.

23 *μετανοοῦντος* ALLE (*qui agit poenitentiam*).

24 *καθαράν* MLLE: *καθαρῶς* A, corrected by Hilgenfeld.

25 *συμφέρον* A.

27 *δέ σοι* AE. L² omits *δέ* and L¹ has only *quid multum* for the whole phrase.

29 The papyrus has a point between *δεῖ* and *καθώς* — probably an accidental spot.

30 A omits *τοῦ*.

31 *παραδούς* MLLE (*qui tradidit*): *παραδιδούς* A. — *καὶ τοῦτο* MAL² (*et hoc gratias age*); cf. E *et propter hoc gratias age*: L¹ *quin potius gratias age*.

P. 32. 7–8 *δυνήσομαι πᾶσαν θλῖψιν* A. *facile . . . sustinebo* LL, *potero patienter ferre* E. — *ὑπενεγκεῖν* A.

δε και τον αγγελον τ[ον
τειμωρητην ϊνα σ̣ε̣
ελαφρωτερον θλε[ι]ψ̣η̣
αλλα ολιγω χρονω̣ θ̣λε[ι̣
βηση και παλιν απ[οκα
τασταθηση εις τον τ[ο
που σου μονον παρα
μ[ε]ινον ταπεινοφρονων
και λειτουργων τω κ̅ω̣̅
θ̣ω [ε]ν καθαρα καρδια σο̣υ
και τα τεκνα σου και ο [ο]ι
κος σου και πορευου ταις
εντολαις μου ας σ[ο]ι εν
τεταλμαι και δυνησε
ται σου η [μ]ετανοια ειναι
ϊσχυρα και καθαρα και ε̣αν 7
ταυτα φυλαξης μετα
του̣ οικ̣ου σου αποστη[σ]ε
τ̣α̣ι π̣α̣σα θλειψις απο σ̣[ο]υ̣

13 ἐλαφροτέρως A; this form of the comparative is illustrated by Crönert, *Mem. Graec. Hercul.* p. 193. — As to the reading of M, the ordinary rule which keeps ο after mute and liquid appears to have been generally observed even in post-classical times (Mayser, p. 297, Robertson, p. 278). But the distinction between ο and ω was fading, and some irregularities occur in consequence (Crönert, p. 19, p. 192).

14 ὀλίγον χρόνον A: *exiguo tempore* LL.

16 Although both the end of l. 16 and the beginning of l. 17 have been slightly injured, I am convinced that the injured letters are τ[ο] and π, not [ο]ι and κ. οἶκον A, τόπον LLE. G.-H. overlooked the fact that the translators had a text differing from A.

20 ALLE omit θεῷ, but the reading of M is scarcely in doubt. The left side of θ is visible, and the left curve of ω is on a small fragment originally attached, but now unfortunately broken off. The combination κύριος θεός seems not to occur elsewhere in Hermas — if so, I have overlooked it. But it was common enough, even in ordinary letters between Christians. It is found in two of the Paniskos letters in the University of Michigan collection (Inv. no. 1362, l. 4 and 1365, l. 6).

σου is omitted by ALLE, and is probably an error for σύ, which seems to be needed and may well be the original text.

22 ἐν ταῖς A.

23 μου ML¹E, om. L²: σου A. — αἷς A.

24 ἐντέταλμαι MLLE: ἐντέλλομαι A.

25–26 A places εἶναι after καθαρά.

27 ταῦτα ML¹ (*haec*), *hoc* E: ταύτας A. L² omits the whole clause.

29 *incommoda* (without *omnia*) L¹.

p. 33

πθ

[και] απο παντων δε α̣[πο]στη
[σε]ται η θλειψι[ς] ος α̣ν [τ]αις
εντολαις μου πορευσεται
ταυταις·

Sim. VIII, 1

η —
εδειξ[ε] μ̣οι ϊτ[εα]ν σκεπαζο[υ] 1
σαν πε[δ]ια και [ο]ρη και υπο τ[ην
[σκ]επ̣η̣[ν] της ι̣τεας παντε[ς
[ελ]ηλυθεισαν οι κεκλημεν[οι
[τ]ω̣ ονοματι $\overline{κου}$· ϊστηκει δ[ε 2
ο αγ̣γελος του $\overline{κυ}$ ενδοξος
[λεια]ν̣ υψηλος παρα την
[ι]τεαν δρεπανον̣ εχων με
[γα] κ̣α[ι] α[π]εκοπτεν [κ]λαδους
[απο της ι]τεας και επεδιδου

P. 33. 1 A inserts *φησίν* after *δέ*: omitted in the versions.

2 A omits *ἡ*. — *omnis vexatio* LL; but MAE agree in omitting *πᾶσα*. — *ὅσοι ἐν ταῖς* A. The versions have pronoun and verb in the plural, but that proves nothing so far as the original text is concerned. M might be read *ὃς ἐν ταῖς*; but the trace of the broken letter seems to me to be the last stroke of *α*, not the horizontal of *ε*. For *ἄν* in a general relative clause with indicative, compare Moulton (*Grammar of N. T. Greek*, Vol. I, p. 168), who cites *ὅταν δώσουσιν*, Rev. 4, 9. See also note on p. 38, l. 5.

3–4 *ταύταις πορευθῶσιν* A.

5 *similitudo octava* LL, *similitudo nona* E: om. A.

6 *ἰτέαν μεγάλην* AE: MLL omit the adjective.

9 *ἐληλύθεισαν* ML[1]: *ἐληλύθασιν* APBerol 6789 L[2]E.

10 *ἐν ὀνόματι* PBerol. — The unusual abbreviation $\overline{κου}$ in M is worth noting, but it may be due to a mere slip on the scribe's part. The *ο* is not complete; and the scribe may have left it unfinished and gone on to *υ* without taking the trouble to erase the *ο*, or may have erased the *ο* carelessly, leaving most of it visible. There is more than the usual space between *κ* and *υ*. — *εἱστήκει* A.

11 The letters *ο αγ* are on a small separate fragment. APBerol omit *ὁ*. — PBerol omits *τοῦ*, L[2]E omit *τοῦ κυρίου*.

12 The scribe of PBerol wrote *ἰσχυρός*, then deleted it and wrote *ὑψηλός*.

14 *ἔκοπτε* A. The reading of PBerol is uncertain, since only the beginnings of lines are preserved in this portion, and the verb was in the middle of its line.

15 The letters *ιδ* have been renewed, also the *ρ* in line 17 below. After *ἐπεδίδου* M has lost the end of this clause and the beginning of the next by homoioteleuton. A reads *τῷ λαῷ τῷ σκεπαζομένῳ ὑπὸ τῆς ἰτέας· μικρὰ δὲ ῥαβδία ἐπεδίδου.* PBerol has some remains of this passage, and E translates it closely. The Latin versions are somewhat condensed.

[α]υ̣τοις ωσ̣[ε]ι πηχιαια· μετα 3
[τ]ο παντας λαβ̣ειν τ[α] ρα[βδια
[ε]θηκε το δρεπανον ο αγ[γε
λος και το δενδρον εκε[ινο
ϋγιες ην οιον και εορ̣[ακειν
αυτο εθαυμαζον δε εγω 4
εν εμαυτω λεγων τοσουτω̣ν
κλαδων κεκομμενων το
δενδρον ϋγιε[ς ε]στιν λε
γει μοι ο ποιμην μ[η] θαυμαζε̣
ει το δενδρον ϋ[γιες] εμει
νεν τοσουτων κλ[α]δ[ω]ν̣ κο
πεντων· αφες δ[ε] φησ[ιν
παντα ϊδης και δηλωθ[η]σε

16 πηχυαῖα A. AL^1E have δέ after μετά: MPBerol L^2 omit it.

20 ἑωράκειν A, lacuna in PBerol. The form ἑόρακα, well known in Attic writers, is found in New Testament MSS, and occasionally in other writings down to the sixth or seventh century, when it disappears (Crönert, *Mem. Graec. Hercul.* p. 272). It seems to be rare in papyri.

22 πῶς τοσούτων AE. The clause λέγων . . . ἐστιν is omitted by LL (though L^1 may have had λέγων), and was probably not in PBerol; see Schmidt's note in *Berliner Klassikertexte*, VI, p. 18.

26 τὸ δένδρον τοῦτο PBerol LL: MAE omit τοῦτο.—διέμεινε PBerol; cf. *permanserit* LL.

28 ἀφ' ἧς δέ A, [. .]ε̣ς̣ φησ[ι (only the tops of ες remain) PBerol, according to Professor Schubart, who has kindly examined it for me. L^1 has *sed expecta, et tunc demonstrabitur tibi*, etc., omitting πάντα ἴδῃς. L^2 *expecta igitur, et cum universa videris, tunc demonstrabitur*, etc. E *sed mane adspiciens, et omnia exponentur tibi.* All omit φησί. Because of these renderings Hilgenfeld inserted ἀλλ' ἀνάμεινον into the text of A before ἀφ' ἧς, and other editors have followed him. But the Berlin papyrus had no room for such a clause, and it is impossible to combat the united negative testimony of this and the other two Greek sources, M and A. Even if it were possible to believe that our Greek texts were descended from an archetype which had lost this clause, a further difficulty would be presented by ἀφ' ἧς, which does not mean *until*, but ἐξ οὗ, *from what time, since*; cf. 1 Maccab. 1, 11, 2 Peter 3, 4, Hermas Sim. *8*, 6, 6 (ἀφ' ἧς ἐλάλησα) and Mand. *4*, 4, 3 where ἡμέρας is expressed with ἀφ' ἧς. One might think of extending the scope of ἀφ' ἧς so that it should introduce a when-clause of the more vivid future type; but the καί is an obstacle.

In view of these difficulties it is best to accept the reading of M as the true text, especially since the Berlin papyrus is now found to support it in the point of chief importance. We then explain ἄφες in this passage as an extension of its use with the first person of the subjunctive, where, beginning with the notion of *let*, *allow*, it becomes virtually a particle which introduces and strengthens the hortatory idea. Jannaris (*Historical Greek Grammar*, § 1914) cites several cases from the N.T. (Matth. 27, 49 may serve as a specimen) and from later authors. He shows that it may occur with the third person, but I have not up to this

ται σοι οτι εστιν· ο αγγελ[ο]ς 5
ο επιδους τω λαω τας ραβ[δ]ους

p. 34

[παλιν] α[π]η[τ]ει απ αυτ[ων
κ[α]θως ελαβον [ο]υτως
εκαλ[ο]υντο πρ[ος α]υτ[ον
[και ει]ς εκα[σ]τος αυτων
ε[π]ε[δ]ιδο[υ τ]ας ρ[α]βδου[ς
ελαμβα[νε δ]ε [ο] αγγελος του
κ̅υ̅ και κα[τε]νοε[ι αυ]τας πα 6
ρα τινων ελαμ[β]α[ν]ε τα[ς
ραβ[δο]υς ξηρας [και β]ε[βρω
μενας ωσε[ι] υπο σητος
εκελευεν ο αγγε[λο]ς τ[ους
τας ραβδους επ[ι]δεδω
κοτα[ς χ]ωρις στα[θηναι
ετ[ερο]ι δε επεδιδ[ου]ν [ξη 7
ρας αλλ ουκ ησαν [βεβρω
μεναι υπο σητος και τ[ο]υ
του[ς] εκελευ[σ]εν χωρις
[ισ]τανεσθαι· ετεροι δε 9

time found another case of ἄφες with the second person. The translators, not fully understanding the idiom, made the mistake of over-translating ἄφες. Apparently they passed from the idea of *leave alone*, *let be*, to that of *wait*, which appears in all the versions.

30 τὸ τί A. Lacuna in PBerol.

31 ἐπιδεδωκώς A. Lacuna in PBerol.

P. 34. 1 PBerol [απητει αυτ]ους. The single accusative of the person to whom a request is addressed is strange, but cf. Matth. 5, 42.

2 καὶ καθώς APBerol. — οὕτω καί AL^1 (*eodem etiam ordine*) and probably PBerol.

5 The first ε is mutilated but virtually certain. ἀπεδίδου A, *reddebat* LL. [απε]διδουν PBerol.

10 ὡς APBerol.

11 ἐκέλευσεν APBerol. L^1 has *iubebat* here and *iussit* l. 17, L^2 *iubebat* in both places, E *iussit* in both.

12 τὰς τοιαύτας ῥάβδους APBerol L^1E: L^2 condenses the sentence and its testimony is uncertain.

13 ἵστασθαι A, ἱστάνεσθαι PBerol. It should be noted, in view of the occurrence of ἱστάνεσθαι at l. 18, that the scribe of M may have had ἱστάνεσθαι in his copy, and may have written στά[νεσθαι] because of the final syllable of χωρίς — a natural haplography.

14 ἐπεδίδοσαν A: PBerol is uncertain. The ending ουν is common; οσαν is to be found in A's text of this passage and in PBerol at l. 27, and in M at p. 44, 8.

[ε]πεδιδουν τας ραβδους
[α]υτων ημιξηρους και
σχισμας εχουσας και ου
τοι χωρ[ι]ς εσταν[οντ]ο·
ετεροι δ[ε] επεδιδ[ου]ν 10
α]υτων δυ[ο] μερη [χλωρ]α
τας ρα[β]δους χλ[ω]ρ[α]ς μεν
το δε τ[ριτο]ν ξηρον
σχισ[μας] δε εχουσα[ς] και
ουτο[ι χω]ρις εσταν[ο]ντο
[ετερο]ι δε επεδιδουν τας 11
ρα[βδ]ους το ημισυ ξηρον
[κ]α[ι] τ[ο] ημισυ χλωρον και

p. 35

[ουτο]ι χωρις ε[σ]τ[ανοντο
[ετε]ροι δε [ε]φερον τ[ας ραβδους 12

18 ἵστασθαι A, ἱστάνεσθαι PBerol. After this word A and PBerol have the sentence ἕτεροι δὲ ἐπεδίδουν ἡμιξήρους· καὶ οὗτοι χωρὶς ἵσταντο (ἱστάνοντο PBerol). The versions also have this sentence. L² strangely renders ἡμιξήρους *pseudo-aridas*. E has *et porrigebant alii socii eorum semiaridas*. One is tempted to explain this as derived from a text in which εταιροι αυτων was written (αι = ε !) and then ετεροι δε added above by the diorthotes; but Professor W. H. Worrell suggests that *socii eorum* in d'Abbadie's Latin version may be a mistranslation of the Ethiopic bīsōmū, *each of them*. The same blunder recurs in § 11.

22 ἵσταντο A. PBerol has only one case in which the beginning of this word (*i.e.* in the imperfect) is not mutilated, viz. § 10, where it reads ἱστάνοντο. Evidence bearing upon the use of ἱστάνω, ἱστάνομαι has been collected by Crönert, p. 262, Mayser, p. 353, Jannaris, § 962, Robertson, p. 316. There is, however, no instance of εστανοντο among the material collected by these authorities. The form ἔστανεν occurs in an inscription in Kaibel, *Epigr. Graeca* 970, 1 and παραστανέτω is found in the Laws of the Iobacchi (Dittenberger, *Sylloge*³, 1109, 75) before 178 A.D. The existence of εστανοντο alongside of ἱστάνεσθαι may be due to a half-conscious recognition of the σταν- forms. In consequence of this confusion the breathing — ἑστάνοντο or ἐστάνοντο — can scarcely be regarded as certain. See Introduction, p. 21.

23–26 ἕτεροι δὲ . . . χωρὶς ἑστάνοντο. These words stood in the original of L²E, but are omitted by AL¹. PBerol had a corresponding passage, of which only ἐχούσας καὶ οὗτοι χωρὶς ἱστάνοντο is left.

The words interlined by the corrector are wrongly placed here, and in fact are entirely unnecessary; for they correspond to the matter of § 12, which is in its proper place (p. 35) and is intact. — χλωρά is represented in the papyrus by a few illegible traces; even the α is not certain.

27 ἐπεδίδοσαν PBerol, which omits τὰς ῥάβδους.

28 A omits τό.

29 [το ημισυ μερ]ος PBerol. L² omits § 11 entirely.

P. 35. 1 ἵσταντο A. Lacuna in PBerol.

2 προσέφερον A and almost certainly

[αυ]των τα δυο μερη τη̣ς ρα[β
δου χλωρα το δ[ε] τρ[ι]τον ξη
[ρο]ν και ο[υ]τ̣ο̣ι̣ [χωρ]ις [εσ]τ̣[α]νον
[το] ετε[ρο]ι δ̣[ε επ]εδ̣[ι]δουν τα̣ 13
[δ]υο με[ρ]η̣ ξηρ[α τ]ο δε τριτον
[χ]λ̣ω[ρον] κ̣α̣ι ου[το]ι χωρις εστ̣[α
[νο]ν[το] ε̣τεροι δε επεδιδου[ν 14
[τα]ς ρ[α]βδους αυτ̣ων παρα
[με]ικρον ολας χλωρας ελαχι
[σ]τ̣α δ̣ε̣ των ραβδων αυτω[ν
[ξη]ρ̣α ην αυτο το ακρον
[σχ]ισ[μα]ς δε ειχον εν αυταις
[και ο]υ̣τ̣ο̣ι χωρις ε[σ]τανοντο
[ετερω]ν δε ην ελαχιστον 15
[χλ]ωρον τα δε λο̣ιπ[α] μερη
των ραβ[δω]ν ξηρα και ου
τοι χω[ρ]ις ε[σ]τανοντο· ετ[ε 16
ροι δε η̣ρχοντο τας ραβδ[ους
χλωρας φεροντες ως ελ[α
βον παρα του αγγελου τ̣[ο δε
πλειον μερος του οχλου τοι̣
αυτας ραβδους ε[π]εδιδου
ο δε αγγελος επι [το]υτοις
εχαρη λειαν και [ο]υτοι χ̣ω
ρις ε̣στανοντο· [ετ]ε̣[ρ]οι δε 17
επεδιδουν χλωρας κ̣α̣ι πα
ραφυαδας εχουσ[ας] και ου

PBerol (which has a short line even if one inserts προσ), *adferebant* L^1: *porrigebant* (*i.e.* ἐπεδίδουν) L^2E.

5 ἵσταντο A. The beginning of the word in PBerol is lost.

6–9 L^2 omits § 13 entirely.

8 ἵσταντο A.

11 *paulo minus aridas* L^1, a slip of the scribe; cf. L^2 *paulo minus totas virides*.

12–13 ἐλάχιστον . . . ξηρόν ALLE.

14 L^2 omits the whole line.—The ι of σχισμάς was found on a very small separate fragment.

15 ἵσταντο A here and in 19.

17 A omits μέρη.

21 L^2 omits χλωράς.

22 L^1 omits παρὰ τοῦ ἀγγέλου.

24 ἐπεδίδουν A.

27 ἵσταντο A.

27–32 ἕτεροι . . . ἐγένετο om. A. The

τοι χωρις εστανοντο·
και επι τουτο̣ις ο αγγε̣λος
λειαν ϊλαρος εγενετο·

p. 36

[επεδιδο]υ[ν δε ετεροι τας 18
[ραβδ]ο̣υ̣[ς] α̣υτω[ν χλωρας
κ̣αι π̣α̣ρ̣α̣φ̣υ[αδας] ε[χου
σας [α]ι δ̣ε π̣α̣ρα[φυαδες
α̣υ̣τ̣ων [ωσ]ε̣ι̣ κ̣[αρπον τι
να ειχο̣ν [κα]ι̣ λει̣[αν ιλαροι
ησαν οι α[ν]δ̣ρες [εκεινοι
ω̣ν̣ αι ραβδο[ι] τ[οια]υ̣τ̣α̣ι̣
ευ̣ρε̣θησαν [κ]α̣ι̣ [ο] α̣[γγε
λος επι τουτο̣ις [ηγαλλια
το και ο ποιμην [συν αυ
τω λειαν ϊλαρος [ην] ε̣[πι
τουτο[ις] εκελευ[σε δε ο αγ 2, 1
γελος τ̣[ο]υ̣ κ̅υ̅ στ[εφ]α̣[νους
ενεχθ[η]ναι [κ]α̣ι ε[νεχθησαν
στεφανοι ωσει [ε]κ̣ φο̣ι̣ν̣[ι
[κ]ων γεγονοτες και εστ̣ε
[φ]ανωσε τους ανδρας
τους επιδεδωκοτας τας
ρ̣αβδους τας παραφυαδας
εχουσ̣ας και καρπ[ον] τινα

versions indicate no variations from M unless, possibly, they had in 28 τὰς ῥάβδους χλωράς. All express *virgas*.

P. 36. 1 There is a trace of a numeral in the upper margin. — After υ there is a trace which does not much resemble ν. The whole upper part of the page is terribly torn and frayed. — ἕτεροι δὲ ἐπεδίδουν A.

5 ὡσεί MA: om. LLE. — τινά MALL: om. E.

7 ἄνδρες M and probably L^1, ἄνθρωποι A and E(?), *ipsi* L^2.

10 There are traces after τούτοις, but none legible.

11 σὺν αὐτῷ ML^1E: om. AL^2.

13 Perhaps better ἐκέλευσεν; an upright trace three spaces after the last uninjured letter may be part of ν.

14 A omits τοῦ. — The α is on a minute fragment.

15 ἠνέχθησαν A. For the omission of the temporal augment, see Mayser, p. 336, Crönert, p. 206.

20 τὰς ἐχούσας τὰς παραφυάδας A.

και απ[ε]λυσεν αυτ[ο]υς εις
τον πυργον· και α[λλ]ους̣ 2
δε απελυσεν εις τον̣ πυρ̣
γον τ̣ο[υς] τας ραβδους
επι̣δεδωκοτας τ̣α̣ς̣ παρα̣
φυαδας εχουσας καρ̣π[ο]ν̣
δε μη εχουσας δους αυτοις
σφραγ̣ε̣ιδα ϊματισμον δε 3

p. 37

ϙγ

[τον] α̣υτον ειχον παντες λευ
[κο]ν̣ ωσει χειονα οι πορευ[ο]με
ν̣[οι] εις το̣ν πυργον και τους 4
τας ραβδους επιδεδωκοτας
χλωρας ως ελαβον απελυσεν
δους αυτοις ϊματισμον λευ
κον και [σ]φραγειδα· μετα 5
το ταυ̣[τ]α τελεσαι τον αγγε
λον λε[γ]ε̣ι̣ τω ποιμενι εγω
υ[π]αγω̣ σ̣υ δε τουτους απο
λυ̣σον̣ εις τα τειχη καθως
[τ]ι̣ς̣ α̣ξ̣ιος εστιν κατοικειν
κατ̣αν̣ο̣η̣σον δε τας ραβδους

23 καὶ τοὺς ἄλλους δέ A, also E *et illos alios quoque* (*illos* = τούς). The Latin versions seem to have read καὶ αὐτοὺς δέ. In view of the injury to the papyrus one might be tempted to read αὐτούς rather than ἄλλους in M; but if the former had been written, the tail of υ should be visible below the perforation, which is not the case, and the slight trace which remains is nearest to λ in appearance.

24 ἀπέστειλεν A. L[1] has *iussit ire* in 22, *misit* here, L[2] *iussit ire* in both places, E *misit* in both.

25 τὰς ῥάβδους MLL: τὰς ῥάβδους τὰς χλωράς AE (*totas virides*).

26 A has καί for τάς.

28 A adds τὰς παραφυάδας after ἐχούσας; cf. E *sed sine fructu in surculis*.

29 σφραγῖδας A: σφραγῖδα LLE.

P. 37. 1 πάντες εἶχον A. L[1] omits πάντες.

6 λευκόν MLLE: om. A.

7 σφραγῖδα ME: σφραγῖδας AL[2]. L[1] has *data eis veste candida, et sic illos dimisit*, where *sic illos* probably represents *sigillis*; cf. L[2] *datis eis sigillis et vestem candidam*.

9 A trace of the second ε was found on a minute fragment now broken off and lost.

10 ἀπολύσεις A: L[1] *dimitte*, L[2] *cura dimittere*, E *introduc*.

11 καθὼς ἄξιός ἐστί τις A.

α[υτ]ων επιμελως και ουτως
[απ]ολυσον βλεπε μη τις σε
[παρε]λθη και φησιν εγω αυ
[τους επ]ι το θυσιαστηριον δο
κιμασω· ταυτα ειπων τω
ποιμενι απηλθεν μετα το 6
απελθειν τον αγγελον λε
γει μοι [ο] ποιμην λαβωμεν
παρα παντων τας ραβδους
και φυτευσωμεν αυτας
ει τινες εξ αυτων δυνησον
ται ζησαι· λεγω αυτω κ̅ε̅
τα ξηρα ταυτα πως δυνα
ται ζησαι· αποκριθεις μοι 7
λεγει το δενδρον τουτο
ἴτεα εστιν και φιλοζωον
το γενος εαν φυτευθωσι
και μεικραν ικμαδα λα
βωσι αι ραβδοι αυται ζησον
ται πολλαι εξ αυτων ειτα δε

15 After ἀπόλυσον A adds ἐπιμελῶς δὲ κατανόησον, and this seems to have been in the original of E also. It is omitted by ML[2]. L[1] reads *dimitte . . . consideratis prius virgis eorum. diligenter tamen ne quis te fallat considera.* This may show that L[1] did not have ἐπιμελῶς in the first instance (corresponding to l. 14 of M); but it agreed with A in having ἐπιμελῶς δὲ κατανόησον, which the translator construed with the following words. The second κατανόησον seems to have displaced βλέπε in the original of L[1].

16 A omits this καί and adds ἐάν δέ τίς σε παρέλθῃ with LL (*si quid* L[2]). E omits the whole clause. L[1] adds *inquit* after *si quis te praeterierit*. If the archetype read φησί in this place also, the loss of the clause in M was probably due to homoioteleuton (φησι), and the καί in l. 16 of M may be a means of improving the sentence-connection after the loss had taken place.

It is possible that the Latin versions of ll. 15–16 reveal another feature of the original text. L[2] has, after its translation of the clause ending ἀπόλυσον (15), *sed vide ne quis te fallat.* L[1], incorporating this with the preceding (see note on 15), has *diligenter tamen ne quis te fallat considera.* Perhaps the original text was βλέπε μή τίς σε λάθῃ, φησίν. ἐὰν δέ τίς σε παρέλθῃ, φησίν, ἐγὼ κτλ. This supposition seems to provide an original from which all the texts might derive by natural courses.

19 μετά ML[1]: καὶ μετά AL[2]E.

22 A omits παρά, and so also E (*horum omnium*).

24 L[1] omits τινὲς ἐξ αὐτῶν.

25–27 L[2] omits λέγω . . . ζῆσαι.

26 δύνανται A.

30 ἐὰν οὖν AL[1] (*si plantatae ergo fuerint*): *et si* L[2], *et simulac* E.

31 λαμβάνωσιν A: *acceperint* LL.

32 αὗται MLLE: om. A.

p. 38

ϙδ

πειρασω[[μεν]] και υδωρ α̣[υ
ταις παραχεω εαν τις̣ [αυ
των δυνηθη ζησαι [συν
χαρησομαι αυταις εαν
δε μη ζησεται ο̣υχ ευρε
θησομαι εγω αμελης·
εκελευσεν με [ο π]οιμην 8
καλεσαι καθως [τι]ς αυτων
εσταθη ηλθον τ̣α[γ]μα̣τ̣α
ταγματα και επ̣εδι̣δουν
τας ραβδους τω̣ π̣[ο]ιμ̣[ενι]·
ελαμβανεν δε ο̣ π[ο]ιμ̣ην τας̣
ραβδους και κατ[α] τα[γμα
τα εφυτευεν αυτας μ̣[ε
τα το φυτευσ̣α̣ι̣ αυτ[ας
υδωρ αυταις̣ π̣[ο]λ̣υ παρε
χεεν ωστε απ̣ο του ὑδα
τος μη φαινεσθαι τας ραβ
δους μετα το ποτισαι αυ 9
τον τας ραβδους λεγει

P. 38. 1 The ending *μεν* is deleted with several strokes of the pen, apparently by the first hand. πειράσωμεν AE (*temptemus*): *temptabo* LL.

2 παραχέειν A (with καί before ὕδωρ, as in M): but *et suffundam* LL, *et irrigemus* E.

3 There are uncertain traces which belong to the last syllable.

4 αὐταῖς MAE: *ei* L[1], *illi* L[2].

5 ζήσῃ A. For the future indicative with ἐάν, see Vis. *1*, 3, 2 (א), Mand. *4*, 3, 7, *5*, 1, 2; also Mayser, II, p. 285, Robertson, p. 1009 f.

7 ἐκέλευσε δέ μοι A. The versions have a connective — *deinde* LL, *et* E.

8 *vocare eos; et sicut steterunt* L[1].

12 The letters εν were added by a later hand (the second?), ε crowded into the space between the previous ν and δ, then ν above the line.

14 ἐφύτευσεν A and apparently the versions, but M and A agree in ἐλάμβανεν (l. 12). — καὶ μετά ALLE.

15 αὐτάς ME, *omnes* LL: om. A.

17–18 ὥστε . . . ῥάβδους MA. The versions seem to have had a fuller text, perhaps, as G.-H. suggest, σκεπασθῆναι καὶ μὴ φαίνεσθαι. L[1] *ita ut tegerentur ab aqua neque ab ea exstarent*, L[2] *sic ut tegerentur ab aqua neque extarent*, E *ita ut aqua eas operiret neque visae essent*.

19 καὶ μετά ALLE (*quod cum fecisset* L[2]).

μοι αγωμεν και μετα ολι
γας ημερας επανελθωμεν
και επισκεψωμεθα τας
ρ̣αβδους ταυτας ο γαρ κ̅ς̅
του δενδρου το̣υτου θε
λει παντας ζη̣ν τους
λαμβανοντα̣ς̣ απ αυτου
κλαδον ελπιζω δε καγω

p. 39

[ο]τ̣ι λαβοντα τα ραβδια ταυ
[τ]α̣ ϊκμαδα και ποτισθεντα
υδατι ζησεται το πλειστον
μερος· λεγω αυτω κ̅ε̅ το δεν 3, 1
δρον τουτο τι εστιν γνωρι
σον μοι απορουμαι γαρ περι
αυτου τ[ο]σουτων κλαδων
κοπεν̣[τ]ων υγιες εστιν τ[ο
δενδρον και ολως ουδεν
φαινεται κε̣κομμενον απ αυ
του εν τουτω ουν απορουμαι
ακουε φησιν το δενδρον 2
τουτο το μεγα το σκεπαζον
πεδια και ορη και πασαν
την γην νομος θ̅υ̅ εστιν
δ̣οθεις εις ολον τον κοσμον

21 ἄγωμεν M with the versions (*eamus* LL, *veni eamus* E), confirming Anger's conjecture. A omits the word.

24 ταύτας MLL: πάσας A, *omnes has* E. — ὁ γὰρ κτίσας τὸ δένδρον τοῦτο A and the versions (*qui creavit*).

27 λαβόντας A and the versions (*qui acceperunt* LL, *qui acceperint* E). — ἀπ' αὐτοῦ MLL (*ex ea*): ἐκ τοῦ δένδρου τούτου A, *ex hac arbore* E.

28 κλάδον M alone: κλάδους AL^2 (*ramos*), *virgas* (ῥάβδους?) L^1E.

P. 39. 3 ζήσονται A.

4 μέρος αὐτῶν A; cf. L^2 *plurimas ex eis*, E *multae ex iis*: *plurimas* L^1.

5–6 γνώρισόν μοι τί ἐστιν A.

7 ὅτι τοσούτων A and the versions: M has omitted ὅτι by an error.

9 ὅλως ML^1 (*nec omnino quicquam*), perhaps E (*nec quidquam unquam . . . decisum esse*). A omits ὅλως, L^2 omits καὶ ὅλως . . . ἀποροῦμαι.

16 δοθείς (without article) M and perhaps LL (*lex est dei data*): ὁ δοθείς A, *lex domini est, quae data est* E.

[ο] δε νομος ουτος ο υ̅ι̅ς̅ του
θ̅υ̅ εστιν ο κηρυχθεις εις
τα περατα της γης οι δε υπο
την σκεπην λαοι οντες οι
ακουσαντες του κηρυγμα
τος και πιστευσαντες αυτω
ο δε αγγελος ο μεγας και εν 3
δοξος μιχαηλ [[εστιν]] εχων
την εξουσιαν τουτου του
λαου και διακυβερνων αυ
τος γαρ εστιν ο διδων αυτοις
τον νομον εις τας καρδιας
των πιστευοντων επισκε
πτεται ουν αυτους οἰς εδω
κε τον νομον ει αρα τετη
[ρ]ηκασιν αυτον· βλεπεις 4

17 υἱὸς θεοῦ A, omitting both articles.

18 A omits ὁ, and so perhaps LL (*lex filius dei est praedicatus*: L² *praedicaturus*, an error). E may have had the article, like M (*filius domini, qui . . . praedicatus est*).

22 εἰς αὐτόν A.

24 ἐστίν was deleted with several strokes, apparently by the first hand. A heavy point and a short line above ε seem to be due to a later hand; I do not understand their meaning. *est* is expressed by L¹E: AL² omit. — ὁ ἔχων A, probably rightly.

26 διακυβερνῶν without expressed object MA. The versions have *eos*, whence Hilgenfeld inserted αὐτούς in the Greek text. οὗτος A, *hic* LL, *is* E. αὐτός, the reading of M, may be regarded as an example of the nominative of the pronoun used in a manner approaching the demonstrative value which it has in Modern Greek. Compare Luke 19, 2, Hebr. 13, 17, and Hermas Mand. *4*, 1, 11, *9*, 3, Sim. *5*, 6, 4 (M). This use has been discussed by Radermacher, *Neutestamentliche Grammatik*² p. 77, Robertson, p. 290 and p. 679 f., Jannaris, § 1399, Hatzidakis, *Einleitung in die neugriech. Gram.* p. 208.

27 διδούς A. διδων is apparently διδῶν, from διδῶ. Crönert (p. 250, n. 3) cites a number of examples from papyri and late authors. — αὐτοῖς MA: *legem eius* E, whence G.-H. wrote αὐτοῦ.

30 αὐτός A: αὐτούς LLE, whence Hilgenfeld adopted this reading, now confirmed by M. Here also αὐτούς seems to have demonstrative value.

31 The third hand of M has written κε in the second and third spaces of the line; the first is now occupied by a small perforation. The original writing was κεν, and κε was written after the first space had been perforated and the other letters injured by abrasion.

τὸν νόμον MLL, *legem eius* E: A omits.

32 βλέπεις MA, *vide* E. Most MSS of L¹ have *videns*, and *cognoscens* for γνώσῃ of A (cf. p. 40, l. 5 and note). A corrector of the Carlsruhe MS erased the *n* in both cases. The Bodleian MS has *videns . . . cognoscet*. L² omits βλέπεις . . . ῥάβδους.

p. 40

ϙϛ

δε ενος εκαστου τας ρ[αβ
δους αι δε ραβδοι ο νο[μος
εστιν· βλεπεις ουν π[ο̣λ
λας εκ των ραβδων ηχρ[ει
ωμενας ϊδε αυτους παν
τας τους μη τηρησαντας
τον νομον και [ο]ψη ενος
εκαστου την κ̣ατοικι
αν· λεγω αυτω $\overline{κε}$ δια τι 5
ους μεν απελυσ̣εν εις τον
πυργον οὓς δε σοι κατε
λειπεν· οσοι φησι παρε
βησαν τον νομον ὃν ελα
βον παρ αυτου εις την
εμην εξουσιαν αυτους
κατελειπεν εις μετανοι
αν οσοι δε ηδη ευ̣ηρε
στηκαν τω νομω και τε
τηρηκαν αυτον υπο την
ιδιαν εξουσιαν αυτους
εχει· τινες ουν φημι $\overline{κε}$ 6

P. 40 In the lower half of this page a number of letters have been renewed by a later hand (the third, apparently) after the original writing had become indistinct through handling; so εμ (15), κατ (16), τη (19), the second ι (20), εχει (21), εισι (22), γον (24), εγ (25). In l. 18 στη was rewritten in such a way that the first two letters stand on the line, but η is above the remains of the original letter.

2 γάρ (for δέ) ALLE.

4 πολλὰς ἐκ τῶν ῥάβδων MLLE (E has mistranslated the rest of the sentence): πολλὰς ῥάβδους A.

5 γνώσῃ δὲ αὐτούς A. The strange reading of M is probably derived from an original in which γνωσϊ was written for γνώσῃ. The scribe's eye passed from the sigma of ἠχρειωμένας to the sigma of γνωσϊ, omitting all of this word but ϊ, which attached itself to δέ. — *cognosces* L[2]; for L[1], see note on p. 39, 32. — αὐτοὺς πάντας MAL[1]: L[2]E omit πάντας.

6 E omits μή.

7 ὄψει A.

12 κατέλειπεν is for κατέλιπεν: κατέλειψεν A. For the latter form see Reinhold, *De graecitate patrum* (1898), p. 75.

15–16 κατέλιπεν αὐτούς A.

17–19 εὐηρέστησαν A, but the perfect τετηρήκασιν below! For the forms in -καν, cf. Mayser, p. 323.

20 ἔχει αὐτούς A.

ειϲιν οι εϲτεφανωμενοι
και ειϲ τον πυργον υπα
γοντεϲ· αποκριθειϲ μοι
λ̣εγει οι εϲτεφανωμενοι
ουτοι ειϲιν οι μετα του
διαβολου παλαιϲαντεϲ
και νεικηϲαντεϲ αυτον
ο̣υ̣τ̣[ο]ι̣ οι υπερ του νομου
παθοντεϲ οι δε ετεροι 7

p. 41

ϙϛ

[και] αυτοι οι ταϲ ραβδουϲ χλω
[ραϲ] επιδεδωκοτεϲ και παρα
καρπον δε μη εχ̣[ου
[φ]υα̣δ̣αϲ εχουϲαι υπερ του ϲ[αι
νομου θλειβεντεϲ μη πα
θοντεϲ. μηδε αρνηϲαμε
νοι τον νομον αυτων·
οι δε χλωρ̣αϲ επιδεδωκοτεϲ. 8
οιαϲ ελαβον ϲέμνοι και δι̣και
οι και λειαν πορευθεντε[ϲ
εν καθαρα καρδια και ταϲ εν
τολαϲ του $\overline{κυ}$ πεφυλακοτεϲ
τα δε λοιπα γνωϲη οταν κα
τανοηϲω ταϲ ραβδουϲ ταυ
ταϲ ταϲ πεφυτευμεναϲ και
πεποτιϲμεναϲ· μετα ημε 4, 1

24–28 ἀποκριθεὶς . . . αὐτόν om. A. The Latin versions do not translate ἀποκριθείς: *et respondit et dixit mihi* E.

29 οὗτοί εἰσιν ALL. E has a loose version (*eum vicerunt, qui coronati sunt ob religionem suam*), but seems to have agreed with M in omitting εἰσί. — αὐτοί in place of οὗτοι is a possible reading of the papyrus.

30 The Latin versions omit ἕτεροι.

P. 41. 1 The versions take no account of καὶ αὐτοί. A omits οἱ. — χλωρὰς τὰς ῥάβδους A.

3 ἐχούσας all other sources, rightly. — καρπὸν δὲ μὴ ἐχούσας is read by all others. The insertion is due to the corrector (the second hand). — οἱ ὑπέρ AL²E : ML¹ omit οἱ.

5 A adds δέ after παθόντες, and this was the reading of the versions. M is again in error.

11 A omits τοῦ.

15 μετά ML¹ : καὶ μετά AL²E.

ρ̣ας [ο]λιγας ηλθομεν εις τον
τοπον και εκαθισεν ο ποιμην
εις τον τοπον του αγγελου
του μεγαλου καγω παρεστα
θην αυτω λεγει μοι περιζω
σαι [ω]μολινον και διακονει
μοι περιεζωσαμην εγω ωμο
λινον εκ σακκου γεγονος κα
θαρον ϊδων με περιεζωσμε 2
νον και ετοιμον οντα τω δια
κονειν αυτω καλει φησιν
τους ανδρας ων εισιν αι ραβ
δοι πεφυτευμεναι κατα
τα ταγματα ως τις επεδω
κεν τας ραβδους· απηλθον

p. 42

ϥη

εις το πεδιον και εκαλ̣[εσα
παντας και εσταθη.[

19 τοῦ μεγάλου MLL: om. AE.

20 καὶ λέγει AL²E; cf. L¹ *tunc ait.*

21–23 καὶ . . . ὠμόλινον om. A (homoiot.).

23 καθαρόν om. L². The letters ονοσκ in this line and εζωσμ in the next were retraced by the third hand.

24 ἰδὼν δέ με AL¹E (L²?).

25 τοῦ A. ἕτοιμος is more often used with πρός or εἰς and the accusative case. The genitive and infinitive are found in Acts 23, 15, and this construction is frequent in LXX (Robertson, p. 1068, p. 1077).

29 τὸ τάγμα A and probably the versions: *suo ordine* L², *suoque ordine* (for *suo quemque ordine*?) L¹, *ex ordine* E. — ὅστις A: M confirms Hilgenfeld's correction. *sicut* LLE. — ἔδωκε A: *porrexerunt* L¹ (*-rant* L²), which usually corresponds to ἐπέδωκαν.

30 καὶ ἀπῆλθον AE, *et duxit me* L¹. L² omits the clause.

P. 42. 2 The reading is doubtful. After ἐστάθη the only remaining trace is a point on the base line, which is more likely to have belonged to a letter made of straight lines than to a round letter like sigma. The space would accommodate four or five letters. ἐστάθη[σαν τάγμα]τα therefore seems impossible; and because of the objection to reading the trace after η as σ, ἐστάθη[σαν κα]τά and ἐστάθη[σαν εἰς] τά are unsatisfactory. I incline to accept ἐστάθη π[άντα] τὰ τάγματα as most likely. A has ἔστησαν πάντα τὰ τάγματα, which G.-H. emend to ἔστησαν τάγματα τάγματα. L¹ reads *qui etiam universi constiterunt agminibus suis*, which suggests πάντες εἰς τὰ τάγματα, as does the Ethiopic *et steterunt omnes ex ordine.* L² *qui cum venissent et locis suis stetissent.*

τα ταγματα λεγει δε [α]υ̣ 3
τοις εκαστος εκτεινατω
τας ραβδους τας ϊδιας
και φερετω προς με·
πρωτοι επεδω[κ]α̣ν οι τας 4
ξηρας και κεκομμενας
εσχηκοτες ωσαυτως ευ
ρεθησαν ξηραι και κεκ[ο]μ̣
μεναι εκελευσεν αυτου[ς
χωρις στηναι· ειτα επε 5
δωκαν τας ραβδους [ο]ι
τας ξηρας και μη κεκομ
μενας εχοντες τινες
εξ αυτων επεδωκ[αν
τας ραβδους χλωρας τι
νες δε ξηρας και κεκομ
μενας υπο σητο[ς] τους
επιδεδωκοτας χλωρας
εκελευσεν χωρις στη̣ναι·
τους δε ξηρας και κεκομ
μενας μετα των πρωτων
εκελευσεν στηναι· ειτα 6
επεδωκαν οι τας ημισους

3 λέγει δέ ML^1E: A omits δέ, L^2 modifies the construction.

4–5 ἕκαστος τὰς ἰδίας ῥάβδους ἐκτιλάτω A, *extrahat* LL, *vos omnes evellite* E. M's reading is explained by the similarity which exists between λ and the first two strokes of uncial ν.

9 καὶ οἱ οὕτως A, corrected by editors to καὶ ὡσαύτως with the aid of *eque* (i.e. *aeque*) which appears in some MSS of L^1; most read *et quae*. Dibelius preferred καὶ οὕτως. L^2 omits the clause. E has *sicut antea non inventae sunt aridae et comestae*, where *non* is an error; but E seems to have had no conjunction.

12 [στῆν]αι A, σταθῆναι G.–H.

13 A omits τὰς ῥάβδους, and so L^1; L^2 and E translate as if these words were in the participial clause, not direct object of ἐπέδωκαν. The testimony of the versions is of little value in such cases.

15 τινές (without conjunction) MLLE: A adds δέ.

19 ὑπὸ σητός ME: ὡς ὑπὸ σητός ALL.

20 ἐπιδεδωκότας οὖν AE (*quidem*): L^1 omits the conjunction, L^2 condenses and paraphrases the sentence.

21 σταθῆναι A.

23 κεκομμένας ἐπιδεδωκότας AL^1.—ἐκέλευσε μετὰ τῶν πρώτων A.

24 σταθῆναι A.

25–26 ἡμιξήρους A. Herwerden (*Lexi-*

ξηρους και σχισμας εχου
σας πολλοι εξ αυτων χλω
ρας επεδωκαν και μη εχου
σας σχισμας· τινες δε χλω
ρας και παραφυαδας εχου

p. 43

ϙθ

[σας κ]αι εις τας παραφυαδας
[καρ]πους οιας εσχον οι εις τον
[π]υ[ρ]γον πορευθεντες εστε
φανωμενοι· τινες δε επεδω
καν ξηρας και βεβρωμενας
τινες δε ξηρας και αβρωτους
τινες οιαι ησαν ημιξηροι και
σχισμας εχουσας εκελευσεν
αυτους εκαστον αυτων χω
[ρ]ις στηναι τους μεν προς τα
ιδια ταγματα τους δε χωρις
ειτα επεδιδουν οι χλωρας 5, 1
μεν εχοντες σχισμας δε
εχουσας ουτοι παντες χλω
ρα[ς] επεδωκαν και εστησαν
εις το ϊδιον ταγμα· εχαρη
ο ποιμην επι τουτοις οτι παν

con Suppletorium s. v. αἱμισέων) cites evidence from inscriptions for the forms ἥμισος, ἥμισσος; see also Mayser, p. 295, Jannaris, § 401 b. A document in the Berlin collection has the phrase ψειλοὺς τόπους δύο ἡμίσους (BGU 112, l. 15; the reference in Jannaris is wrong).

27 καὶ πολλοί AE: LL omit καί.

P. 43. 2 οἵους A, *fructum . . . qualem* E: *sicut* LL. The reading of M may be right. The relative clause should qualify not only the fruits, but the entire branches. — εἶχον AE (*habebant*): *habuerunt* L². L¹ omits the verb.

7 τινές ML²E: τινὲς δέ AL¹. E omits οἷαι ἦσαν.

8 ἔχουσαι A. ἐχούσας may be due to σχισμάς; but LL suggest ἡμιξήρους . . . ἐχούσας.

9 ἕνα ἕκαστον A.

12 τὰς ῥάβδους χλωράς A. The versions all express ῥάβδους, but this does not prove that the noun stood in their originals.

16 ἐχάρη δέ AL²E: L¹, like M, omits the connective.

τες ηλλοιωθησαν και απε
θοντο τα σχισματα αυτων
επεδωκαν δε και οι το ημι 2
συ ξηρον το δε ημισυ χλω
ρον τινων ευρεθησαν αι
ραβδοι ολοτελεις χλωραι
τινων ημιξηροι τινων
ξηραι και βεβρωμεναι τι
νων δε χλωραι και παραφυα
δας εχουσαι ουτοι παντες
απελυθησαν εκαστος προς
το ταγμα αυτου· ειτα επε 3
δωκαν οι τα δυο μερη χλωρα

p. 44 ρ̣

εσχηκοτες το δε· τρι̣[τον
ξηρον πολλοι δε εξ [αυτων
χλωρας επεδωκαν [πολ
λοι δε ημιξηρους ετ[ε]ρ̣[οι
δε ξηρας και βεβρωμενα[ς
ουτοι παντες απεσταλη
σαν εκαστος εις το ϊδιον
ταγμα· ετεροι δε επεδιδο 4

19 ἀπέθεντο A. The form ἀπέθοντο is known from Ptolemaic papyri and occurs in Christian writings; Mayser, p. 367, Crönert, p. 278, Reinhold, *De graecitate patrum* p. 94. — τὰς σχισμάς A.

21 χλωρὸν . . . ξηρόν ALL (E om. the χλωρόν clause): ἔχοντες after ξηρόν ALLE.

22 τινῶν οὖν A. L[1] has no connective, L[2] has modified the construction. E has *et*.

23 ὁλοτελεῖς MAL[1]E: om. L[2].

24–25 τινῶν (second) . . . βεβρωμέναι om. L[1]. The clauses are confused in E.

P. 44. 1 ἔχοντες A.

2 ALLE omit δέ.

6 ἔστησαν εἰς (omitting ἕκαστος) A, *et hi omnes in suo agmine unusquisque steterunt* L[2]: *hi omnes dimissi sunt in suum quisque agmen* L[1], agreeing exactly with M. *et omnes dimissi sunt ad socios suos* E.

8 A has omitted the whole of § 4 (ll. 8–17). The text of M is in general agreement with LL, but they show that the scribe of M omitted, after ξηράς (l. 13), the words καὶ βεβρωμένας, τινὲς δὲ ἡμιξήρους. In l. 14 L[1]E seem to have read ὀλίγοι δέ. The source of L[2] approached fairly nearly to the text of M. In 13–15 L[2] has *aliqui semiaridas et scissuras minimas habentes, alii virides tradiderunt*. This may represent an original καὶ σχισμὰς ἐχούσας ἐλαχίστας, τινὲς δέ κτλ., or it may be that at some stage in the tradition represented by L[2] ἐλάχιστοι

σαν τας ραβδους αυτων
τα δυο μερη ξηρα̣ το δε τ[ρι
τον χλωρ̣ον πολλοι εξ [αυ
των επεδωκαν ημιξηρ[ο]υς
τινες δε [ξη]ρ̣α̣[ς] και σχι
σμας εχουσας ελαχισ̣τοι
δε χλωρας επεδωκ̣αν ου
τοι παντες εστησαν ε̣[ι]ς το
ϊδιον ταγμα· επεδω[κα]ν̣ 5
δε οι τας ραβδους χλωρ̣α̣[ς
εσχηκοτες ελαχιστον [δ]ε̣
ξηρον και σχισμας εχου
σας εκ τουτων τινες
χλωρας επεδωκαν τι
νες δε χλωρας και παρα
φυαδας εχουσας και καρ 6
πον εν ταις παραφυασιν
και ετεραι χλωραι ολαι
επι ταυταις ταις ραβδοις
εχαρη ο ποιμην μεγαλως
οτι ουτως ευρεθησαν
απηλθον και ουτοι εκαστος
εις το ϊδιον ταγμα·

was misread ἐλαχίστας, and τινές was then inserted to improve the sense. It should also be noted that at the beginning of § 4 L² agrees closely with M, reading *alii vero porrigebant*, while L¹ has *deinde porrigebant qui habuerunt*.

17 L¹ omits § 5 entire.

18 ῥάβδους αὐτῶν A, *virgas suas* L².

19–20 The Ethiopic translator has *extrema pars arida*, as if he had read ἔσχατον for ἐλάχιστον. Similarly *extrema pars viridis* in § 6, a passage which M has omitted; see note on 24.

20 A omits ξηρόν, which was supplied by G.-H.

24 After ἐχούσας A reads ἀπῆλθον καὶ οὗτοι εἰς τὸ τάγμα αὐτῶν. εἶτα ἀπέδωκαν οἱ ἐλάχιστον ἔχοντες χλωρόν, τὰ δὲ λοιπὰ μέρη ξηρά. τούτων αἱ ῥάβδοι εὑρέθησαν τὸ πλεῖστον μέρος χλωραὶ καὶ παραφυάδας ἔχουσαι καὶ καρπόν κτλ. The eye of the scribe of M passed from ἐχούσας to ἔχουσαι, so that he omitted the first part of § 6. The versions agree fairly closely with A.

26 καὶ ἕτεραι MAE: *et reliquae* L¹, *et caeterorum virgae* L².

28 λίαν μεγάλως A.

30 καί ML¹E, δέ A.

31 A space sufficient for four or five letters is vacant after τάγμα.

p. 45

[μετα τ]ο παντων κατανοησαι 6, 1
[τας ρ]αβδους τον ποιμενα λε
[γει μο]ι ειπον σοι οτι το δενδρον
τ[ουτ]ο φιλοζωον εστιν βλε
πεις φησι ποσοι μετενοησαν
και εσωθησαν· βλεπω φημι
κε ἵνα ειδης φησιν την πολυ
σπλα[γ]χνιαν του κυ οτι μεγα
λη και ε[ν]δοξος εστιν και επε
δ[ω]κεν [π]να τοις αξιοις ουσι μ[ε
τανοιας οτι ουν φημι κε παν 2
[τ]ες ου μετεν[ο]ησαν· ὧν ειδεν
[φη]σιν ο κς τη[ν] καρδ[ι]αν μελ
[λουσαν] κ[αθαραν γενεσθαι
[και δουλε]υει[ν] αυτω [εξ ο]λης
[καρδια]ς τουτοις δεδω[κ]ε τ[η]
[μετ]ανοιαν ὧν δε ειδε την
[δολι]οτητα και πονηριαν και
[με]λλοντας εν υποκρισει ει
[ν]αι εκεινοις ουκ εδωκεν μη
ποτε παλιν βλασφημησωσιν

P. 45. 7 *vidisti* E, as if omitting ἵνα and reading εἶδες. — πολυευσπλαγχνίαν A; cf. p. 11, l. 24 above.

9 ἔδωκε A rightly. M has been affected by the numerous examples of the compound in the foregoing parable.

11 οὗτοι οὖν A (which Anger emended to διατί οὖν), *quare ergo* LL, *quomodo* E. The reading of M, which is evidently right, was corrupted into οὗτοι οὖν. For ὅτι as direct interrogative, cf. Robertson, p. 729 f., Jannaris, § 2038, Radermacher, p. 78, citing John 8, 25 and Baur's comment *ad loc.*

12 E omits οὐ.

13 ὁ κύριος ML[1]E, *deus* L[2]: om. A.

16 ἔδωκε A. — The stroke indicating final ν is visible at the end of the line.

18–19 . . . πονηρίαν, μελλόντων ἐν ὑποκρίσει μετανοεῖν A. *et animadvertit fallaciter ad se reversuros* L[1], supporting the text of M so far as the construction is concerned, but reading μετανοεῖν with A. L[2] has *alios enim animadvertit fallaciter ad se reversuros*, but omits τὴν δολιότητα καὶ πονηρίαν. The Ethiopic version is padded, but its original seems to have agreed with A; *quod sub oculis hominum . . . poenitentiam acturi sint.*

20 οὐκ ἔδωκε μετάνοιαν A (and LLE?).

21 βεβηλώσωσι τὸ ὄνομα αὐτοῦ A; cf. E *ne rursus deinceps nomen eius blasphemarent.* LL support M: *ne quando rursus legem eius nefandis maledicerent verbis* L[1], and so with insignificant variations L[2].

τον νομον αυτου· λεγω αυ 3
τω $\overline{\kappa\epsilon}$ νυν μοι επιλυ[σον τους
τας ραβδους αποδε[δωκοτας
ποταπος τις αυτων [εστιν
και την τουτων κα[τοικιαν
ϊνα ακουσαντες οι πι[στευσαν
τες και ειληφοτες τη[ν σφρα
γειδα και τεθλακοτες [αυτην
και μη τηρησαντ[ες υγιη επι
γνοντες τα εαυ[των εργα με
τανοησωσιν λαβ[οντες υπο
σ[ου] σφραγειδ[α και δοξα
[σωσι τον $\overline{\kappa\nu}$ οτι εσπλαγχνι]

p. 46

• •

σθη επ αυτοις και εξ[απε
στειλεν σε του ανα[καινι
σαι τα $\overline{\pi\nu\alpha}$ αυτων
ακουε φησιν ων αι ραβδο[ι 4
ξηραι και βεβρωμεναι υπο
σητος ουτοι εισιν αποστα
ται και προδοται της εκ
κλησιας και βλ[ασ]φημη
σαντες ε[ν] ται[ς αμ]αρτια[ι]ς

23 νῦν οὖν A. The versions take no account of οὖν.—δήλωσον (for ἐπίλυσον) ALL (*demonstra*). The Latin versions regularly render ἐπιλύω by *exsolvo* (L^1 has *absolvo* once). E (*explica*) is uncertain.

24 ἀποδεδωκότας MLL (*reddiderunt*): ἐπιδεδωκότας AE (*porrexerunt*).

27 L^1 has *ut auditis his et creditis hi qui non custodierunt*, etc., which perhaps represents ἀκούσαντες καὶ πιστεύσαντες οἱ εἰληφότες κτλ. L^2 is corrupt here.

33 καί AL^2: before λαβόντες L^1.

34 Several traces are visible, but none can be assigned to definite letters. The line above κν is clear.

P. 46. Traces of a numeral are visible at the head of the page.

1 ἐπ' αὐτούς A.—ἀπέστειλε A.

5 ὑπὸ σητός MAE: *velut a tinea* LL; cf. *8*, 4, 5.

6 ALLE read εὑρέθησαν after σητός.—οἱ ἀποστάται A.

αυτων το̣ν $\overline{κυ}$ [ετι] δ̣ε̣ κα̣ι
επαισχυνθεντες [το] ο̣[νο
μα [τ]ου $\overline{κυ}$ [το επ]ι̣κ̣λη̣θε̣ν
ε̣π̣ αυ̣του[ς ουτο]ι̣ [ουν εις
τ[ελ]ος απεθαν[ον τω $\overline{θω}$
βλεπεις οτι ουδε ε̣[ις αυ
των μετενοησε κ̣[αιπερ
ακουσαντες τα ρ[ηματα
α ελαλησας αυτοις̣ α [σοι
ενετειλαμην απο των
τοιουτων ουν η̣ ζωη απ[ε
[στη] οι δε [[τας ραβδους]]
[τας] ξηρας και ασηπτους
[επι]δεδωκοτες και ουτο[ι
[εγγ]υς αυτων ησαν γαρ υπο
[κρι]ται και διδαχας ετερας
[εισ]φ̣εροντες εκστρεφον
[τες τ]ο̣υ̣ς δουλους του $\overline{θυ}$
[μαλιστα] δε τους ημαρτη
[κοτας μη] αφιοντες αυ
[τους μετα]ν̣οειν αλλα ταις
[διδαχαις τα]ι̣ς μωραις π̣[ει
[θοντες α]υ̣τ̣[ου]ς ουτοι ο̣[υν

12 A omits τοῦ.

14 ἀπέθανον MLLE: ἀπώλοντο A.

15 βλέπεις δέ A, *atque etiam vides* L[1]. L[2] has a conjunction, but the construction has been changed. *et ecce vide* E.

16 A trace after μετενόησε could belong either to final ν or to κ. — καὶ παρακούσαντες A, corrected to καίπερ by Anger.

20 οὖν ML[1]E: om. AL[2]. POx 1599, which begins here, has an obliterated word after τοιούτων — perhaps the same word repeated — but omits οὖν.

21 There is a little space vacant before οἱ. — τὰς ῥάβδους is deleted with points above the letters, probably a correction by the diorthotes. The words are omitted by POxAL[1]E. L[2] has *virgas*.

23 POx punctuates after οὗτοι.

24 γάρ MALLE: om. POx.

25 ἑτέρας MPOx (διδαχὰς εἰσφέροντες ἑτέρας) E (*duplicem doctrinam*): ξένας A, *pravas* LL.

26 καὶ ἐκστρέφοντες APOxL[1]E: L[2] may have agreed with M in omitting καί.

28 μάλιστα δὲ πάλιν POx without support. — ἡμαρτηκότες POx.

29 ἀφιέντες A, ἀφέντες POx. For the form in ο, cf. Crönert, p. 258, n. 3, Jannaris, § 960.

30 μετανοεῖν αὐτούς A: POx has the same order as M.

31 Even the π of πείθοντες is very doubtful in M. *detinentes* L[1], *detinebant* L[2], *seducunt* E.

p. 47

[εχουσιν] ελπιδα του μετανοησαι
[βλεπει]ς δε εξ αυτων πολλους 6
[μετα]νενοηκοτας αφοτε ελα
[λησας] αυτοις τας εντολας μου
[κα]ι ετι δε μετανοησωσιν επει
[απωλ]εσαν την ζωην αυτω[ν
[οσοι δε] μετενοησαν εξ αυτ[ων
[αγαθοι] ε[γενοντο και εγενετο
[η κατοικια αυτων εις τα τειχη]
[τα πρωτα τινες] δε και ε[ις τον
[πυργον ανεβησ]αν βλεπ[εις ουν
[φησιν οτι η μετ]ανοια τ[ων αμαρ
[τωλων ζωην ε]χει το δ[ε μη με
[τανοησαι θανα]τον· οσ[οι δε 7, 1
[ημιξηρο]υ[ς επ]εδωκαν [κ]ατα
[αυτας σχι]σματα ειχον ακουε

P. 47. 1 αι is on a small separate fragment.

2 πολλοὺς ἐξ αὐτῶν A: POx omits πολλούς.

3 καί before μετανενοηκότας A, perhaps before πολλούς L[1] (*atque etiam multos vides*): POxL[2]E have no καί. — μετανενοηκότες POx; cf. note on p. 46, 28. — ἀφότε MPOx: ἀφ' ἧς A.

4 On account of the length of the space I restore ἐλάλησας with POxLL: ἐλάλησα A, *nuntiatum est* E.

5 καὶ ἔτι μετανοήσουσιν A, καὶ ἔτι μετανοήσωσιν POx. For the use of the subjunctive as future, which on account of the agreement of M and POx we must take to be original, see Mayser, Vol. II, p. 235, Jannaris, p. 555, Robertson, p. 928 ff., and Reinhold, *De graecitate patrum* pp. 101–103, 104–105. After μετανοήσωσιν M lacks a clause which A gives as ὅσοι δὲ οὐ μετανοήσουσιν. The ἐπεί in M's text seems to have been added to remedy a defective connection. This may indicate that the error of omission goes back to the original from which M was copied. — POx has ὅσοι δὲ οὐ μετενόησαν.

6 ἀπώλεσαν MA: *amittent* LL. — ζωήν MA, ψυχήν POx, *vitam* LLE.

8 ἀγαθοὶ ἐγένοντο καί om. L[1].

13 ἔχει MALLE: εἶχεν POx.

15 The reading of M is not free from doubt. In the first space after ἐπέδωκαν the writing has been destroyed entirely, then there is a fairly good α, then a trace which could belong to the lower part of τ, then an α which is clear; after that there are no traces, although the margin is some distance away. In writing κατά, I assume that καί was lost before it because of the similar beginnings of the two words. For κατά in this vague use, see Robertson, p. 608, Radermacher, p. 139, and especially G. Kuhring, *De praepositionum Graecarum in chartis Aegyptiis usu* (Bonn, 1906), p. 12, § 2. κατά evidently encroached upon the functions of ἐν and other prepositions; cf. l. 17 below. — For κατὰ αὐτάς, A and POx read καὶ ἐν αὐταῖς.

16 σχισμάς APOx.

[περι αυτω]ν οσον ησαν κατ αυ
[τους αι ραβ]δοι ημιξηροι διψυ
[χοι εισιν ο]υτε γαρ ζωσιν ουτε
[τεθνηκασ]ιν· οι δε ημιξηρους 2
εχ[οντες κα]ι εν αυταις σχισ[μα
τα ουτοι δ[ιψ]υχοι εισιν και κ[α
ταλ[α]λοι μηδεποτε ειρηνευ
οντες εν αλληλοις αλλα διχο
στατου[ντ]ες παντοτε και του
τοι[ς] φ[ησ]ιν ετι κειται μετα
νοια βλεπεις φησιν ηδη τι
νας εξ αυτων μετανενοηκο
[τ]ας και ετι ελπις εστι[ν αυ
τοις μετανοιας οσοι ουν φη 3
σι[ν] εξ αυτων μετανενο[η
κασιν την κατοικιαν εις το[ν

17 καὶ περὶ αὐτῶν A: καί is omitted by MPOxLLE. — ὅσον is apparently an error for ὅσων (APOxLLE). — A reads ὅσων ἦσαν αἱ ῥάβδοι καθὰ τὸ αὐτὸ ἡμίξηροι, POx ὅσων ἦσαν αἱ ῥάβδαι ἡμιξήρους (*sic*). Lake supposed καθὰ τὸ αὐτό to be a gloss which had been incorporated in the text of A; but M seems to show that a phrase with κατά belonged to the original. If the reading of M was κατ' αὐτούς, as I think, we have another peculiar use of the preposition, the phrase being equivalent to ἐξ αὐτῶν. The versions take no account of the phrase, agreeing with POx in this respect. L[1], it is true, has *tantummodo*; but that does not appear to have any relation to anything in the existing Greek sources.

19 οὔτε: a later hand, apparently the third, added another ε above the original one, though it is quite legible.

21–22 σχισμάς A. — καὶ δίψυχοι καὶ κατάλαλοί εἰσι A. L[1]E have *et . . . et*. POx, which omits 19–22 (οὔτε . . . εἰσίν) by homoioteleuton, must have agreed with M in the position of εἰσίν.

23 μηδέποτε MPOxE (*nunquam*): καὶ μηδέ A (μηδέποτε Hilgenfeld), *et numquam* LL.

24 ἀλλήλοις: ἑαυτοῖς APOx.

25 καὶ τούτοις MPOxL[1]: ἀλλὰ καὶ τούτοις AE, *nam et his* L[2].

26 ἔτι κεῖται MLL (*adhuc*): ἐπίκειται APOx, also probably E, which does not translate ἔτι, cf. p. 26, 14.

27 τινὰς ἤδη POx, *iam aliquos* L[2]: AL[1]E omit ἤδη.

28 LL apparently read μετανοοῦντας.

29 Only the tops of the dotted letters are left. — The length of lines 28 and 30 suggests that αὐτοῖς alone, rather than ἐν αὐτοῖς, would fill 29 to a natural length; cf. E *et adhuc habere spem poenitentiae*. However, both A and POx have ἐν αὐτοῖς. LL omit the clause. A has the order καὶ ἔτι, φησίν, ἔστιν ἐν αὐτοῖς ἐλπὶς μετανοίας. POx and E omit φησίν, with M.

30 ὅσοι οὖν, φησίν MPOx, *quicumque enim* L[2]: καὶ ὅσοι, φησίν A, *omnes qui* E.

31 τὴν κατοικίαν . . . ἐξ αὐτῶν (p. 48, 2) om. POx.

p. 48

πυργον εχ[ο]υ[σ]ιν [οσοι δε
εξ αυτων βραδυτ[ερον με
τανοησουσιν εις τα τ[ειχη
κατοικησουσιν οσοι [δε
ου μετανοησουσιν α[λλα
ετ[ι] ενμενουσιν εν τ[αις
π[ρ]αξεσιν α[υ]των [θανα
[τω α]ποθ[α]ν[ουνται

(Four lines are lost.)

αγ[α]θ[οι εγενοντο εχοντες 4
δε [ζηλον εν αλληλοις τι
να [πε]ρι πρωτ[ειων και πε
ρι δοξης τινος α[λλα παν
τες ο[υ]τοι αφρον[ες εισιν
εν α[λ]ληλ[ο]ις εχ[οντες πε

P. 48. 1 ἔχουσιν MLLE: ἕξουσιν A.

3 In the seventh space of the line the scribe apparently started the letter ω, then changed it to ο. The horizontal which formed the bottom of the flat ω now connects ο and υ in what looks like an intentional ligature but is really nothing of the sort.

μετανενοήκασιν A, and such must have been the reading of the copy from which POx is derived; for it passes from μετανενοήκασιν above (p. 47, 31) directly to βραδύτερον and has no verb corresponding to μετανοήσουσιν of M. *gesserunt* L[1]: *egerint* L[2]E (supporting M or the equivalent μετανοήσωσιν).

4 κατοικήσωσιν POx, *habitabunt* LL: *habitationem habent* E. — οἳ δέ POx.

5 μετανοήσωσι POx, *qui autem non egerint* L[2], *egerunt* L[1]E: μετανοοῦσι A.

6 ἔτι M without support; all others omit the word. — The fifth letter of the line is injured but scarcely doubtful, although in three other instances ν becomes μ before a labial. ℵ has ἐνμίνατε (Vis. 2, 2, 7) etc.; see Mayser, p. 233. — We should accent ἐνμενοῦσιν in view of the preceding future; A has ἐμμένουσι (with μετανοοῦσιν preceding); cf. E *et opera sua delinquere nolunt*. L[1] has *permanserunt*, as *egerunt* before; cf. note on l. 5. — POx omits ἀλλὰ ἔτι ἐνμενοῦσιν ἐν; A also omits ἐν. For lines 4–8 L[2] has only *qui autem non egerint, comburentur* — in which last word the translator seems to have allowed the vividness of his eschatological imagination to override his sense of duty towards the original.

14 δέ MPOxLLE: om. A. — ζῆλόν τινα ἐν ἀλλήλοις APOx. *quandam invidiam et zelum* L[1], *aemulationes* (omitting τινά) L[2] and so also E (*invidias*).

16 δόξας POx. — τινός MAL[2] (*de principatu et vita et dignitate quadam*, where *et vita* is a corrupt addition): om. POxL[1]E.

17 μωροί APOx. The Latin versions have *fatui*, which may represent either μωροί or ἄφρονες.

18 Neither here nor in l. 19 was there

ρι πρω̣τειων [αλλα και ου 5
τοι ακουσαν[τες] τω[ν] ε̣ν
τολων μου αγαθ[οι] οντες
εκαθαρισαν εαυτους και
μετενοησαν τα[χυ] εγενε
το η κα̣τοικ̣ια αυ[τ]ω̣[ν] ε̣ι̣[ς
τον πυργον εαν [δ]ε τις αυ
των παλιν επιστραφη
επι την διχοστασιαν
εκβ̣λ̣ηθησεται εκ του πυρ
γου και απολεσει την [ζ]ω
ην α̣υ̣τ̣ο̣υ η ζωη παντ̣[ων 6

p. 49

[εστι των] τ̣α̣[ς] εντολας του
[$\overline{κυ}$ τη]ρουντων εν ταις εντο
[λαις π]ε̣ρι πρωτειων η δοξης
[ουκ ε]σ̣τιν αλλα περι μακ[ροθυ
[μιας] και ταπεινοφροσ[υνης
[ανδ]ρος εν τοις το[ιουτοις

room for ζῆλον in the lost parts at the ends of the lines. One might think of dropping the copula εἰσίν at the end of l. 17 and inserting ζῆλον there; but it is more likely that M agreed with A, which omits ζῆλον. Compare Mand. 2, 2, ἕξεις κατὰ τοῦ ἀδελφοῦ σου.

POx omits the phrase ἔχοντες περὶ πρωτείων and ζῆλον along with it (supposing it ever to have stood in the original). L[1] has *habent inter se aemulationem*, E *inter se habent invidias*, L[2] *certantur*; all have words corresponding to περὶ πρωτείων.

24 ἐγένετο οὖν APOxL[1]: *et* E. L[2] either read καί or freely modified the structure of the sentence. — κατοίκησις APOx.

25 αὐτῶν MPOxLLE: om. A.

26 ἐπιστραφῇ MPOx: ἐπιστρέψῃ A.

27 εἰς APOx, *in* E: *ad* LL.

28 ἐκκολληθήσεται POx — a corruption due to a cursive stage in its tradition. — ἀπό ALL (*a*): *e* E. POx omits the preposition.

30 πάντων MAPOxE: om. LL.

P. 49. 2 τηρούντων MPOx: φυλασσόντων A. — POx has a different order, τῶν τηρούντων τὰς ἐντολάς.

3 ἐν ταῖς ἐντολαῖς δέ A. POx has καὶ τὰς ἐντολὰς δέ, which, though corrupt, attests the connective. — ἤ περί APOx. For the irregularity as to the use or the neglect of the second preposition, cf. Mand. 5, 2, 2. — δόξης τινός ALL (*aliqua*): τινός is not found in MPOxE.

5 A and POx have a second περί. — ταπεινοφροσύνης MPOx: ταπεινοφρονήσεως A.

6 POx has ἐν τοῖς δέ and omits οὖν.

[ουν η] ζω[η] του κ̅υ̅ [εν τοις διχο
[σταταις δε κ]αι παρ[ανομοις
[θανατος οι] δε [**8,** 1

(About nine lines are lost.)

[με]τενοη[σαν οσοι γουν μετε 2
νοησαν ει[ς τον πυργον η κα
τοικ[ι]α αυτων τινες δε εξ [α]υ
των ε[ι]ς τελος απεστησαν
ουτοι ουν μετανοιαν ουκε
τι εχουσιν δια τας πραγμα
τειας γαρ αυτων εβλασφη
μησαν τον κ̅ν̅ και απηρνη
σαντο αυτον απωλεσαν την
ζωην αυτων δια την πον[η
ριαν ην επραξαν πολλοι δε 3
εξ αυτων εδιψυχησαν ου
τοι ετι εχουσι μετανοιαν

p. 50

εαν ταχυ [μ]ε[τανοησω
σιν και εστα[ι η κατοικια
αυτων εις τον [πυργον
εαν δε βραδυτε[ρον με
[τα]ν[ο]ησωσιν κατ[οικη
[σουσι]ν εις τα τειχ[η εαν

7–8 ἐν τοῖς διχοστάτοις δέ A, ἐν δὲ τοῖς διχοστάτοις POx; διχοστάταις edd.

19 γοῦν A: οὖν POx. γοῦν does not occur elsewhere in Hermas.

20–21 ἡ κατοικία αὐτῶν εἰς τὸν πύργον APOx. ἐξ: om. APOx and probably LL.

23 οὐκέτι: οὐκ APOxLLE. — The letters οι in μετάνοιαν are connected — one of the few ligatures in this papyrus.

24 A places γάρ after διά.

27 αὐτόν MPOxLL: E does not express the object. A has λοιπόν with the following sentence, for which Hilgenfeld conjectured αὐτόν. — ἀπώλεσαν οὖν APOxL^1: *et* L^2, *et propterea* E.

31 οὗτοι ἔτι MA: οὗτοι οὖν ἔτι POx. *adhuc et his est regressus* L^1, *quibus adhuc . . . regressio est* L^2, *et ii quoque adhuc poenitentiam habent* E.

P. 50. 2–3 αὐτῶν ἡ κατοικία A.

[δε μη] μ̣ετ̣[αν]οησω[σιν
[και] ο̣υτο̣[ι απωλεσαν την

(About nine lines are lost.)

]. . . [
ο]υτο[ι] τη[ν 5
ζωην εις τελ[ο]ς απωλεσαν
τινες δε εξ αυτων εδιψυ
χησαν και εδιχοστατη
σαν τουτοις ουν ετι εστιν
μετανοια εαν ταχυ μετα
νοησωσιν και μη επιμει
νωσιν ταις ηδοναις αυτω̄
εαν δε επιμεινωσιν εν
ταις πραξεσιν αυτων και
αυτοι θανατον εαυτοις
εργαζονται·

p. 51

[οι δε επιδεδωκοτε]ς τας ραβ 9, 1
[δους τα μεν δυ]ο̣ μερη ξηρα το δε
[τριτον χλ]ω̣ρον [ο]υτοι εισιν πι
[στοι μεν] γεγονοτες πλουτη
[σαντες] δε και γενομεν[ο]ι ενδο
[ξοτερ]οι π[α]ρα τοις εθ[ν]εσιν

8 *αὐτοί* A, with the demonstrative sense to which attention was called above, Sim. *8*, 3, 3, p. 39, 26. But the imperfect letter in M cannot be *α*. *et isti* L², om. L¹E.

18 There are illegible traces of three or four letters.

19–20 οὗτοι τὸ ζῆν εἰς τέλος ἀπώλεσαν A: *hi igitur in totum amiserunt vitam* L¹, *qui et in finem amiserunt vitam* L², *ii autem in perpetuum vitam suam perdiderunt* E. The variations of the versions are due to different interpretations of εἰς τέλος; see Preuschen's *Wörterbuch zum N. T.*², col. 1299.

23 ἔτι ML¹E (*adhuc*): om. AL².

27 ἐν: om. A.

29 *αὐτοί* M, doubtless in the demonstrative sense, which, however, the Ethiopic translator did not understand; his version is *mortem deinceps sibi ipsi consciscent*. καὶ οὗτοι A, *et isti* L². L¹ does not translate this pronoun.

30 ἐργάζονται: κατεργάζονται A. *adquirunt* L¹: L² (*acquirent*) and E (*consciscent*) seem to have read ἐργάσονται.

P. 51. 5 ἐνδοξότεροι MLL: ἔνδοξοι A, om. E.

[υπε]ρηφανιαν μεγαλην ενε
[δυσαν]το και ενκατελε[ιπον
[την αληθεια]ν και ουκ ε[κολ
[ληθησαν τοις δ]ικαι[οις αλ
[λα μετα των εθ]ν[ων συνεζησαν
[και αυτη η οδος] αυτο[ις] ηδυ
[τερα εγενετο απο] δε του θ̄ῡ
[ουκ απεστησαν αλλ] εμειναν
[εν τη . . .]στια μη εργαζο
[μενοι δε τ]α εργα της πιστεω[ς
[πολλοι ουν] εξ αυτων μετεν[ο 2
[ησαν κ]αι εγενετο η κατοικια
[αυτ]ων εις τον πυργον· ετερ[οι 3
δε ει[ς] τελος μετα των εθνων
[σ]υνζωντες και φερομενο[ι
[ται]ς κενοδοξιαις απεστησ[αν
[α]πο του θ̄ῡ και επραξαν τας
πραξεις των εθνων ουτοι
ουν μετα των εθνων ελογι
σθησαν· ετεροι δε εξ αυτω[ν 4
εδ[ι]ψυχησαν μη ελπιζον[τες

8 After ἐνεδύσαντο A adds καὶ ὑψηλόφρονες ἐγένοντο; cf. L[1] *et sublimia coeperunt spirare*, E *et se ipsos extulerunt*. L[2] has the strange rendering *et semitam suam asperam fecerunt*. — κατέλιπον A.

12–13 ἡδυτέρα αὐτοῖς A. — ἐγένετο AE: ἐφαίνετο (*visa est*) LL and Hilgenfeld.

14 ἐνέμειναν A: the space in M is not sufficient for this.

15–16 A reads τῃ πίστει without ἐν. The space in M seems to require the preposition. However, the reading of M was certainly not ἐν τῇ πίστει. One might think of θεια, *i.e.* [αλη]θεια, comparing l. 9. But the supposed θ would stand farther from ε than is natural, and the trace tentatively assigned to ε would not agree with the usual form of that letter. The traces are much more like στια. It seems scarcely possible that a form so barbarous and so without parallel as πιστίᾳ for πίστει could have been written. Perhaps the scribe, reading carelessly, thought that the sense required ἀπιστίᾳ and wrote it. This might easily happen if he did not observe the δέ in l. 16. As a matter of fact, A does not read δέ there; but the space in M requires it, and the versions had it — *sed* L[1], *autem* L[2], *quamvis* E.

18 κατοίκησις A.

19 ἐν τῷ πύργῳ A.

21 φερόμενοι ML[1] (*evecti*) L[2] (*ducti*); cf. E *quos secuti sunt in superbia sua*: φθειρόμενοι A.

22 A adds τῶν ἐθνῶν after κενοδοξίαις and so L[2] (*gentium*), L[1] (*eorum*); cf. E, cited in the preceding note.

25 οὖν MLL (*ergo*), *autem* E: A omits.

[σωθ]ηναι δια [τας] πραξεις α[ς
[επ]ρ̣αξαν· ετερο̣[ι] δε εδιψυ
χ[η]σ̣α̣ν και σχισματα εν αυ
τ̣ο̣ι̣ς εποιησαντο τουτοις
ο̣υ̣[ν κ]αι τοις διψυχησασιν

p. 52

δια τα̣ς [πρ]α̣ξ̣ε̣[ις αυτων
μετανοια ετι ε[στιν αλ
λ η μετανοια αυ[των ταχι
[ν]η̣ χρηζει ει[ναι ινα η
[κατο]ι̣κια γενη̣[τ]α̣ι̣ [αυ
[των] εις τον π[υ]ργον
[τω]ν̣ δε [μη] μετ̣ανο[ουν
[τω]ν̣ αλλα [ε]π̣[ιμενον
[των ταις] η̣δ̣[οναις ο
[θανατος εγγυς οι δε τας] **10, 1**
[ραβδους επιδεδωκοτες]
[χ]λ̣ω̣ρ̣α̣ς̣ [αυτα δε τα ακρα
ξ̣ηρα κ̣α̣ι̣ [σχισμας εχον
τα ουτοι πα[ντοτε αγα
θοι πιστοι κα[ι ενδοξοι
παρα τω $\overline{\theta\omega}$ ε[γενοντο
ελαχιστον δε ημ̣[αρ
τον δια μεικρας ε[πι]θ̣υ̣
μιας και μ̣εικρατ[ατ]α̣ κα
τ αλληλων εχ̣οντ[ε]ς αλ̣
λ̣α ακουσαντες μο[υ] των̣

30 ἑαυτοῖς A.

31 ἐποίησαν A.

32 καί: om. A. But several MSS of L[1] have *his igitur et his qui* (vv. ll. *his igitur et hi qui*, *his igitur qui*), and L[2]'s *utrisque ergo adhuc regressio est* points in the same direction. E, however, agrees with A: *hi autem qui . . . dubitaverunt.*

P. 52. 4 χρῄζει: ὀφείλει A.

5 αὐτῶν γένηται A.

15 ἀγαθοὶ καὶ πιστοί A.

17 ἐξήμαρτον A.

18 L[1] has *inanes* (κενάς) for μικράς.

19 μικρά AE, *minimas disputationes* LL. If μεικράτατα was the reading of M, the first α is due to assimilation, cf. Mayser, I, p. 61. μεικρά τινα is a possible interpretation of the traces.

ρηματων το πλει[σ]τον
μερ[ο]ς ταχυ μετε[νο]ησαν
και εγενετο η κατ[ο]ικια αυ
των εις τον [π]υργον τι 2
νες δε ε[ξ αυ]των εδιψ[υ
χησαν διχοστασιας με[ι
ζονας εποιησαν εν του
τοις ουν ετι εστιν ελπις

p. 53

[μετανοιας οτ]ι αγαθοι παντο[τε
[εγενοντο] δυσκολως δε τις
[αυτων αποθ]ανειται·
[οι δε τας ραβδο]υς επιδεδω 3
[κοτες ξηρας] ελαχ[ιστ]ον δε
[χλωρον ουτο]ι εισιν πιστευ
[σαντες μονο]ν τα δε εργα της
[ανομιας ε]ργασαμενοι ουδε το
[τε δε απ]εστησαν [α]πο του $\overline{\theta\upsilon}$
[και το] ονομα η[δεως] εβαστα

27 After ἐδιψύχησαν M has omitted by an error τινὲς δὲ διψυχήσαντες (A). From L[2] (*quidam autem ex his dubia mente evaserunt et dissensiones moverunt*) and E (. . . *dubitaverunt et maiores contentiones moliuntur*), one might suppose that M had lost only καί. But L[1] had the longer text, and L[2] and E may have condensed it. — διχοστασίας μείζονας ME, *dissensiones* (without adjective) LL: διχοστασίαν μείζονα A.

29 ἔτι MLL: om. E. — ἔνεστιν A (ἔτι ἐστίν Anger). — μετανοίας ἐλπίς A.

P. 53. 3 There is a vacant space after ἀποθανεῖται.

4 ῥάβδους αὐτῶν A and the versions (*suas*). — ξηρὰς ἐπιδεδωκότες A.

6 χλωρὸν ἐχούσας A. After this phrase the versions may have read αὐτὸ τὸ ἄκρον, as in Sim. *8*, 1, 14: *exceptis cacuminibus earum quae sola erant viridia* LL, *aridas cum extrema parte viridi* E; but there is also a possibility that the translators misread ἐλάχιστον (l. 5) as ἔσχατον, or that the latter actually stood in their originals. Compare Sim. *8*, 5, 5 (p. 44, 19). — εἰσιν οἱ A. But the translators took εἰσιν πιστεύσαντες simply as a periphrasis for the perfect tense and rendered it *crediderunt*. For such periphrastic forms, see Jannaris, §§ 2106–7, Moulton, *Grammar*, Vol. I, p. 225 ff.

7 Measurement of the space shows that M agreed with AE (*tantummodo*) in reading μόνον here, not μέν with LL (*quidem*).

8 οὐδὲ τότε: οὐδέποτε A rightly, *numquam* LL, *non* E.

9 ἀπὸ τοῦ θεοῦ ἀπέστησαν A.

10 LL add *semper*, CE *in se*.

[σαν και η]δεως [εις το]υς [οι]κο[υς
[αυτων] υπεδ[εξαν]το τ[ους
[δουλους] του θυ ακουσ[αντες
[ουν] ταυτην την μεταν[οιαν]
[αδισ]τα[κ]τως μετενο[ησαν
[κ]αι [ε]ργαζονται πασαν [αρετης
[δι]καιοσυνην τινες δ[ε εξ αυ 4
[τ]ων και παθουνται κ[αι ηδε
[ως θλειβον]ται γεινωσκ[οντες
[τας πραξ]εις αυτων ᾶς ε[πρα
[ξα]ν τουτων ουν παντ[ων
[η κα]τοικια εις τον πυργον
[εσται και] μετα το συντελεσαι 11, 1
[αυτον τ]α[ς ε]πιλυσεις πασω[ν
[τω]ν [ρ]αβδων λεγει μοι υπ[α
[γε κα]ι πα[σ]ι λε[γε ι]να μετα[νο
[ησω]σι και ζησωσι τω θω [οτι
[ο κς εσ]πλ[α]γχνισθη και επ[εμ

11 ἡδέως after αὐτῶν (12) A: om. CE.

16 ἀρετῆς δικαιοσύνην: ἀρετὴν καὶ δικαιοσύνην A. Line 16 is unusually long even with the reading given above, and it is impossible to think that ἀρετὴν καί was the reading of M. The best manuscripts of L[1], according to Professor Turner, have *virtutem aequitatis;* but Hilgenfeld reports the Dresden and Vatican MSS as reading *virtutis aequitatem*, and this is the reading of the second hand of the Lambeth MS. The variant *virtutem aequitatem* also occurs, as in the Carlsruhe MS and the first hand of the Lambeth MS. L[2] has *virtutem aequitatis*, C likewise; E *bona opera et iustitiam*. Mand. *1*, 2 and Sim. *6*, 1, 4 argue for ἀρετὴν δικαιοσύνης.

18–19 A difficult passage. The reading παθοῦνται is plain, and I have supplied ἡδέως θλείβονται from the Latin *libenter patiuntur*. A has only τινὲς δὲ ἐξ αὐτῶν καὶ φοβοῦνται γινώσκοντες κτλ. The form παθεῖται occurs also in 2 Clem. 7, 5 (I owe this reference to Mr. L. I. Highby), where editors treat it as a future, though the preceding sentence shows that it is possible to take it as a present. παθοῦνται is future in Ps.-Callisthenes ch. 40 (codex C, where the older recension has παθήσονται), similarly παθεῖται in an inscription from Orta-Keui (J. H. S. VIII, 388). The form παθοῦμαι was apparently suggested by ἡδυπαθῶ, δυσπαθῶ, προσπαθῶ, or by such futures as ἀποθανοῦμαι.

L[1] reads *mortem obierunt* (error for *obeunt?*) *et libenter patiuntur*, L[2] *compressi libenter patiuntur*. Mr. Highby points out that in Sim. *8*, 3, 7 μὴ παθόντες δέ is rendered by L[1] *non obierunt vero mortem.* — The Coptic, though mutilated, agrees closely with L[1], while E has *se ipsos afflixerunt*, which apparently does duty for both verbs.

21–23 τούτων . . . ἔσται om. LL.

27 ζήσωνται A.

28 ἔπεμψέ με σπλαγχνισθείς A. The testimony of the versions is not conclusive in such cases. L[1]E use participles — *motus dominus . . . misit, dominus misertus mihi mandavit*; but L[2] has *dominus misertus est*

[ψε με] δουναι πασι την μετα
[νοιαν κ]αι περι τινων μη ον
[των αξ]ιων σωθηναι δια τα
εργα [αυτ]ων αλλα μακροθυμος
[ων ο κ̅ς̅ θ]ε[λ]ει την κλησιν τ̅η̅

p. 54

γενομενην δ[ια του υιου αυ
του σωθηνα[ι λεγω αυτω 2
κ̅ε̅ ελπιζω ο[τι παντες
ακουσαντε[ς αυτα μετα
νοησουσιν [πειθομαι γαρ
οτι ἑις εκασ[τος τα ιδια
εργα επιγνους [και φοβη
θεις τ[ον] θ̅ν̅ μετ[ανοησει
αποκ[ριθει]ς μοι λεγ[ει 3
[οσ]οι [φησι]ν μετ[ανοησω
[σι]ν εξ [ολης] καρδ[ιας αυ
[τω]ν και [κ]αθαρισω[σιν
[εαυ]τους απο των πον[η
[ριων] αυτων των προει
[ρημ]ενων και μηκετι
[προ]σθωσι μηδεν ταις

et misit me, and the Coptic also employs two parallel independent verbs.

29 πᾶσι δοῦναι A.

30 καὶ περί: καίπερ A and the versions rightly.

31 σωθῆναι MLL, *digni qui vivant* E: om. A.

P. 54. 1 γενομένην ML[1]E: γινομένην A and perhaps L[2].

2 σῴζεσθαι A.

10 The reading is doubtful as far as ε. A trace at the beginning of the line may be the rough breathing. — A omits μετανοήσωσιν here and καί below (12); all the versions had these words.

12 καθαρίσουσιν A.

14 M confirms A's reading αὐτῶν, which G.-H. had wrongly changed to πασῶν, comparing L[1] (*ab omni nequitia*) L[2] (*ab omnibus operibus nequitiae*). But *omnis* is probably only a translator's way of heightening emphasis. Neither the Coptic nor the Ethiopic version has anything corresponding to πασῶν. It should be observed that both C and E use a demonstrative with the word for wickedness, which seems to show that they took αὐτῶν not for a possessive genitive, but for a demonstrative in agreement with πονηριῶν.

16 μηδὲν προσθῶσι A.

[αμ]αρτιαις αυτων λημ
[ψ]ονται ϊασιν π[αρα του κ̅υ̅
των προτερων α[μαρτι
ων εαν μη διψυχ[ησω
[σ]ιν επι ταις εντο[λαις
[τ]αυταις και ζησοντ[αι
[τω] θ̅ω̅ οσοι δε προσθ[ω
[σι τ]α[ι]ς α[μαρ]τιαις αυ[των
[και] πορευσοντα[ι] ται[ς επι
[θυμ]ιαις του αιω[ν]ος τ[ου
[τ]ου κατακρινουσιν ε[αν
τους εις θανατον [συ δε πο 4
[ρε]υου εν ταις εντ[ολαις μου
και ζηση· κα[ι] ος α[ν] π[ο
ρευσετ[αι] εν α[υταις

p. 55 Sim. IX, 1

(About twelve lines are lost.)

[του θ̅υ̅ εστιν επειδη γαρ α]σθε 2
[νεστερος τη σαρκι ης ο]υκ εδη
[λωθη σοι δι αγγελου οτε] ουν
[ενεδυναμωθης δια το]υ π̅ν̅ς̅
[και ισχυσας τη ισχυ]ει σου
[ωστε δυνασθαι σε] αγγελον
[ιδειν τοτε μεν ο]υν εδηλω

17 λήψονται A.

18 If we read παρα κ̅υ̅ only, the line will be nearer the length of its neighbors.

23 A omits ὅσοι δὲ . . . εἰς θάνατον (28). The versions (LLE — there is a gap in C) follow the text of M closely.

24 This line is so injured that nothing is free from doubt.

27 The Latin translators took κατακρίνουσι for a future and rendered it *damnabunt*: *morti se ipsos subditos faciunt* E.

30 ζήσῃ MLLCE: ζῆθι A. — L[1] adds *deo*, L[2] *cum deo*: om. MACE. — A omits from καὶ ὃς ἂν to the end of § 4.

P. 55. 6 ὥστε δύνασθαί σε οἱ ἄγγελοι A. Hilgenfeld emended οἱ ἄγγελοι to καὶ ἄγγελον, following L[1] *etiam nuntium*. However, L[2]E have nothing corresponding to καί, and M probably agreed with them; for l. 6 projects no farther into the margin than l. 5 and l. 7, as it must have done had καί been written.

7 ἐδηλώθη: ἐφανερώθη A. *ostensa est* LL, *apparuit* E.

[θη σοι δια της εκκ]λησιας η οι
[κοδομη του πυργο]υ̣ καλως και
[σεμνως παντα ω]ς υπο παρθε
[νου εωρακας ν]υν δε υπο
[αγγελου βλεπεις] δια του αν
[του μεν $\overline{\pi\nu\varsigma}$ δει] δε σε ακρει 3
[βεστερον υπ εμου] παντα ϊδειν
[εις τουτο γαρ εδοθη]ν̣ υπο του
[ενδοξου αγγελου] εις τ̣ο̣ν ο̣ι
[κον σου κατοικησαι ινα] δυνα
[τως παντα ιδης μηδε]ν δει

p. 56

(About thirteen lines are lost.)

[μη εχον· το δε τριτον ακαν] 5
θω̣ν [και τριβολων πληρες
το [δε τεταρτον βοτανας εχον 6
ημ̣[ιξηρους τα μεν επανω
τ̣ω[ν βοτανων χλωρα τα δε
προς̣ [ταις ριζαις ξηρα τινες
δε βοτ[αναι οταν ο ηλιος επι
κεκαυ[κει ξηραι εγεινοντο
το δε π̣ε̣[μπτον ορος ην τραχυ 7
λειαν β[οτανας δε ειχε χλω
ρας· το [δε εκτον ορος ολον

14–15 παρ' ἐμοῦ ἀκριβέστερον πάντα μαθεῖν A. Since M has ἰδεῖν, ὑπ' ἐμοῦ seems to be demanded; cf. l. 10. L[1] reads *sed oportet te omnia diligenter videre*, L[2] *oportet enim te diligentius omnia a me discere*, E *et oportet te exacte omnia ab eo discere*—a curious division among the authorities. Line 14 projects into the right margin two letter-spaces, so that it is impossible, so far as M is concerned, either to read ἀκριβῶς or to omit ὑπ' ἐμοῦ.—A has καὶ ἐδόθην in 15, but there is not room for καί in M, nor do the versions render it.

P. 56. 7 After ἐγίνοντο A reads τὸ δὲ ὄρος τραχὺ λίαν ἦν, βοτάνας ἔχον ξηράς. τὸ δὲ πέμπτον ὄρος ἔχον βοτάνας χλωράς, καὶ τραχὺ ὄν. G.–H. omitted the first sentence and adopted the second. It is possible that the first clause belongs to the description of the fourth mountain, but more probable, I think, that the text of A is a mixture of two versions of the description of the fifth mountain, with ξηράς wrongly substituted for χλωράς. The versions support the text of M: LL *quintus mons asperrimus* (*asper* L[2]) *erat, sed virides habebat herbas*, E *quintus mons viridis et asperrimus erat.*

σχισμω̣[ν εγεμεν ας μεν με
γαλας α[ς δε μεικρας ειχον
δε βο[τανας αι σχισμαι ου
λει[αν δε ησαν ευθαλεις αι
βοτ[αναι μαλλον δε ως με

p. 57

μαραμμεν[αι] ησαν· το δε εβδο̣μ̣ο̣ν 8
ορος ειχεν [βο]τανας ϊλαρας κα[ι
ο̣λον το [ορος] ε̣υ̣θ̣ηνουν ην κα[ι
παν γενο[ς] κτηνων και ορνεων
ε̣νεμε[το] ε̣ι̣ς το ορος εκεινο
και οσ[ο]ν εβοσκετο τα κτηνη
και τα πετεινα μαλλον και μαλ
λον αι β[ο]ταναι του ορους εκει
ν̣ο̣υ̣ ε̣θ[αλ]λον· το δε ογδοον
ο̣ρος πη[γω]ν̣ πληρες ην και παν
γενο̣ς της κτισεως του κ̅υ̅
[εποτιζε]τ̣ο εκ των πηγων του
[ορους εκειν]ο̣υ· το δε ενατον 9
[ορος ολως υ]δωρ ουκ ειχεν και
[ολον ερημωδες η]ν ειχεν δε εν
[αυτω θηρια ερπετα θ]α̣νασιμα

11 σχισμῶν ὅλον A. — The ω is partly destroyed in M, but the identity of the letter is virtually certain. Despite the genitive, M continued with ἃς μὲν . . . ἃς δέ, an irregularity which is the more natural because of the obsolescence of the simple genitive with verbs of fullness. See Jannaris, § 1319, and Apoc. 17, 3. — ὧν μὲν μικρῶν, ὧν δὲ μεγάλων A, and the versions agree in this order of the adjectives as against M.

P. 57. 1 μεμαρασμέναι A, which G-H. corrected to μεμαραμμέναι, citing Vis. *3*, 11, 2. In that passage ℵ has the latter form and A the former.

5 ἐνέμοντο A.

6 ἐβόσκοντο A.

12 ἐποτίζοντο A.

16–17 In reconstructing the lower part of this fragment the probable length of the lines has to be considered. Taking l. 15, with 23 letters, as a starting-point, we note that 16 is of equal length with 15, and 17 is about a space and a half shorter. Now A reads εἶχε δὲ ἐν αὐτῷ θηρία καὶ ἑρπετὰ θανάσιμα διαφθείροντα ἀνθρώπους. θηρία καί cannot be fitted into l. 16 of M; but if we take ἑρπετά as adjective (cf. the new L. and S.), we have a text of the right length and one from which all the others might have been derived. L^1 reads *sed et mortiferas serpentes habebat et hominibus perniciosas*. L^2 has *et mortiferas serpentes habebat*

[διαφθειροντα ανθρωπο]υς

(Thirteen or fourteen lines are lost.)

p. 58

ρ[ι]δ

[το δε δωδεκα] 10
τ[ον ο]λον ην λευκον και η
προσοψις του ορους ϊλαρα
λειαν και ευπρεπεστατον
ην εν αυτω το ορος· εις 2, 1
μεσον δε του πεδ[ιου] εδει
ξε μοι πετραν μεγαλην
λευκην εκ του πεδιου ανα
βεβηκυϊαν η δε πετρα
υψηλοτερα ην των ορεων
τετραγωνος δε ωστε δυνα
σθαι ολον τον κοσμον χω
ρησαι παλαια δε ην η π[ετρα 2
εκεινη πυλην ε[κκεκομ
μενην ε[χουσ]α ω[ς προσφατος

(About sixteen lines are lost.)

p. 59

[λινους χιτω]νας και περιεζω 4
[σμεναι ησαν] ευπρεπως εξω
[τους ωμους] εχουσαι τους δε
[ξιους ως με]λλουσαι φορτιον

hominibus omnibus perniciosas (Is *omnibus* a dittography of the preceding word?). E reads *et in eo erant ferae venenum hominibus letiferum habentes*.

P. 58. 1 The words τὸ δὲ δωδέκα- were on the preceding page and are printed here only to give the connection. — ὄρος is expressed by all the other authorities.

2 τοῦ ὄρους: αὐτοῦ A. The versions do not repeat *mons*, but that proves nothing.

2–3 ἱλαρὰ ἦν A. λείαν ML^1 (*hilarissimum*) E (*splendens valde*): om. AL^2. — At the end of the line the scribe seems to have written τα, then erased α and written ον.

4 A also reads ἐν αὐτῷ, which G.-H. emended to ἑαυτῷ following L^1 *ipse sibi mons summum praestabat decorem*, L^2 *sibique mons ille summum praebebat decorem*. E has *et mons ipse speciosus erat*.

10 δέ MLLE: PAmh and A omit.

P. 59. 2 ἦσαν is in PAmh and is required by the space in M: om. A.

[τι βασταζε]ιν̣ ως ετοιμαι
[ησαν λειαν γαρ] ϊλαραι ησαν
[και προθυμοι με]τα το ϊδειν με 5
[ταυτα εθα]υμα[ζο]ν εν εμαυτω
[οτι μεγ]α̣λ̣α̣ και ενδ[οξα] πραγμα
τ̣[α εβλεπ]ο̣ν και παλ̣[ιν] ηπορου
μην επι ταις παρθενοις οτι
τρυφεραι ουτως ανδρειως
ειστηκεισαν ως μελλουσαι
ολον τον ου[ρ]ανον βασταζει͞
λεγει μοι ο ποιμην τι εν σεαυ 6
τω διαλογιζη και απορη κα[ι
εν σεαυτω λυπην επισπα[σαι
[ο]σα γαρ ου δυνη νοησα[ι μη επι
χειρι ως συνετος ων α̣[λλ ερω
τα παρα [του] κ͞υ ϊνα λ[αβων συν
εσιν νοη[σ]ης αυτα τ̣[α οπισω 7
σου ϊδειν [ο]υ δυνη τα [δε εμ
προσθεν [σο]υ βλεπ[εις α ουν
ϊδειν ου δυνη σεαυ[τον μη
σ̣τρεβλου ἃ βλεπεις [δε εκει
νων κατακυριευε κ̣[αι περι των
[λο]ιπων μ̣η περιεργα̣[ζου παντα

P. 59. 5 ὡς: οὕτως PAmh A. *sic* LL, *et paratae erant* E. — ἕτοιμοι A.

10 ἔβλεπον: βλέπω A. *quod . . . viderem* L[1], *quod . . . videbam* L[2], *quod . . . videram* E. — διηπόρουν A.

12 τρυφεραὶ οὕτως οὖσαι ἀνδρείως A. Possibly the original was τρυφεραὶ οὖσαι οὕτως ἀνδρείως.

14 βασταζει͞ = βαστάζειν.

15 λέγει: καὶ λέγει AL[2] (*autem*) E (*et*), also L[1], which, however, interpolates a clause, *et cum haec intra me disputarem, ait*.

16 διαπορῇ A.

17 A omits ἐν; M has probably been affected by ἐν in l. 15. — M may have written ἐπισπᾷ only, not ἐπισπᾶσαι (A), for even without the last syllable the line is almost as long as the foregoing one.

19 ὡς: om. A and probably E.

20 ἐρώτα τὸν κύριον A, *roga dominum* LLE.

21 νοῇς A.

24 δύνασαι A, but δύνῃ above (22). δύνῃ is more common in Hermas, but δύνασαι is found in Vis. *3*, 8, 5; see Mayser, p. 355, Reinhold, p. 95. — After δύνασαι A adds ἔασον and so E (*missum fac*): om. ML[1] (L[2]?). — καὶ μὴ στρέβλου σεαυτόν A. E seems not to have had this καί.

25 ἃ δὲ βλέπεις A.

[δε σοι δει]ξω εμβλ[επε ουν τοις
[λοιποις ειδον] ἑξ α̣[νδρας ε 3, 1
[ληλυθοτας υψη]λου[ς και εν

p. 60

ρ[

δοξους και ομ[οιους τη ιδεα
εκαλεσαν δε π[ληθος τι αν
δρων κακειν[οι δε οι ελη
λυθοτες υψη[λοι ανδρες
και λειαν κ̣[αλοι και δυνα
τοι ησαν [και εκελευσαν αυ
τους ο[ι εξ α]ν̣δ̣ρ̣ε̣[ς οικοδο
με[ιν ε]πανω τ[ης πετρας
πυργον τινα η̣ν̣ δ[ε μεγας
θορυβος των ανδρ[ων εκει
νων των εληλυθο[των οικο
δομειν τον πυ[ργον ωδε
κ̣ακει περιτ̣[ρεχοντων κυ

28 After this σοι A adds ἐγὼ δηλώσω ὅσα ἐάν σοι, which M probably omitted by homoioteleuton. L^2 also has a shorter text, *ego enim tibi omnia demonstrabo*, where, however, *demonstrabo* may represent either δηλώσω or δείξω. A is supported by L^1 (*ego autem tibi cuncta monstrabo quaecumque ostendero*) and E (*nam omnia quae tibi ostendi, ego tibi exponam*).

30 ἐληλυθότας: om. C.

P. 60 1 τῇ ἰδέᾳ: om. C(E?).

2 καὶ ἐκάλεσαν (omitting δέ) A.

3 C appears to have lost some words between κἀκεῖνοι and ἐπάνω (8).

4 A has ἦσαν after ὑψηλοί, not after δυνατοί (6).

5 λείαν M, *satis* L^2, *admodum* E: om. AL^1.

8 It is unfortunate that the right-hand margin has been destroyed, since we are left in doubt about the genitive after ἐπάνω. A reads ἐπάνω τῆς πέτρας and so E: L^1 *super eam portam*, L^2 *supra petram illam . . . et super portam ipsam*. G.–H. accepted the double phrase ἐπάνω τῆς πέτρας καὶ ἐπάνω τῆς πύλης, considering it to be warranted by Sim. *9*, 4, 2, ἡ οἰκοδομὴ δὲ τοῦ πύργου ἐγένετο ἐπὶ τὴν πέτραν τὴν μεγάλην καὶ ἐπάνω τῆς πύλης; and Dibelius also is of this opinion. There is room in M for only one of the phrases. I incline to think that ἐπάνω τῆς πύλης is a gloss derived from *9*, 4, 2, where greater particularity in the description was natural. The gloss displaced the older text in L^1, and was superadded in the original of L^2. Leipoldt restores πυλη in the Coptic text, but I do not understand why, seeing that the word is in a lacuna.

9 A omits μέγας here, placing it after ἐκείνων (11).

13 κἀκεῖσε A.

κλω της πυλης αι δ[ε παρθε 2
νοι εστηκυιαι πε[ρι την
πυλην ελεγον τοι[ς ανδρα
[σι] σπ[ε]υδειν δει[ν ο]ικο[δο
[μηθ]ηνα[ι] τον π[υ]ργ[ον εκ
[πεπ]ετακει[σ]αν δε [τας χει
[ρας αι] παρθενοι [ως μελλουσαι
[τι λα]μβανειν [παρα
[των α]νδρων οι [δε εξ αν 3
[δρες ε]κελευον εκ βυθ[ου
[τινος λ]ιθους αν[αβαινειν
[και υ]παγειν ει[ς την οικο
[δομη]ν του πυ[ργου ανε
[βησα]ν δε λιθοι [

(One leaf is lost.)

p. 61

ρ]ιθ

[κιλ]αι[ς λε]λατομημ[ε]νοι υπο 4, 5

14–16 C omits αἱ δὲ . . . τὴν πύλην.

15 There is a short horizontal stroke above υ which may be intended for the circumflex accent. — περὶ τὴν πύλην: κύκλῳ τῆς πύλης A. περί in a purely local sense is rare in Hermas; besides this place I find only Sim. *9*, 7, 6, *9*, 12, 7, while there are more than ten cases of κύκλῳ with the genitive.

17 σπεύδειν δεῖν ML[1] (*iubebant eis aedificationem turris accelerari oportere*): AL[2]CE omit δεῖν. Opinions may differ as to the question whether the presence of δεῖν in the one group is due to dittography or its absence from the other is due to haplography. To my mind the text is harder, and so more likely to be changed, with δεῖν than without it.

18 τὸν πύργον οἰκοδομεῖσθαι A. The beginning of the line in M is much damaged and the traces uncertain; but what remains cannot be read οἰκοδομεῖσθαι.

20 If M agreed with A, this line was much longer than its neighbors, and must have run far into the margin. Line 19 has 20 letters, l. 21 only 15, l. 22, 17, while l. 20 has 24. There is, of course, much irregularity in this respect throughout the papyrus; but a difference of nine letters between two consecutive lines is surprising. The position of the left-hand margin has been established by comparing the position of letters in these lines with the position of those vertically above them in the portion where the left margin is intact; so that μέλλουσαι cannot be divided between l. 20 and l. 21. One might suggest that μέλλουσαι was carelessly omitted, with a consequent change of ὡς to ὥστε; but the versions evidently read μέλλουσαι just as A does.

21 τι: om. C.

[των αν]δρων και επεδιδοντο
[ταις παρ]θ[ε]νοις αι δε παρθενοι
[διεφερο]ν [α]υτους δια της πυ
[λης κα]ι επεδιδουν εις την οι
[κοδομ]ην του πυργου και οταν
[εις τη]ν οικοδομην ετεθησ[αν
[οι] λιθοι οι ποικιλοι ομοι[ο]ι εγε
[νο]ντο λευκοι και τας χροι
[α]ς τας προτερας ηλλασ[σον
[τι]νες δε λιθοι επεδιδον[το 6
[υ]πο των ανδρων εις τη[ν οι
[κ]οδομην και ουκ εγειν[οντο
[λαμ]προι αλλ' [ο]ιοι ετεθη[σαν
[τοιου]τοι και ησαν ου γαρ [ησαν
[απο τ]ων παρθενων επιδε[δο
[μ]ενοι ουτοι ουν οι λιθοι απρε
πεις ησαν εν τη οικοδομη του
πυργου· ϊδον δε οι ̄ε̄ξ ανδρες 7
[τ]ους λ[ι]θους τουτους απρεπεις
[τη] οικοδομη και εκελευσαν
[αυ]του[ς] αρθ[η]ναι και απενεχ

(Eight lines are lost.)

p. 62

ρενεγκα[σαι αυ]τ[ο]υς ε[πιδω 8
σε[τ] εις τ[η]ν [οι]κοδομη[ν εαν

P. 61. 10 χρόας A. προτέρας MLL (*priores*) E (*colorem proprium*): ποικίλας A.

15 ἦσαν MLL (*permanebant*) E: εὑρέθησαν A.

16 ἀπό is supplied from A. Editors have proposed ὑπό.

17 After ἐπιδεδομένοι A adds οὐδὲ διὰ τῆς πύλης παρενηνεγμένοι, and so E (*per portam introducentes*). The Latin translators take no account of ἐπιδεδομένοι nor of οὐδέ, which follows in A: L[1] *quoniam non erant a virginibus per portam translati*, and L[2] similarly.

19 ϊδον (for εἶδον) δέ M: ἰδόντες δέ A (omitting καί in 21), LL *quos* (*quod* L[2]) *cum animadvertissent*, E *quos cum viderent*.

20 τούτους: τούς A.

21 τῇ: ἐν τῇ A, *in aedificatione* E. The Latin translators do not render ἀπρεπεῖς (ἐν) τῇ οἰκοδομῇ. — καί: om. A.

22 ἀπενεχ[θῆναι] ML[1] (*referri*): ἀπαχθῆναι A; cf. E *reduci*. *poni* L[2].

P. 62. There is a trace of a numeral at the top of this page, possibly belonging to ρ.

1–2 The text of M was markedly differ-

γαρ φησ[ι]ν δια̣ τ[ω]ν χ[ειρων
των π̣[α]ρ̣[θεν]ω̣[ν] τουτ̣[ων
μη διενε̣χ̣θω[σι] δια της [πυ
λης τας χρ̣ο̣ας αυτων α[λ
λαξαι ου δυνανται μη
κοπι̣ατε ουν φησ[ι]ν ει̣ς
ματην ετελεσ̣θη εκειν[η 5, 1

ent from that of A at this point, but because of the loss of the right-hand margin and some perforations at the beginning of l. 2, it is impossible to restore it with certainty. ρενεγκα, however, is certain; the sharp angle of α is clearly visible. A subjunctive form is therefore impossible, and since there is not room for καί before αὐτούς, and the surviving letters show that it was not after αὐτούς, the participle παρενέγκασαι seems to be required. The fact that the Latin translators employ a participial construction — *ut hae virgines translatos porrigant* — suggests that they found a participle in their Greek original, but this is not conclusive.

Either ἐπιδιδῶσιν (the reading of A) or ἐπιδῶσιν would be possible so far as considerations of space are involved, but neither can be reconciled with the traces at the beginning of l. 2. Now if the subjunctive forms cannot be accepted, it seems necessary to suppose that M differed still further from the text of A. A reads — going back to the beginning of the clause — τίθετε δὲ αὐτοὺς παρὰ τὸν πύργον, ἵνα αἱ παρθένοι διὰ τῆς πύλης παρενέγκωσιν αὐτοὺς καὶ ἐπιδιδῶσιν εἰς τὴν οἰκοδομήν. If M read καί instead of ἵνα, παρενέγκασαι for παρενέγκωσιν, and an imperative or a future used as imperative of ἐπιδιδωμι instead of the subjunctive, the result would be a loose, homely construction with a sudden change of the persons addressed: "You (men) set them by the tower, and you maidens bring them (*or*, are to bring them) through the gate and give them over for the building." We must now consider the traces at the beginning of line 2 with this possibility in view.

The first letter, of which only the top remains, is probably sigma. There is a very flat curve with a slight thickening of the line, marking the junction with the down-stroke — a form of this letter which is common in the papyrus. This trace cannot be read as tau. The long top of that letter would have shown itself unmistakably on the intact portion of the papyrus, even if part of it were lost. The second trace is almost certainly the left-hand lower part of ε. To judge it from a photograph, θ might be considered possible; but close inspection of the original decides for ε. Whatever stood in the third place has been entirely destroyed by the perforation.

If this reading be correct, neither ἐπιδίδοτε nor ἐπιδότε can be considered, and we are left with the possibility that the reading was ε[πιδω]σε̣[τ]', which may have lost ε by haplography, since the scribe seems not to elide the final vowels of verbs. It may be regarded as a future with the force of a command; but as Jannaris (§ 949) remarks, when the aorist subjunctive became δώσω (cf. Mand. 3, 2), the imperative inevitably became δῶσε; and as is well known the imperative δώσ(ε)τε is common in modern Greek.

In connection with this textual problem, it may be worth while to note that *et . . . porrigant* is reported by Dressel and Hilgenfeld as the reading of the Vatican Manuscript of L[1]. This is not considered one of the best sources for the Old Latin version, and the *et* may be due only to a scribe's carelessness. On the other hand, *et* was more likely to be changed to *ut* in such a sentence than *ut* to *et*.

3 φησίν MA: om. LLE.
5 παρενεχθῶσι A.
8 φησίν: φασίν A, om. LLE.
9 καὶ ἐτελέσθη ALLE. — τῇ ἡμέρᾳ ἐκείνῃ A.

τη ημερα η οικοδομη ο[υ
[κ α]ποτ[ε]λ̣ε̣σ̣θη δε ο πυργ[ος
[ε]μελλε γ̣α[ρ] π̣αλ̣ι̣ν εποικο̣
[δ]ο̣μ̣εισθαι· εγεν̣ε̣το δε
α̣νοχη τις της οικοδομη̣[ς
εκελευσαν δε αυτου̣ς
οι ε̄ξ ανδρες το̣υς οικ[ο
δομουντας ανα̣χ̣ωρη
σαι και ωσει αναπαηναι
ταις δε̣ παρ[θ]ενο̣ις επε
ταξαν απο τ[ο]υ πυργου
μ̣η̣ [αναχ]ωρει̣ν εδ[ο]κει
[δε μοι τας] π̣[αρθενους

(The rest of the page is lost.)

11 ἀποτελέσθῃ: ἀπετελέσθη A. M's reading illustrates the loss of syllabic augment in compound verbs, which is fairly common in Egyptian papyri; cf. Mayser, p. 333.

13 ἐγένετο δέ: καὶ ἐγένετο A.

14 τις ML[1] (*quaedam dilatio*): om. AL[2]E.

15 αὐτούς: om. A.

18 After ἀναχωρῆσαι A adds μικρὸν πάντας: om. MLLE.—ὡσεί ML[1]: om. AL[2]E. LL seem to have read ἀναπαῆναί τι; cf. L[1] *quiescere aliquid*, L[2] *aliquantum requiescere*.—ἀναπαῆναι: ἀναπαυθῆναι A. Compare Vis. *1*, 3, 3 (παῆναι ℵ, παυθῆναι A), *3*, 9, 1 (παῆναι ℵ, παῦσαι A), also P. Oxy. 1172, 9. ἀναπαήσονται occurs in Apoc. 14, 13.

21 ἀναχωρῆσαι A.

SUPPLEMENTARY NOTES AND CORRIGENDA

Most of the following supplementary matter is based upon comments made by two younger coworkers, Mr. H. C. Youtie, Research Associate in Papyrology, and Mr. C. E. Demaray, a former pupil. It is to be regretted that at the time when their suggestions were offered the printing was so far advanced that not all of them could be incorporated in the notes.

The references are to the pages and lines of the papyrus.

P. 3, 12. The context of sections 2–4 of the fourth similitude favors φανεροί more strongly than is allowed in the note. Cf. φανεροὶ ἔσονται οἱ δουλεύοντες τῷ θεῷ (p. 2, 26), τῶν δικαίων οἱ καρποὶ φανεροὶ ἔσονται (p. 3, 2–4). So in section 3 it is by burning with fire that the wicked will be revealed. The ὅτι clause following is epexegetical. (C. E. D.)

P. 6, 15. If ἀποδημήσων was the reading of M, it is the only example of the future participle in Hermas, and this participle is rare in all the Apostolic Fathers. Perhaps ἀποδημῶν was used in a future sense such as is sometimes found in ἔρχομαι and πορεύομαι. The corruption through ἐκδημῶν to ἔντιμον would be more easily explained in this way. (C. E. D.)

P. 22, 4. ἐκπλέξαι MA, *se explicare* LL. It is uncertain whether the Greek text has lost ἑαυτά through the negligence of a scribe, or presents a colloquial ellipsis of the object. The verb is rare and is transitive elsewhere. L. and S. cite only Alex. Rhet. *Fig.* 2, 1; but cf. P. Tebt. 314, 6, 315, 21 and 29, P. Oxy. 1490, 6. (C. E. D.)

P. 25, 31. The words in the lower margin should be read κ(αι) τιμωριας and may be a gloss intended by the writer to be inserted after βασάνου (29). Just after that word and above the line there is a mark of some sort in ink like that used in the marginal gloss.

P. 26, 18. δηλαυγῶς occurs in the great Paris magical papyrus (P. IV in Preisendanz), lines 775 and 1033. Cf. Crönert's comment in Wessely's *Studien zur Palaeographie und Papyruskunde*, IV, p. 101.

P. 28, 3–5 note. In the reading of L^2, insert *delitiosus* before *homo.*

P. 46, 14. The support of LL is claimed for M because ἀπόλλυμι is rendered by *amitto*, *perdo*, *pereo*, and other words, but apparently not by *morior*. (H. C. Y.)

P. 46, 25. It is probable that LL support the reading of M. ἕτερος often implies κακός; cf. L. and S. s.v. ἕτερος III, 2, and ἑτεροδιδασκαλεῖν, 1 Tim. 1, 3. (H. C. Y.)

P. 47, 17. The text of E is confused: *quorum virgae semiaridae sunt, ii ipsi quoque semiaridi sunt.* It is possible that *quoque* represents κατὰ τὸ αὐτό, but the translator may have had καὶ αὐτοί in his copy. In any case ἡμίξηροι must have been repeated. The ὅσον of M may represent an original ὅσων.

P. 48, 30—p. 49, 3. L[1] reads *vita enim eorum qui custodiunt mandata domini in mandatis consistit, non in principatu aut aliqua dignitate.* This supports M in the omission of the conjunction (p. 49, 3, where L[2] has *autem*, E *nam*), and indicates that in the original of L[1] ἐστί must have stood after τηρούντων. (H. C. Y.)

P. 59, 15. The Latin versions may have been made from copies that had before λέγει a participle referring to Hermas. One might expect διαλογιζομένου μου ταῦτα (about one line, which could have been omitted by accident), for the syntax of Hermas is so loose that he would scarcely have used the dative anticipating μοι (15); but it is also possible that here, as elsewhere, he used the nominative in an irregular anacoluthic construction, διαλογιζόμενος ταῦτα or διαλογιζόμενος ἐν ἐμαυτῷ. This would perhaps account for L[1], *pastor autem considerans me ita ait;* the translator referred the participle to the Shepherd and modified the rest of the text accordingly. (H. C. Y.)

P. 60, 14–16. Attention should have been called to the fact that the omission in C is most easily explained if its copy agreed with A in reading κύκλῳ τῆς πύλης in 15–16. The loss would then result from homoioteleuton. (H. C. Y.)

There is some doubt whether the scribe of this manuscript ever omitted the stroke above abbreviated *nomina sacra,* unless by an occasional oversight. There are several places where it cannot be seen, but in most of them the papyrus is injured. It would therefore have been better to print the stroke above all such abbreviations.

A FRAGMENT OF THE MANDATES

A FRAGMENT OF THE MANDATES

P. Mich. 130
Inv. 44-H

This fragment is one of a considerable number that came to the University along with a large lot of papyri purchased in 1921. Because of their small size and unpromising appearance these scraps were put aside for some time, until a fortunate circumstance led Professor F. E. Robbins to examine them in the early part of the year 1926. He observed that this particular piece was part of a Christian text, and called my attention to it on the chance that it might prove to be a fragment of Hermas. Its identity was soon established; and an account of the piece was published some months afterwards in *The Harvard Theological Review* XX (1927), 105–116 (Plates I, II). Since the appearance of that article, suggestions and criticisms of various friendly readers, especially Professor A. S. Hunt and Professor W. Crönert, have led me to revise my previous views about certain readings and restorations. To Professor Hunt I am further obliged for giving me the benefit of his expert judgment as to the date of the writing.

The fragment is irregular in shape, its greatest height being 12.1 cm., its greatest breadth 8.7 cm. The papyrus is of fairly good quality, originally well smoothed, at least on the recto side, thin, and of light color. The piece has been torn and badly crumpled, and the surface of the verso has been injured in several places. On the recto are the ends of some entries regarding the size of different tracts of land. The occurrence of the word αἰγιαλοῦ, shore-land, shows that the document came from the Fayum. The writing may be assigned to the third quarter of the second century.

On the verso is a passage from the Mandates of Hermas (*2*, 6–*3*, 1), written in a not very regular upright semicursive hand, which may be safely assigned to the last years of the second century. A few details about the forms of the letters may be worth mentioning. Eta is of the *h*-shape, with a rather tall first stroke. The horizontal forms a sharp angle with the last stroke, which descends from it in a pronounced curve and then turns up towards the right. A similar curve is used in the last stroke of pi. Upsilon branches widely, and does not extend below the line; in one instance it is quite small and its stem curves up sharply to the right. Omicron is of medium size, with the breadth exceeding the height. Sigma is nearly closed, and the top is usually flat; in two places the flat top is prolonged to fill out unused space. In one case (in ἔνδοξος, l. 6) sigma is a narrow downward facing curve like an inverted U; but it is not, as I stated in *The Harvard Theological Review*, p. 107, connected with the following letter. The appearance of linking which then misled me is due partly to the long top-stroke of the following pi, and partly to a slight depression in the surface of the papyrus. I am also now convinced by the criticisms of Professor Hunt and my colleague Professor Sanders that I was wrong in then reporting the first two letters of the text as ος. The traces could perhaps be interpreted as omicron and a sigma of the downward-turned form like that in l. 6; but it would then be necessary to suppose the sigma to be linked with the following epsilon, which seems to be without parallel. I therefore read στ̣, and assume that the insertion of τ is an error on the part of the scribe, who was probably influenced by the στ of the next word.

A single sign, a short horizontal stroke, seems to serve several purposes. In l. 3 it does duty as an acute accent, in l. 4 as a smooth breathing or perhaps a grave accent, and in the other five places where it occurs it is the rough breathing. A similar vague use of a horizontal stroke is to be found in the Berlin cursive papyrus of Genesis; see *University of Michigan Studies, Humanistic Series*, vol. XXI, p. 239. In lines 7 and 12 a point on the base line is apparently used to separate concurrent vowels. It might be regarded as a minor punctuation in the first instance, but in the second no pause is possible. Thompson (*Introduction to Greek and Latin Palaeography*, p. 62) mentions a use of the apostrophe "to distinguish two concurrent vowels."

In l. 7, θεῷ is written in full; but if κυρίου occurred in the first sentence, as in the other texts, it must have been abbreviated.

The writing consists of the first sixteen lines of one column, containing the end of Mand. 2 and the heading and first few words of Mand. 3, and the first letters of six lines (4–9) of a second column. Enough of the upper margin is left to prove that line 1 was really the first of the page. The original height of the column is somewhat doubtful, since the remaining letters of Column 2 do not give entirely satisfactory evidence. It is true that these letters occur in the right sequence about the middle of the second section of Mand. 3 (line 19 in Gebhardt-Harnack), but the intervals between them do not work out as well as might be desired. If the surviving letters are rightly placed, all of the lines except the third (line 6) would be shorter than the average line in Column 1, while line 6 would be considerably longer than the rest. It will be understood, therefore, that the reconstruction of Column 2 printed below is most uncertain. However, assuming it to be right, the columns would have contained about 28 lines. There is nothing to indicate the original length of the manuscript. Since the writing is not a book-hand and appears on the verso of a discarded document, it may have contained only a few chapters copied for the writer's personal use. At the most we might suppose that it contained all the Mandates, which could have been copied on a roll of moderate length.

In its text this fragment exhibits many discrepancies from the other authorities, which are by no means in close accord among themselves, and which are all — with the possible exception of the mutilated Sinaiticus — open to the suspicion of corruption. Under such circumstances our text, peculiar as it is, should receive careful consideration, especially in view of its antiquity; for it was written scarcely more than two generations after the commonly accepted date of Hermas, and is thus the oldest known manuscript. The irregularities in sentence connection and in syntax show that this piece has not been subjected to the sort of correction which, as the Michigan codex proves, was later applied to the text of Hermas. How far these irregularities, as well as other peculiar points, may be due to the carelessness or the caprice of an untrained scribe is hard to decide in the absence of harmonious testimony from the other manuscripts and the versions.

COLUMN 1

[αθωο]ς̣{τ} εστιν [ως γαρ ελαβε πα
[ρα κ̅υ̅] εγενετο η̣ [διακο]ν̣ε̣ι̣α̣ α
[πλο]υσιο̄τητι μη διακριναν
[τος] τινι δωσιν η̄ μη δωσιν
[εγε]νετο η̄ διακονεια ᾱπλως
[τελ]εσθεισ̣α ενδοξος παρα
[τω] θεω . ω[ς ο]υτως ᾱπλως
[δια]κονουντος φυλα̣σ̣σ̣ε ουν
[ταυ]την την εντολην ην
[σοι] εδωκα ϊνα τ̄ μεταν[οια

[σου] και η̄ του οικου σο[υ εν
[απλο]τητι . ευρεθη κα[ι κα
[θαρα κ]αι ακακ[ος] κ̣α̣ι̣ α̣[μι
[αντο]ς
[ ]ε̣[ν]τ̣ολη[
[παλ]ιν λεγει μ[οι

COLUMN 2

[ην ε]
λ̣[αβον ελαβον γαρ παρ αυ
το[υ π̅ν̅α̅ αψευστον του
το̣[εαν ψευδες αποδωσωσιν ε
μ̣[ιαναν την εντολην
τ[ου κ̅υ̅ και εγινοντο
α̣[ποστερηται

In the Athos manuscript the corresponding passage (Mand. 2, 6–7) reads as follows:

ὁ οὖν διδοὺς ἀθῷός ἐστιν· ὡς γὰρ ἔλαβεν παρὰ τοῦ κυρίου τὴν διακονίαν ἐτ[έλε]σε μὴ διακρίνων τί δῷ. ἐγένετο οὖν ἡ διακονία αὕτη ἁπλῶς τελεσθεῖσα ἔνδοξος παρὰ τῷ θεῷ. ὁ οὖν οὕτως ἁ[πλῶς] διακονῶν τῷ θεῷ ζήσεται. φύλασσε οὖν τὴν ἐντολὴν ταύτην ὥς σοι λελάληκα, ἵνα ἡ μετάνοιά σου καὶ τοῦ οἴκου σου ἐν ἁπλότητι εὑρεθῇ καὶ ἀκ[ακία] καθαρὰ καὶ ἀμίαντος.

This is the transcript made by Professor Lake to accompany his facsimile of the Athos leaves. In one particular I venture to suggest that it should be corrected. The word which he gives as *ἀκ[ακία]* stands at an upper right-hand margin, so that there is no doubt that there would have been room for *ἄκακος* and the abbreviation for *καί*. This would agree, except for a change in the order of words, with the text of the papyrus. It seemed desirable to determine the reading of A more accurately, if possible, and with Professor Lake's permission and the kind assistance of Professor C. H. Turner and the Librarian of Magdalen College, I obtained a new print from the negative. Upon it I read *ακακ[* clearly enough; but, although I have little doubt that *ἄκακος καί* once stood there, I no longer think that any traces in the photograph can be safely referred to the last two letters of ἄκακος or to καί. My previous article is to be corrected on this point.

The second sentence of this passage is quite different in the Sinaiticus, reading ὡς γὰρ ἔλαβεν παρὰ τοῦ κ̅υ̅ τὴν διακονίαν τελέσαι ἁπλῶς αὐτὴν ἐτέλεσεν μηθὲν διακρίνων τίνι δῷ ἢ μὴ δῷ. From there through ζήσεται it agrees with A; but after that word ℵ is mutilated, and nothing remains of this passage but the last two syllables of ἀμίαντος.

The versions also show that from a very early period the text of this passage was far from settled. In the Old Latin, it reads thus:

Qui autem dat innocens erit, sicut enim accepit a domino ministerium consummavit, nihil dubitando cui daret, cui non daret. et fecit hoc ministerium simpliciter gloriosum ad deum. custodi ergo mandatum hoc, sicut tibi locutus sum, ut paenitentia tua simplex inveniatur et possit domui tuae bene fieri, et cor mundum habe.

This is the text which was provisionally established by Professor Turner for his new edition of the Old Latin Hermas. Hilgenfeld reads *dare* (bis) and *gloriose*.

The Palatine version reads:

Ille autem qui dat innoxius erit, cum enim hoc ministerium, quod a domino accipitur, simpliciter apud deum gestum fuerit. quicunque ergo tam simpliciter ministrat, vivit deo. custodi itaque mandatum hoc, sicut tibi dixi, ut poenitentia tua et domus tuae cum simplicitate, et cor tuum sit mundum et indeficiens apud deum.

This is the emended text as it appears in the edition of Gebhardt and Harnack. The readings of the manuscript itself need not concern us, since they throw no light upon the relation of this text to the others. But even in this emended form it is not free from corruptions, and gives clear testimony to the general confusion which existed in the early texts.

In the Ethiopic version also there are manifest corruptions, as its editor observed; the Latin translation of it is as follows:

Is autem qui dedit innocens erit, quia dominus ut ministerium faciat ita fecit, idque simplici corde, non secum distinguens nec dicens, huic dabo et illi non dabo. et ministerium eius factum est honoratum apud dominum, quia simpliciter egit et quia simplici corde ministravit domino et vixit. custodi igitur hoc mandatum sicut locutus sum tibi, ut sit vobis poenitentia et vestri et domus tuae, idque in simplicitate et puritate sine immunditia.

The following details regarding the text of the fragment and its relations to the other sources seem worthy of mention.

Line 1. The τ before εστιν must be due to a slip of some kind, and the letter preceding it is far from certain. It is possible that some other word than ἀθῷος was written.

The first words of the sentence beginning after ἐστιν appear in A and ℵ as ὡς γὰρ ἔλαβεν παρὰ τοῦ κυρίου, which is too long for the available space, even if the sacred name was abbreviated. It is uncertain whether γάρ or τοῦ should be omitted. As to γάρ, it may be observed that laxity in sentence connection is a marked characteristic of the Michigan codex, and that οὖν is omitted from line 5 below. On the other hand Hermas rarely omits the article before θεός and κύριος. The restoration given above is chosen chiefly because line 2 can scarcely have accommodated both τοῦ and $\overline{\kappa\upsilon}$ before ἐγένετο.

Line 2. Since the final α of this line was almost certainly preceded by another α, our text appears to have lacked the ἐν which is usually employed in such phrases by Hermas and the New Testament writers. But the practice of the author may have varied; cf. John 10, 24; 11, 14; 1 Cor. 10, 30; and Schmid, *Atticismus*, IV, p. 616.

Line 3. There can be no doubt that the scribe wrote απλουσιοτητι instead of απλοτητι, but I now regard it as a slip of the pen rather than a hitherto unknown vulgarism, and have therefore restored the ordinary form in line 12. A careful remeasurement of the space there shows that the correct form, though a little short for the space, still fits it better than the longer word. Dr. Crönert suggested that in line 3 the scribe saw his error and cancelled the superfluous letters by placing short dashes (in lieu of the usual dots) above them. But only one dash remains, and it was probably intended for an accent. The photographs which appeared in the previous publication and which prompted Crönert's suggestion, are deceptive here, as sometimes happens. The appearance of ink over two others of the superfluous letters is caused by an unevenness in the surface of the papyrus.

The peculiar twist that is given to this sentence by the use of ἐγένετο and the shift from an active to a virtually passive construction is further emphasized by διακρίναντος. This word was probably felt as a genitive absolute rather than as dependent upon διακονεία; for Hermas shared with the New Testament writers and with others of his time the habit of employing the genitive absolute irregularly. Compare Vis. *1*, 1, 3; *2*, 1, 1; *5*, 4; also Robertson, *Grammar*, pp. 513 and 1131, and Deissmann, *Licht vom Osten*[4], p. 107, n. 5.

Line 4. To the other sources for the text of this passage may be added the not very valuable testimony of Antiochus (*Hom.* 98, col.

1732 Migne). He gives the double indirect question in the form τίνι δῷ ἢ τίνι μὴ δῷ.

The form δωσιν which the papyrus presents here is not easy to explain. The context would lead one to take this as a subjunctive third person singular, but such a form appears to be without parallel in the period of Hermas; Homer's use of δῷσι is of course well known. Crönert suggests that δωσιν is third person plural and that διακριναν[των] should be read. This avoids one difficulty, but raises another in the use of a plural where a singular would be expected. I mention with some hesitation another possibility — if it be that δωσιν could represent δώσειν, and there was a tendency in the Koine to confuse the future and the aorist systems, especially in the infinitive. (Mayser, I, p. 384.) But I have found no example of διακρίνω used with a complementary infinitive. The fact that some manuscripts of L^1 read *dare* may be significant, but is scarcely convincing evidence.

Line 7. The clause ὡς οὕτως ἁπλῶς διακονοῦντος, which may either be referred back to διακονεία in line 5 or treated as another case of the extended use of the genitive absolute, presents a reading quite different from A and ℵ, which agree in giving ὁ οὖν οὕτως ἁπλῶς διακονῶν τῷ θεῷ ζήσεται. Antiochus has καὶ οὕτως ἁπλῶς διακονῶν θεῷ ζήσεται. It is to be observed that L^1 did not translate ζήσεται. The whole clause may have been absent from that translator's copy; but since in the form given by the Michigan fragment it is tautologous, it is quite possible that the original of L^1 agreed with the papyrus, and that the translator deliberately omitted the redundant words.

Equally strange is the situation in the Palatine version (L^2). This translator shows no knowledge of the infinitive of purpose τελέσαι which is found in ℵ, nor of the clause which appears in that manuscript as μηθὲν διακρίνων τίνι δῷ ἢ μὴ δῷ. Perhaps this may be explained by assuming that the Palatine translator had before him (as in the Michigan fragment, line 2) ἐγένετο ἡ διακονεία instead of ἐτέλεσε or αὐτὴν ἐτέλεσεν, and that he passed from this, misled by the recurrence of ἐγένετο in line 5, directly to ἁπλῶς τελεσθεῖσα κ.τ.λ., where, however, he omitted ἔνδοξος. On such a supposition his text might be reconstructed as follows: ὡς γὰρ ἔλαβε παρὰ τοῦ κυρίου, ἐγένετο ἡ διακονεία, ἁπλῶς τελεσθεῖσα παρὰ τῷ θεῷ. This is mere hypothesis; but I can see no more likely explanation of the facts.

Lines 8–10. Here ℵ fails us. Apart from the unimportant variant in the position of ταύτην, it will be noted that the papyrus stands alone in presenting ἥν σοι ἔδωκα instead of ὡς σοι λελάληκα, which was read by all other authorities. The former reading is at least as good as the latter; compare Sim. *5*, 5, 3 with *8*, 6, 6.

Lines 11–14. The repetition of the article in line 11, as if to support the dependent genitive τοῦ οἴκου, is probably rare in all periods of Greek literature. Grammarians cite Isocrates 2, 4, πότερόν ἐστιν ἄξιον ἑλέσθαι τὸν βίον τὸν τῶν ἰδιωτευόντων μέν, ἐπιεικῶς δὲ πραττόντων, ἢ τὸν τῶν τυραννευόντων; and Plato, *Epist.* 8, p. 354 E, μετρία ἡ θεῷ δουλεία, ἄμετρος δὲ ἡ τοῖς ἀνθρώποις. After εὑρεθῇ, the original of L[1] seems to have been either corrupt or quite different. I find no ready explanation for the words *et possit domui tuae bene fieri*, nor can I account for the omission in L[2] of a word corresponding to εὑρεθῇ.

The last clause again reveals considerable confusion in the text. L[2] ignores ἄκακος, L[1] both ἄκακος and ἀμίαντος. Athous had, as I think, καὶ ἄκακος καὶ καθαρὰ καὶ ἀμίαντος, thus showing only a difference in word-order as compared with the papyrus fragment. The Ethiopic translator read ἐν ἁπλότητι, also, probably, καθαρὰ καὶ ἀμίαντος. The seat of corruption appears to be the word ἄκακος, which had disappeared from the original of the Ethiopic translation, and which, it may be, became so illegible in certain copies as to be replaced by ἡ καρδία — whence *cor* in the Latin versions. Now that the evidence of the new fragment is joined to that of the Athos manuscript, there can no longer be any reason for introducing ἡ καρδία into an edition of the Greek text, as Gebhardt and Harnack did. It must be remembered of course that they had only Simonides' copy of the Athos leaves, and that it is particularly bad in this passage.

Line 15. The right-hand side of the papyrus is torn away after ἐ[ν]τ̣ολη. Under the last letter of this word there is a horizontal stroke, which is nearer to this line than to line 16. Professor Sanders has shown me, in the Washington papyrus codex of the Minor Prophets, headings which are framed in, as it were, by horizontal strokes.

INDEX

This list comprises peculiar grammatical forms and constructions discussed in the notes, and some words introduced into the text of Hermas by the papyri here edited. The references are to the pages and lines of the papyrus codex, except two that are preceded by "Fr." These refer to the lines of the fragment of the Mandates.

PLATE I

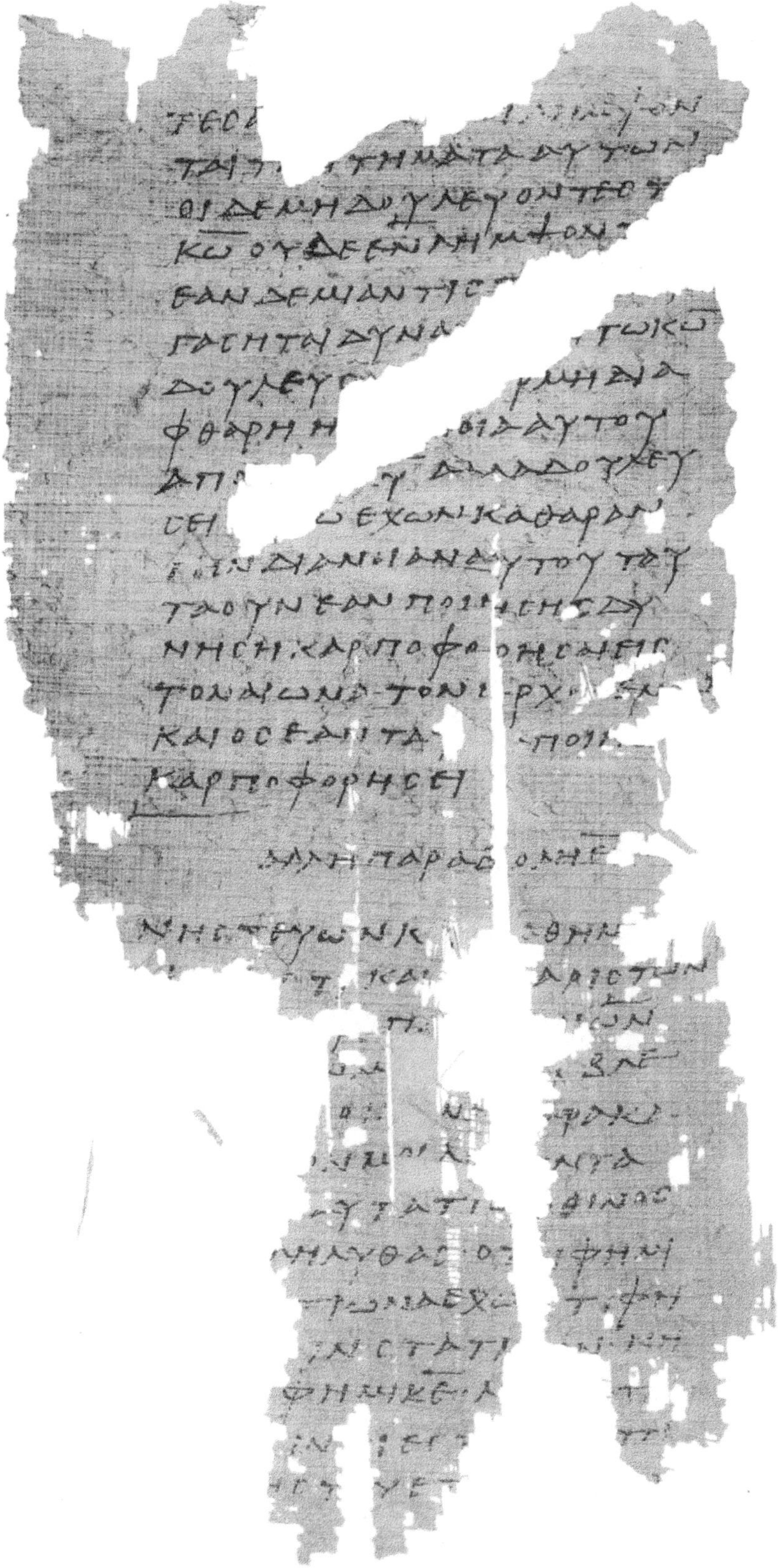

SIMILITUDE 4, 6—5, 1, 2
(Page 4)

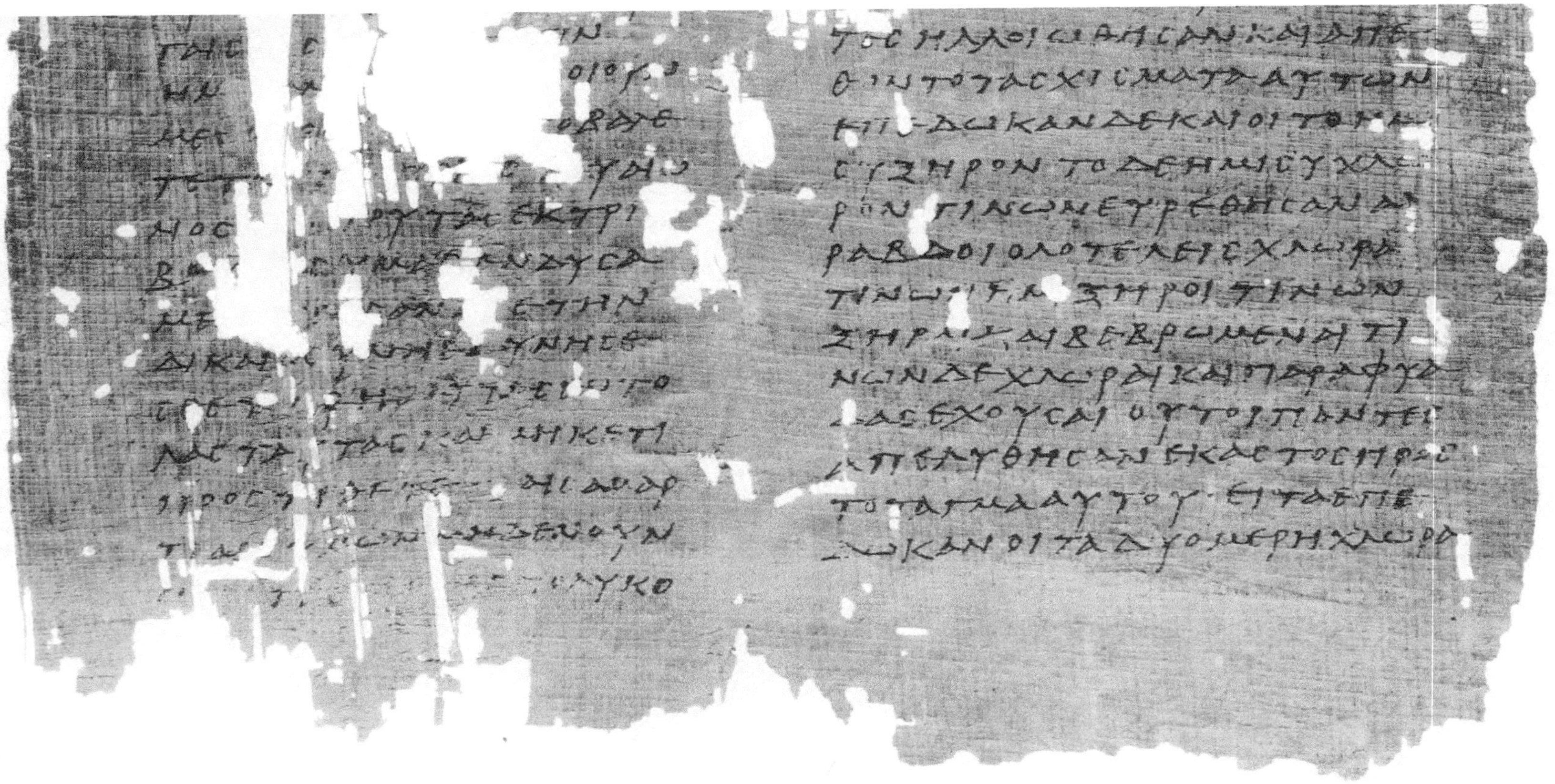

SIMILITUDE 6, 1, 1–4
(Page 18)

SIMILITUDE 8, 4, 6—5, 3
(Page 43)

PLATE III

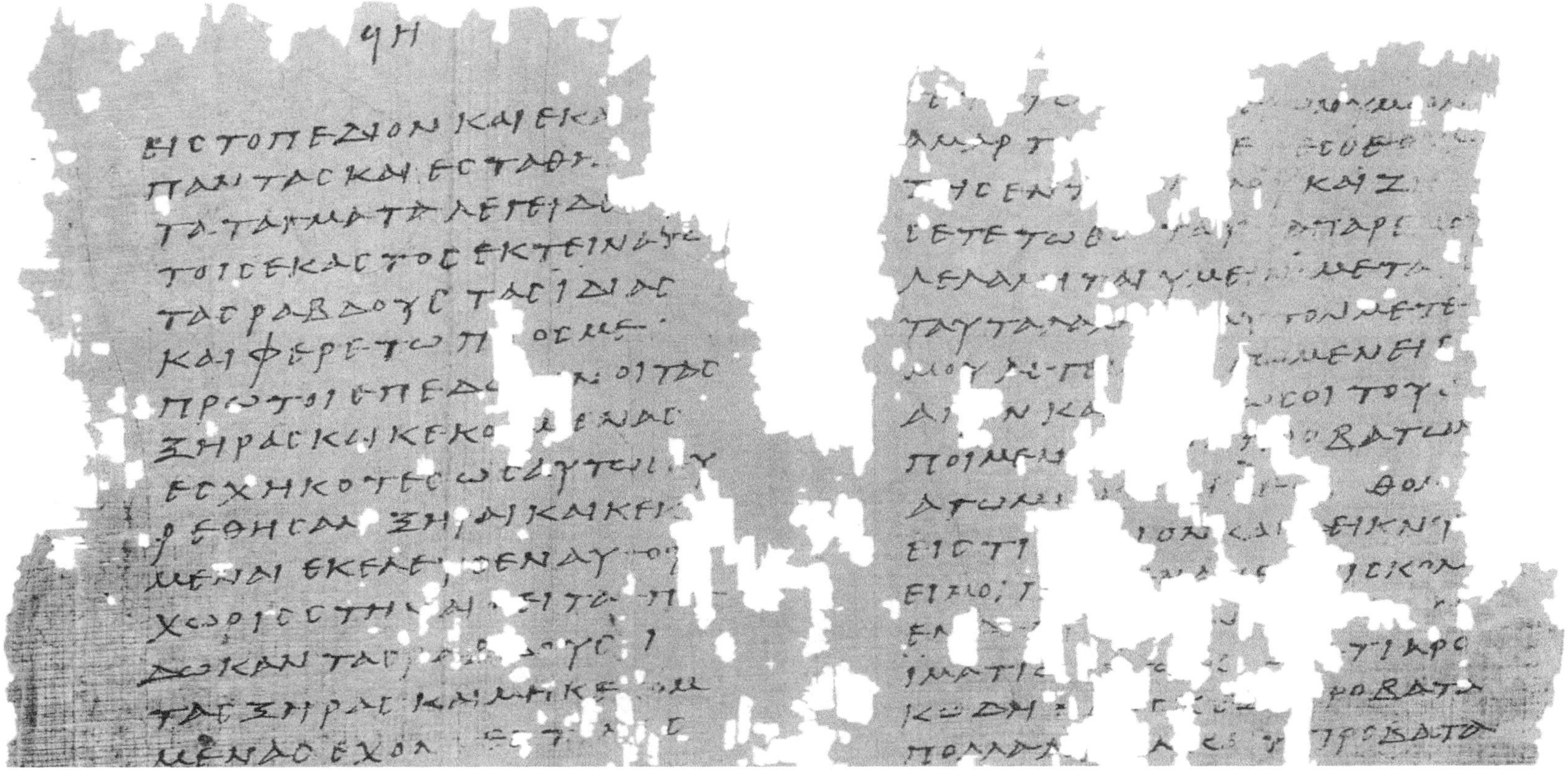

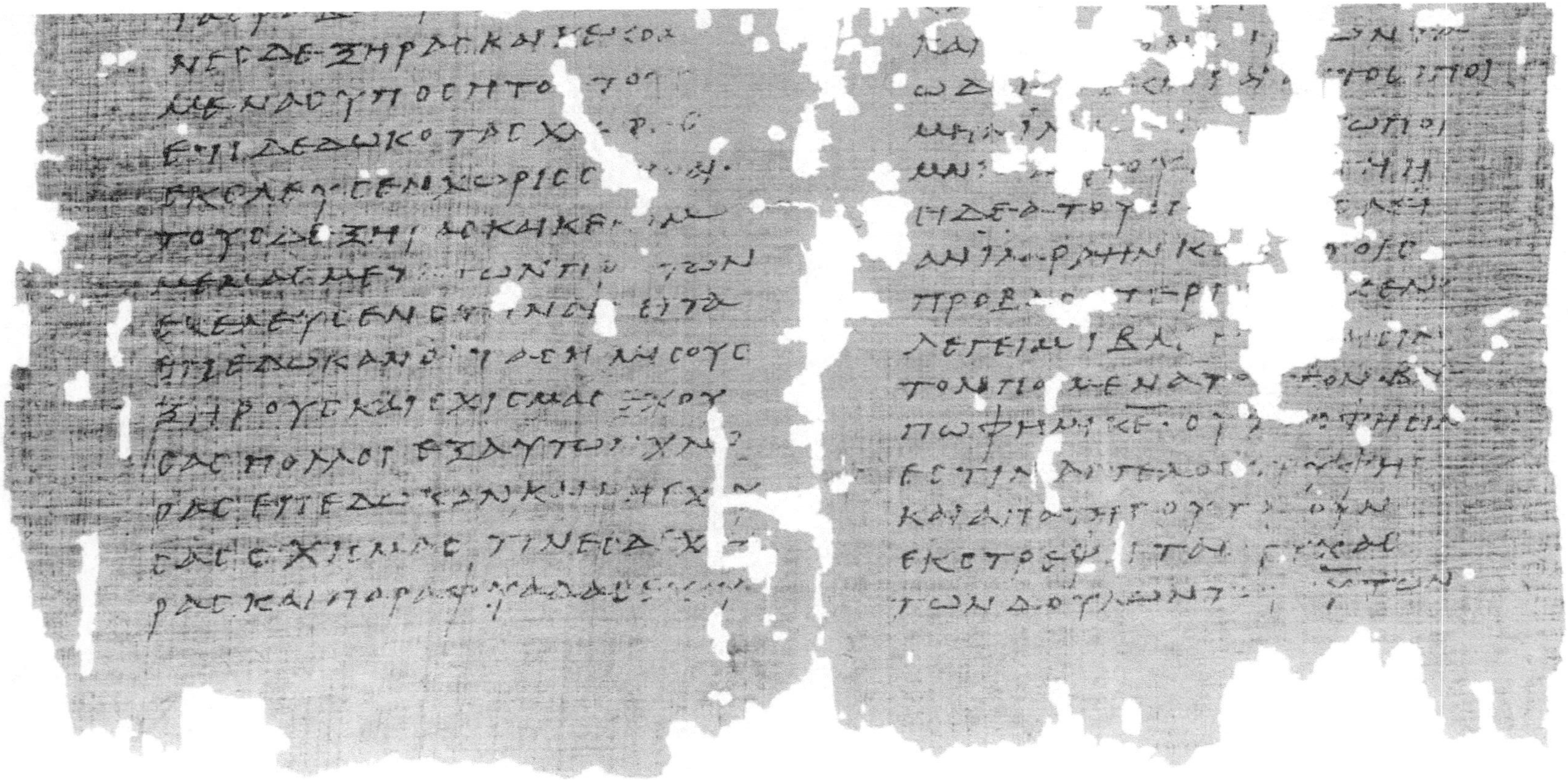

SIMILITUDE 8, 4, 2–6
(Page 42)

SIMILITUDE 6, 1, 4—2, 1
(Page 19)

PLATE IV

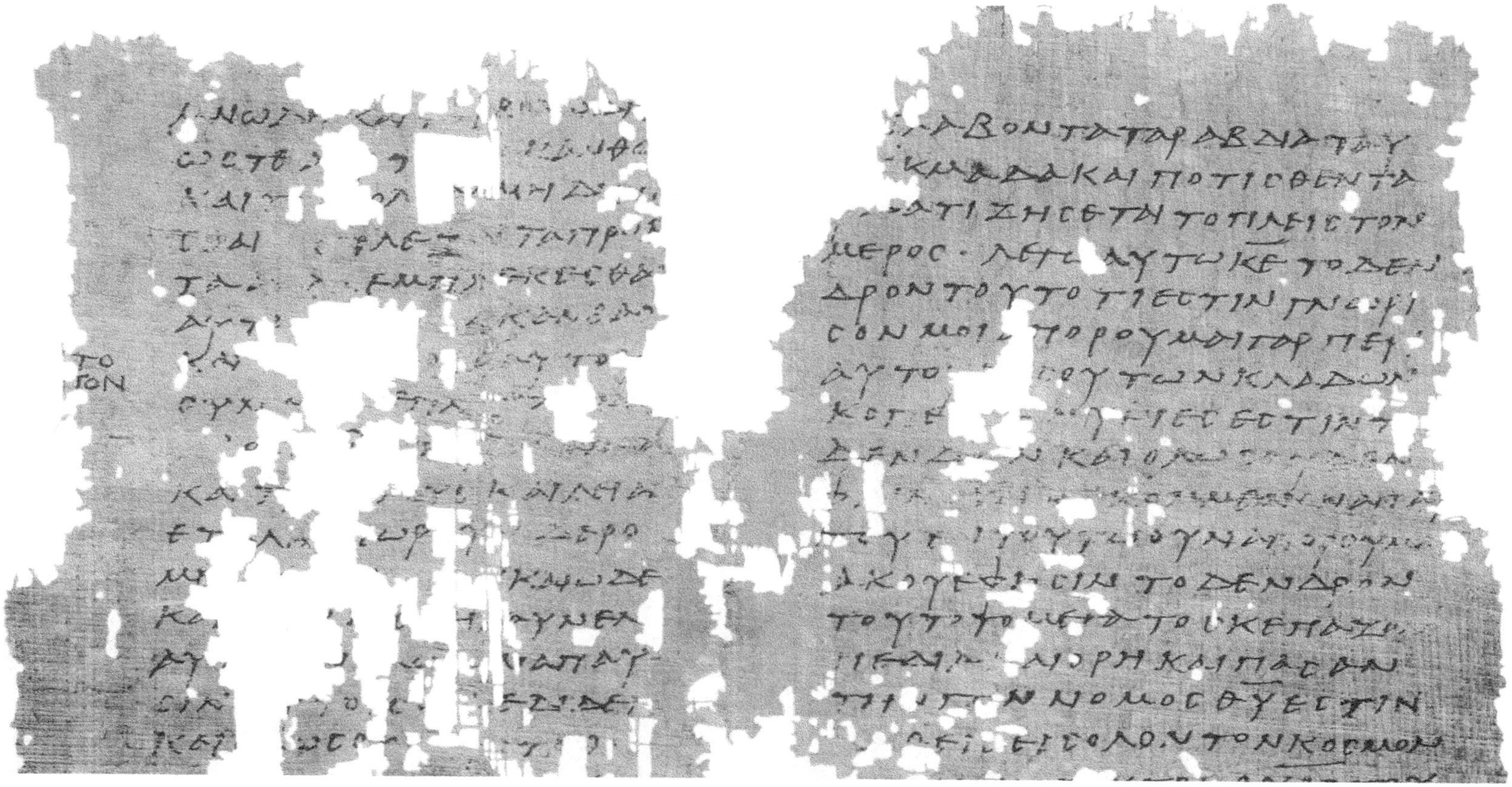

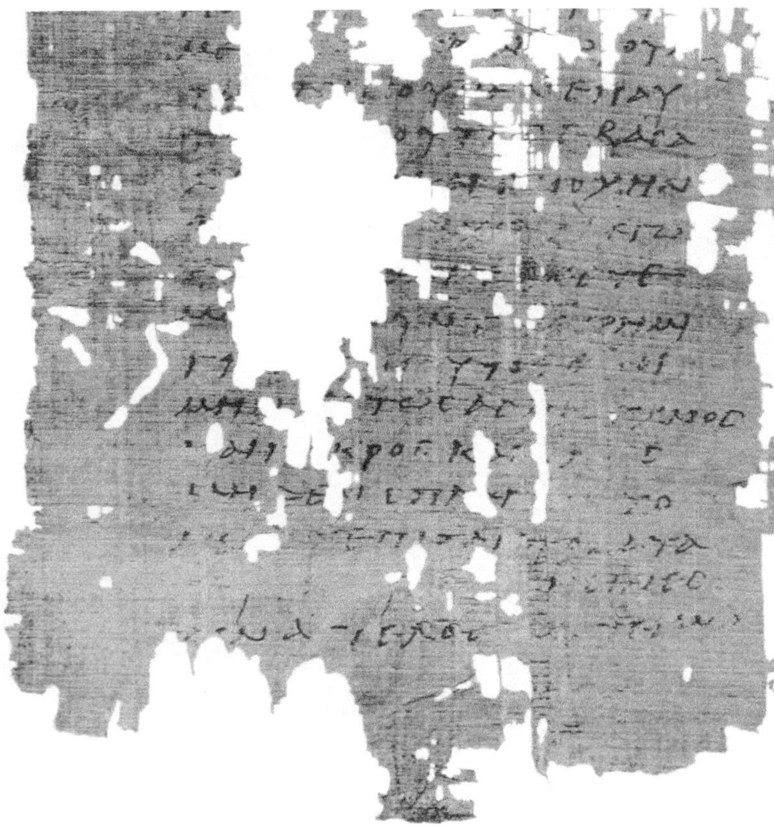

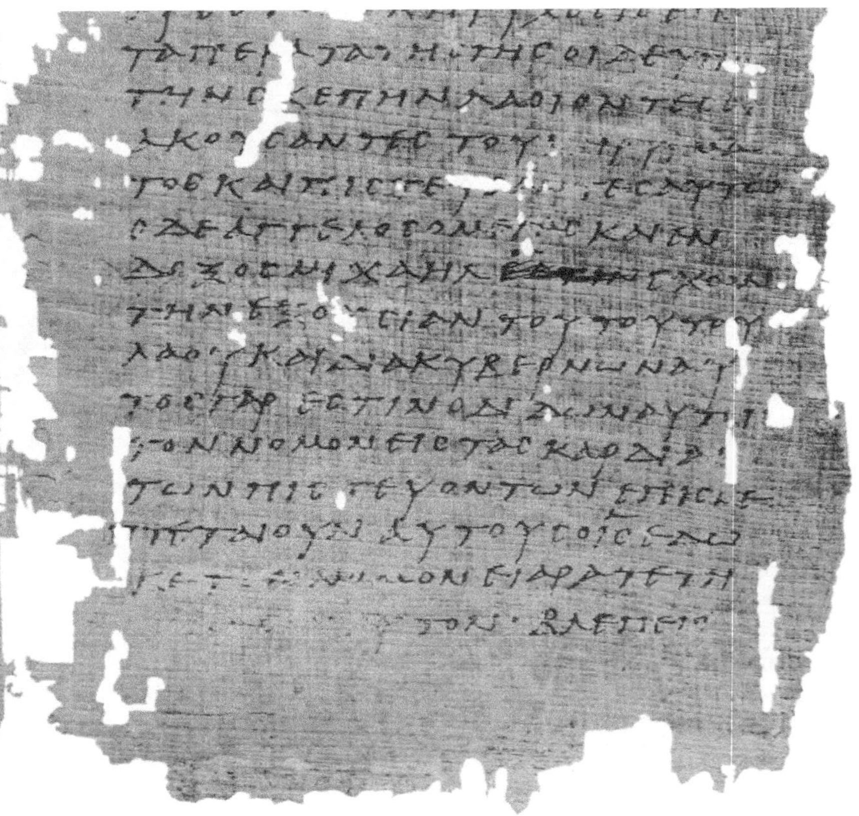

SIMILITUDE 6, 2, 6—3, 2
(Page 22)

SIMILITUDE 8, 2, 9—3, 4
(Page 39)

PLATE V

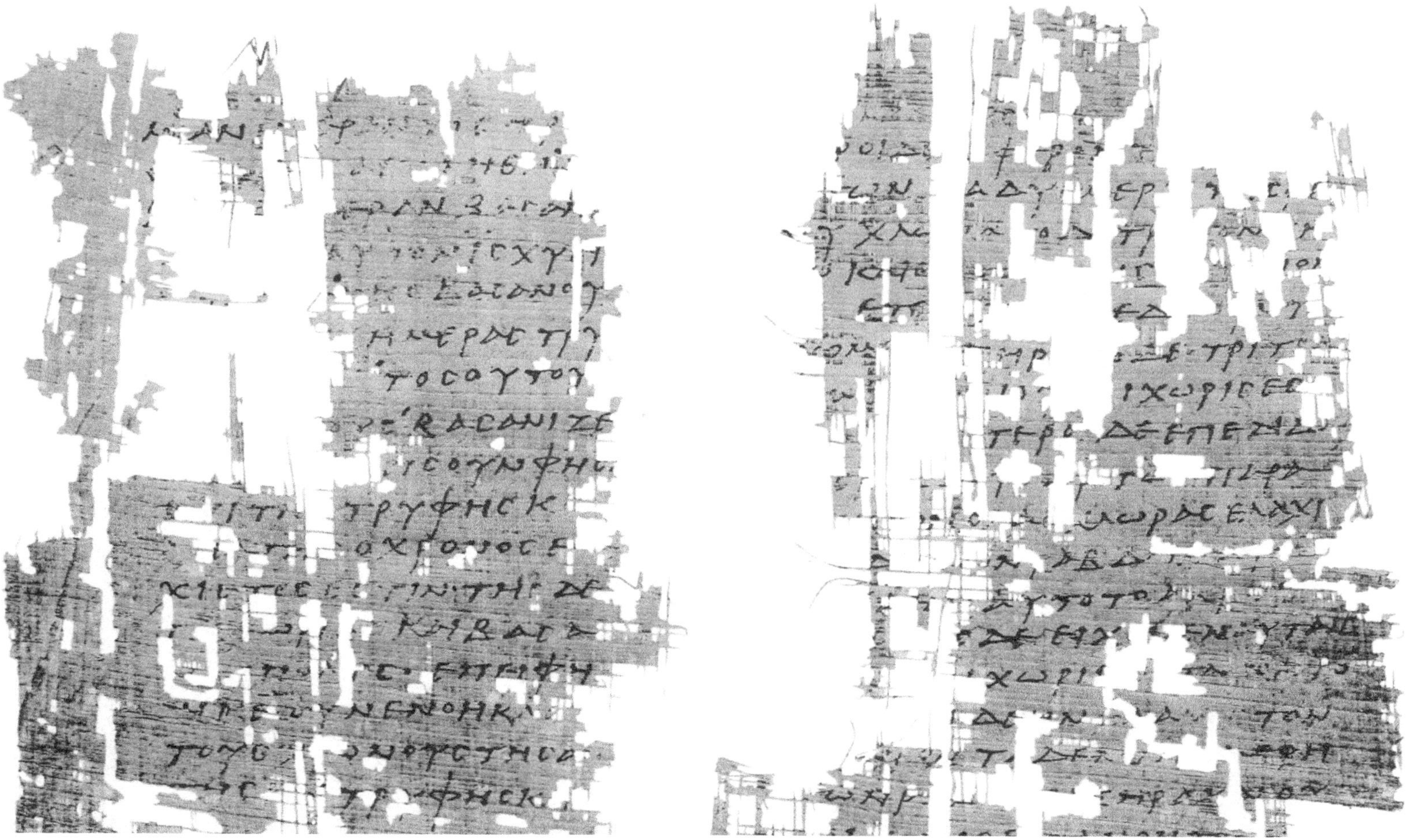

SIMILITUDE 6, 4, 4—5, 2
(Page 26)

SIMILITUDE 8, 1, 11–17
(Page 35)

University of Michigan Studies

Vol. VIII. The Old Testament Manuscripts in the Freer Collection. By Henry A. Sanders. With 9 plates. Pp. viii + 357. $3.50.

Parts Sold Separately in Paper Covers:

Part I. The Washington Manuscript of Deuteronomy and Joshua. With 3 folding plates. Pp. vi + 104. $1.25.

Part II. The Washington Manuscript of the Psalms. With 1 single plate and 5 folding plates. Pp. viii + 105–357. $2.00.

Vol. IX. The New Testament Manuscripts in the Freer Collection. By Henry A. Sanders. With 8 plates. Pp. x + 323. $3.50.

Parts Sold Separately in Paper Covers:

Part I. The Washington Manuscript of the Four Gospels. With 5 plates. Pp. vii + 247. $2.00.

Part II. The Washington Manuscript of the Epistles of Paul. With 3 plates. Pp. vii + 249–315. $1.25.

Vol. X. The Coptic Manuscripts in the Freer Collection. By W. H. Worrell. With 12 plates. Pp. xxvi + 396. $4.75.

Parts Sold Separately in Paper Covers:

Part I. The Coptic Psalter. The Coptic Text in the Sahidic Dialect, with an Introduction, and with 6 plates showing pages of the Manuscript and Fragments in Facsimile. Pp. xxvi + 112. $2.00.

Part II. A Homily on the Archangel Gabriel by Celestinus, Archbishop of Rome, and a Homily on the Virgin by Theophilus, Archbishop of Alexandria, from Manuscript Fragments in the Freer Collection and the British Museum. The Coptic Text, with an Introduction and Translation, and with 6 plates showing pages of the Manuscripts in Facsimile. Pp. 113–396. $2.50.

Vol. XI. Contributions to the History of Science. By Louis C. Karpinski and John G. Winter. With 11 plates. Pp. xi + 283. $3.50.

Parts Sold Separately:

Part I. Robert of Chester's Latin Translation of the Algebra of Al-Khowarizmi. With an Introduction, Critical Notes, and an English Version. By Louis C. Karpinski. With 4 plates and 25 diagrams. Pp. vii + 164. $2.00.

Part II. The Prodromus of Nicolaus Steno's Latin Dissertation on a Solid Body Enclosed by Process of Nature within a Solid. Translated into English by John G. Winter, with a Foreword by William H. Hobbs. With 7 plates. Pp. vii + 169–283. $1.30.

Orders should be addressed to The Librarian, University of Michigan, Ann Arbor, Michigan.

University of Michigan Studies

Vol. XII. Studies in East Christian and Roman Art. By Charles R. Morey, and Walter Dennison. (*Out of print.*)

Parts Sold Separately:

Part I. East Christian Paintings in the Freer Collection. By Charles R. Morey. (*Out of print.*)

Part II. A Gold Treasure of the Late Roman Period from Egypt. By Walter Dennison. With 54 plates and 57 illustrations in the text. Pp. 89–175. $2.50.

Vol. XIII. Fragments from the Cairo Genizah in the Freer Collection. By Richard Gottheil and William H. Worrell. Text, with Translation, Notes and an Introduction. With 52 plates. Pp. xxxi + 273. $4.00.

Vol. XIV. Two Studies in Later Roman and Byzantine Administration. By Arthur E. R. Boak and James E. Dunlap. Pp. x + 324. $2.25.

Parts Sold Separately in Paper Covers:

Part I. The Master of the Offices in the Later Roman and Byzantine Empires. By Arthur E. R. Boak. Pp. x + 160. $1.00.

Part II. The Office of the Grand Chamberlain in the Later Roman and Byzantine Empires. By James E. Dunlap. Pp. 161–324. $1.00.

Vol. XV. Greek Themes in Modern Musical Settings. By Albert A. Stanley. (*Out of print.*)

Parts Sold Separately in Paper Covers:

Part I. Incidental Music to Percy Mackaye's Drama of Sappho and Phaon. Pp. 1–68. $.90.

Part II. Music to the Alcestis of Euripides with English Text. Pp. 71–120 $.80.

Part III. Music for the Iphigenia among the Taurians by Euripides, with Greek Text. Pp. 123–214. $.75.

Part IV. Two Fragments of Ancient Greek Music. Pp. 217–225. $.30.

Part V. Music to Cantica of the Menaechmi of Plautus. Pp. 229–263. $.50.

Part VI. Attis: A Symphonic Poem. Pp. 265–384. $1.00.

Vol. XVI. Nicomachus of Gerasa: Introduction to Arithmetic. Translated into English by Martin Luther D'Ooge, with Studies in Greek Arithmetic by Frank Egleston Robbins and Louis C. Karpinski. (*Out of print.*)

Vols. XVII–XX. Royal Correspondence of the Assyrian Empire. Translated into English with a transliteration of the Text and a Commentary. By Leroy Waterman.

Orders should be addressed to The Librarian, University of Michigan, Ann Arbor, Michigan.

University of Michigan Studies

Vol. XVII. Translation and Transliteration. Pp. x + 490. $4.00.
Vol. XVIII. Translation and Transliteration. Pp. iv + 524. $4.00.
Vol. XIX. Commentary. Pp. x + 377. $4.00.
Vol. XX. Supplement and Indexes. (*In preparation.*)

Vol. XXI. The Minor Prophets in the Freer Collection and the Berlin Fragment of Genesis. By Henry A. Sanders and Carl Schmidt. With 7 plates. Pp. xii + 436. $3.50.

Vol. XXII. A Papyrus Codex of the Shepherd of Hermas, with a Fragment of the Mandates. By Campbell Bonner. Pp. x + 137. With 5 plates. $3.00.

Vol. XXIII. The Complete Commentary of Oecumenius on the Apocalypse: Now printed for the first time from Manuscripts at Messina, Rome, Salonika and Athos. By H. C. Hoskier. Pp. viii + 260. $4.00.

Vol. XXIV (= Michigan Papyri, Vol. I). Zenon Papyri in the University of Michigan Collection. By C. C. Edgar. Pp. xiv + 211. With 6 plates. $3.50.

Vol. XXV. Karanis: Topographical and Architectural Report of Excavations during the Seasons 1924–28. By A. E. R. Boak and E. Peterson. Pp. viii + 69. With 42 plates, 19 plans, and 1 map. $2.00.

Vol. XXVI. Coptic Sounds, by William H. Worrell, with an Appendix by Hide Shohara. (*In press.*)

Vol. XXVII. Athenian Financial Documents of the Fifth Century. By B. D. Meritt. Pp. xiv + 192. $3.50.

Vols. XXVIII–XXIX (= Michigan Papyri, Vols. II–III). Papyri from Tebtunis. By A. E. R. Boak.

Vol. XXVIII (= Michigan Papyri, Vol. II). Pp. xvi + 259. With 4 plates. $3.50.
Vol. XXIX. (*In preparation.*)

Vol. XXX. Karanis: The Temples, Coin Hoards, Botanical and Zoölogical Reports, Seasons 1924–31. Edited by A. E. R. Boak. Pp. xii + 93. With 37 plates, 16 plans, and 4 diagrams. $2.50.

University of Michigan Studies

VOL. XXXI. ANCIENT TEXTILES FROM EGYPT IN THE UNIVERSITY OF MICHIGAN COLLECTION. By Lillian M. Wilson. Pp. x + 77. With 23 plates. $2.50.

VOL. XXXII. PARTHIAN POTTERY FROM SELEUCIA ON THE TIGRIS. By Neilson C. Debevoise. (*In press.*)

FACSIMILES OF MANUSCRIPTS

Size, 40.5 × 35 cm.

FACSIMILE OF THE WASHINGTON MANUSCRIPT OF DEUTERONOMY AND JOSHUA IN THE FREER COLLECTION. With an Introduction by Henry A. Sanders. Pp. x; 201 heliotype plates.

Limited edition, distributed only to Libraries, under certain conditions. A list of libraries containing this Facsimile is given in *University of Michigan Studies, Humanistic Series*, Vol. VIII, pp. 351–353.

Size, 34 × 26 cm.

FACSIMILE OF THE WASHINGTON MANUSCRIPT OF THE FOUR GOSPELS IN THE FREER COLLECTION. With an Introduction by Henry A. Sanders. Pp. x; 372 heliotype plates and 2 colored plates.

Limited edition, distributed only to Libraries, under certain conditions. A list of libraries containing this Facsimile is given in *University of Michigan Studies, Humanistic Series*, Vol. IX, pp. 317–320.

Size, 30.5 × 40.6 cm.

FACSIMILE OF THE WASHINGTON MANUSCRIPT OF THE MINOR PROPHETS IN THE FREER COLLECTION AND THE BERLIN FRAGMENT OF GENESIS, with an Introduction by Henry A. Sanders. With 130 plates.

Limited edition, distributed only to Libraries, under certain conditions. A list of libraries containing this Facsimile is given in *University of Michigan Studies, Humanistic Series*, Vol. XXI, pp. 431–434.

THE JEROME LECTURES

LIFE AND LETTERS IN THE PAPYRI. By John G. Winter. Pp. viii + 308. $3.50.

SCIENTIFIC SERIES

Size, 28 × 18.5 cm. 4°. Bound in cloth

VOL. I. THE CIRCULATION AND SLEEP. By John F. Shepard. Pp. ix + 83, with an Atlas of 63 plates, bound separately. Text and Atlas, $2.50.

VOL. II. STUDIES ON DIVERGENT SERIES AND SUMMABILITY. By Walter B. Ford. Pp. xi + 194. $2.50.

Size, 23.5 × 15.5 cm.

VOL. III. THE GEOLOGY OF THE NETHERLANDS EAST INDIES. By H. A. Brouwer. With 18 plates and 17 text figures. Pp. xii + 160. $3.00.

Orders should be addressed to The Librarian, University of Michigan, Ann Arbor, Michigan.

University of Michigan Publications

Size, 18 × 12 cm. Bound in paper

THE MENAECHMI OF PLAUTUS. The Latin Text, with a Translation by Joseph H. Drake, University of Michigan. Pp. xi + 129. $.60.

LANGUAGE AND LITERATURE

VOL. I. STUDIES IN SHAKESPEARE, MILTON AND DONNE. By Members of the English Department of the University of Michigan. Pp. viii + 232. $2.50.

VOL. II. ELIZABETHAN PROVERB LORE IN LYLY'S 'EUPHUES' AND IN PETTIE'S 'PETITE PALLACE,' WITH PARALLELS FROM SHAKESPEARE. By Morris P. Tilley. Pp. x + 461. $3.50.

VOL. III. THE SOCIAL MODE OF RESTORATION COMEDY. By Kathleen M. Lynch. Pp. x + 242. $2.50.

VOL. IV. STUART POLITICS IN CHAPMAN'S 'TRAGEDY OF CHABOT.' By Norma D. Solve. Pp. x + 176. $2.50.

VOL. V. EL LIBRO DEL CAUALLERO ZIFAR: Part I, Text. By C. P. Wagner. With 9 facsimiles. Pp. xvii + 532. $5.00.

VOL. VI. EL LIBRO DEL CAUALLERO ZIFAR: Part II, Commentary. By C. P. Wagner. (*In preparation.*)

VOL. VII. STRINDBERG'S DRAMATIC EXPRESSIONISM. By C. E. W. L. Dahlström. Pp. xii + 242. $2.50.

VOL. VIII. ESSAYS AND STUDIES IN ENGLISH AND COMPARATIVE LITERATURE. By Members of the English Department of the University of Michigan. Pp. viii + 231. $2.50.

VOL. IX. TOWARD THE UNDERSTANDING OF SHELLEY. By Bennett Weaver. Pp. xii + 258. $2.50.

VOL. X. ESSAYS AND STUDIES IN ENGLISH AND COMPARATIVE LITERATURE. By Members of the English Department of the University of Michigan. Pp. vi + 278. $2.50.

HISTORY AND POLITICAL SCIENCE

The first three volumes of this series were published as "Historical Studies" under the direction of the Department of History. Volumes IV and V were published without numbers.

VOL. I. A HISTORY OF THE PRESIDENT'S CABINET. By Mary Louise Hinsdale. (*Out of print.*)

VOL. II. ENGLISH RULE IN GASCONY, 1199–1259, WITH SPECIAL REFERENCE TO THE TOWNS. By Frank Burr Marsh. Pp. xi + 178. $1.25.

Orders should be addressed to The Librarian, University of Michigan, Ann Arbor, Michigan.

University of Michigan Publications

SECOND PRELIMINARY REPORT UPON THE EXCAVATIONS AT TEL UMAR, IRAQ, CONDUCTED BY THE UNIVERSITY OF MICHIGAN, THE TOLEDO MUSEUM OF ART, AND THE CLEVELAND MUSEUM OF ART. Leroy Waterman, Director. With 26 plates and 12 text figures. Pp. xii + 78. $1.50. Bound in paper.

UNIVERSITY OF MICHIGAN COLLECTIONS

CATALOGUE OF THE STEARNS COLLECTION OF MUSICAL INSTRUMENTS (Second edition). By Albert A. Stanley. With 40 plates. Pp. 276. $4.00.

PAPERS OF THE MICHIGAN ACADEMY OF SCIENCE, ARTS AND LETTERS

(Containing papers submitted at annual meetings)

Editors: EUGENE S. McCARTNEY AND PETER OKKELBERG

Size, 24.2 × 16.5 cm. 8°. Bound in cloth

VOL. I (1921). Pp. xi + 424. $2.00.

VOL. II (1922). Pp. xi + 226. $2.00. Bound in paper, $1.50.

VOL. III (1923). Pp. xii + 473. $3.00. Bound in paper, $2.25.

VOL. IV (1924), PART I. Pp. xii + 631. $3.00. Bound in paper, $2.25.

VOL. IV (1924), PART II. A KEY TO THE SNAKES OF THE UNITED STATES, CANADA AND LOWER CALIFORNIA. By Frank N. Blanchard. With 78 text figures. Pp. xiii + 65. Cloth. $1.75.

VOL. V (1925). Pp. xii + 479. $3.00. Bound in paper, $2.25.

VOL. VI (1926). (Papers in botany only.) Pp. xii + 406. $3.00. Bound in paper, $2.25.

VOL. VII (1926). (No papers in botany.) Pp. xii + 435. $3.00. Bound in paper, $2.25.

VOL. VIII (1927). Pp. xiv + 456. $3.00. Bound in paper, $2.25.

VOL. IX (1928). (Papers in botany and forestry only.) Pp. xiv + 597. $4.00. Bound in paper, $2.25.

VOL. X (1928). (No papers in botany or forestry.) Pp. xvii + 620. $4.00. Bound in paper, $2.25.

VOL. XI (1929). (Papers in botany and zoölogy only.) Pp. xii + 494. $3.50. Bound in paper, $2.25.

Orders should be addressed to The Librarian, University of Michigan, Ann Arbor, Michigan.

University of Michigan Publications

Vol. XII (1929). (No papers in botany or zoölogy.) Pp. xii + 348. $3.00. Bound in paper, $2.25.

Vol. XIII (1930). (Papers in botany and zoölogy only.) Pp. xii + 603. $4.00. Bound in paper, $2.25.

Vol. XIV (1930). (No papers in botany or zoölogy.) Pp. xv + 650. $4.00. Bound in paper, $2.25.

Vol. XV (1931). (Papers in botany, forestry, and zoölogy only.) Pp. x + 511. $3.50. Bound in paper, $2.25.

Vol. XVI (1931). (No papers in botany, forestry, or zoölogy.) Pp. x + 521. $3.50. Bound in paper, $2.25.

Vol. XVII (1932). (Papers in botany, forestry, and zoölogy only.) Pp. x + 738. $4.00. Bound in paper, $2.25.

Vol. XVIII (1932). (No papers in botany, forestry, or zoölogy.) Pp. x + 623. $4.00. Bound in paper, $2.25.

Vol. XIX (1933). (*In press.*)

Orders should be addressed to The Librarian, University of Michigan, Ann Arbor, Michigan.

Printed and bound by CPI Group (UK) Ltd, Croydon, CR0 4YY
09/06/2025
14686147-0004